The Afterlife of Bach's Organ Works

The Afterlife of Bach's Organ Works

Their Reception from the Nineteenth Century to the Present

RUSSELL STINSON

Oxford University Press is a department of the University of Oxford. It furthers
the University's objective of excellence in research, scholarship, and education
by publishing worldwide. Oxford is a registered trade mark of Oxford University
Press in the UK and certain other countries.

Published in the United States of America by Oxford University Press
198 Madison Avenue, New York, NY 10016, United States of America.

© Oxford University Press 2024

All rights reserved. No part of this publication may be reproduced, stored in
a retrieval system, or transmitted, in any form or by any means, without the
prior permission in writing of Oxford University Press, or as expressly permitted
by law, by license, or under terms agreed with the appropriate reproduction
rights organization. Inquiries concerning reproduction outside the scope of the
above should be sent to the Rights Department, Oxford University Press, at the
address above.

You must not circulate this work in any other form
and you must impose this same condition on any acquirer.

CIP data is on file at the Library of Congress

ISBN 978–0–19–768043–8

DOI: 10.1093/oso/9780197680438.001.0001

Printed by Integrated Books International, United States of America

To Abigail and Kenneth

CONTENTS

Abbreviations ix

Introduction 1

1. Studies and Discoveries 6

2. On the Reception of Bach's Organ Works in Nineteenth-Century
   Leipzig: Rochlitz, Becker, Schellenberg, and Their Reviews of Two
   Early Editions 43

3. Karl Gottlieb Freudenberg's *Erinnerungen aus dem Leben eines alten
   Organisten* and Bach Reception in the Nineteenth Century 74

4. Bach Goes to Hollywood: The Use of His Music in Motion
   Pictures 94

5. New Data and New Insights: Ten Case Studies 105

Epilogue 133
Notes 139
References 177
Index 185

ABBREVIATIONS

Bach-Dokumente VI *Ausgewählte Dokumente zum Nachwirken Johann Sebastian Bachs 1801–1850,* ed. Andreas Glöckner, Anselm Hartinger, and Karen Lehmann. Kassel: Bärenreiter, 2007.

BWV Bach-Werke-Verzeichnis = Wolfgang Schmieder, *Thematisch-systematisches Verzeichnis der musikalischen Werke von Johann Sebastian Bach.* Rev. ed. Wiesbaden: Breitkopf & Härtel, 1990.

NBA Neue Bach-Ausgabe = *Johann Sebastian Bach: Neue Ausgabe sämtlicher Werke.* Kassel: Bärenreiter; Leipzig: Deutscher Verlag für Musik, 1954–2007.

Introduction

The goal of this book is simply to better understand how the music of Johann Sebastian Bach has been received by later generations, starting in the early nineteenth century, the era of the so-called Bach revival. In other words, I hope to sharpen our picture of Bach's decisive role in music history over the past two hundred years. The true essence of Bach's art may defy explanation, but it might be described as masterful musical engineering combined with profound expressivity. To paraphrase the nineteenth-century organist Hermann Schellenberg, who is mentioned often in these pages, Bach's music may represent the summit of contrapuntal technique, yet it is just as amazing for its depth of emotion. The book's contents are presented as five independent essays. They are all published here for the first time except for Chapter 3, a preliminary version of which appeared, in German translation, in the 2019 *Bach-Jahrbuch*.[1]

I focus on the organ works for various reasons, not least of which is that, as an organist myself, I know those works the best. Furthermore, the organ is the instrument that best represents Bach as a musician, that is, as a composer *and* performer. And just as the organ is the dominant instrument of Bach's career, so Bach dominates the field of organ music like no other composer dominates any other repertory. The sheer number of his surviving organ compositions (almost three hundred) and the incomparable quality of the music both attest to this fact.

The Afterlife of Bach's Organ Works. Russell Stinson, Oxford University Press. © Oxford University Press 2024.
DOI: 10.1093/oso/9780197680438.003.0001

Anyone reading this book will eventually see that it involves a rather diverse group of musicians and non-musicians—some famous, some forgotten—who in one way or another became champions of Bach's organ works. These individuals performed the music; edited it for publication; promoted it by means of books, articles, and reviews; transcribed it for other media; taught it to their pupils; shared it with their families and friends; and incorporated it into the soundtracks of their motion pictures. They ensured its "afterlife." Accordingly, this book is a history of performance practice, an aesthetic history of musical taste, and a social history. I do not, however, discuss Bach's organ works to the exclusion of his compositions for other media, whether instrumental or vocal, as Chapters 3 and 4 best demonstrate.

The opening chapter is the only one of the five not directly concerned with matters of reception. It begins like a review-essay on two recent monographs in the field, with numerous remarks on issues of musical style, and then centers on a fascinating but neglected Bach source that happens to be housed today in an American archive. The source sheds light on how the nineteenth-century organist Wilhelm Rust conceived his orchestration of the famous Fantasy in G Minor, BWV 542/1, which he conducted in 1881 in his capacity as Leipzig Thomaskantor in Bach's own church. Johannes Brahms had recommended Rust for that exalted position, and Brahms turns up earlier in this chapter as a "receptor" of the music both of Bach (in particular, the Musical Offering, BWV 1079) and of Dietrich Buxtehude. I also consider some overlooked features of the autograph of Bach's *Orgelbüchlein* and offer new data on the nineteenth-century tradition of transcribing Bach's organ works for the piano. As I discuss, Brahms was a leading practitioner of that tradition, and he heard (and conducted) various orchestrations of Bach's organ works throughout his career.

Chapter 2 has a narrower focus. It deals with Hermann Schellenberg, Friedrich Rochlitz, and Carl Ferdinand Becker in their capacity as music critics in the "Sebastianstadt," as Felix Mendelssohn referred to the city of Leipzig. I consider Rochlitz's review of an edition of organ chorales by Bach published between 1803 and 1806, and reviews by Becker and

Introduction

Schellenberg of an edition of free organ works by Bach published in 1845. In reading these critiques, one senses how exciting it must have been to encounter new compositions by Bach at this point in history, even if all three critics voiced negative as well as positive thoughts about the music. For example, Rochlitz, who did not play the organ himself, maintained that Bach's penchant for thick, imitative textures in his organ chorales resulted in music better suited to the eyes than the ears. Becker and Schellenberg were both professional organists, and they objected to pieces in the edition they reviewed that differed from their notion of idiomatic writing for the instrument. Schellenberg's favorite organ work may well have been Bach's Fantasy *and Fugue* in G Minor (BWV 542), which he arranged for organ, four hands, and "double pedal," and which he transcribed for piano, four hands. As I discuss, Schellenberg also heard the organ virtuoso Adolph Friedrich Hesse render this piece on an organ crawl in Leipzig the same year of his review. Hesse succeeded despite a broken tracker on one of the organs he played and frequent ciphers on the other one.

The subject matter of Chapter 3 is the autobiography of the organist Karl Gottlieb Freudenberg (1797–1869) and what it can tell us about Bach reception in the nineteenth century. Happily, this obscure source is a bonanza of information on the topic, with lively anecdotes about how such dignitaries as Mendelssohn, Liszt, and even Beethoven responded to the music of Bach. We also learn in vivid detail about Freudenberg's own experiences as a Bach interpreter, including his triumphant performance of the above-mentioned Fugue in G Minor at an organ jury in Berlin—where he snubbed his distinguished audience by not acknowledging them as he left the building—his victorious rendition of Bach's "St. Anne" Fugue (BWV 552/2) at an organ audition in Breslau, and an altercation he had with his supervisor—in the middle of a worship service—at his church in Breslau. A more poignant story related by Freudenberg involves the Bach chorale that he played at the funeral of one of the children of his Breslau colleague Johann Theodor Mosewius, a fellow Bach enthusiast. The chorale "Was mein Gott will, das g'scheh allzeit" ("What my God wants, may it always happen") was Mosewius's favorite from the St. Matthew Passion, and it obviously took on special significance for him in the context of that service.

Chapter 4 is a bit of a wild card, as the receptors there are not musicians but filmmakers. It explores the appropriation of Bach's music in three (quite violent) blockbuster films of the 1970s and 1990s, starting with the climactic baptism scene at the end of Francis Ford Coppola's *The Godfather*. That scene, despite all the blood, makes brilliant use of two of Bach's most celebrated organ works: the Passacaglia in C Minor, BWV 582; and the Prelude in D Major, BWV 532/1. I then examine a scene from Jonathan Demme's *The Silence of the Lambs* involving the evil-genius protagonist of the film, Hannibal Lecter, and Bach's Goldberg Variations. Lecter's obsession with this mathematically exact opus has since become a common trope in popular culture, for better or worse.[2] The third film is *Schindler's List*, Steven Spielberg's harrowing account of the Holocaust. There, in a nightmarish scene that shows SS troops liquidating a Jewish ghetto, a young Nazi officer executes the opening bars of the prelude to Bach's second English Suite. Spielberg uses the scene as a metaphor for the cultural barbarity and ignorance of the Nazi regime. I then discuss the organist Herbert Haag (1908–1977) as an embodiment of this archetypal character.

The fifth and final chapter consists of ten case studies in the reception of Bach's organ music, including both free works and chorale settings. Special attention is paid to issues of performance practice, musical style, and the art of transcription. It is my conviction that the historical layers imparted to the music by this research open up fresh perspectives on the music for us today. I take into account a wide variety of books, articles, editions, recordings (especially the magnificent compilation known as *Bach 333*), films, and videos. The dramatis personae encompass such disparate figures as Albert Schweitzer and Cosima Wagner, and the performance venues include some of the most historic churches and concert halls in the world.

I was assisted in my work by various colleagues and friends, particularly James A. Brokaw II, Paul Cary, Valerie Woodring Goertzen, Karl Traugott Goldbach, Hugh Morris, Michael Mullen, and Michael Oriatti.

I am indebted to Kristian Ameigh and Jenna Waters for preparing the musical examples. I must also thank the two anonymous reviewers engaged by the press for their many helpful comments on my first draft. A special shout-out goes to Norm Hirschy, Executive Editor at Oxford, for his support of the project from its inception. My greatest debt, once again, is to my wife, Laura, for her encouragement and love.

Two general attributes of the book are its up-to-dateness and the amount of material offered for the first time in English (all translations are my own, unless otherwise indicated). I hope that even the most seasoned Bach aficionado will learn much in reading it, and I welcome anyone intrigued by history's complex reckoning with Bach's music to explore its contents.

Russell Stinson
Winston-Salem, North Carolina
November 2022

1

Studies and Discoveries

Johann Sebastian Bach's compositions for the organ occupy a central place within the Western musical tradition. They are also the subject of a vast musicological literature. Still, despite the number of books, articles, and editions that have been devoted to Bach's organ works, the topic has by no means been exhausted. I will take as my point of departure two recent monographs on Bach in which the organ works are prominently mentioned, and then I will focus on a Bach source from nineteenth-century Germany that has found its way to America.

I

One catalyst for my comments here is *Bach's Musical Universe: The Composer and His Work*, a book by Christoph Wolff published in 2020 by W. W. Norton. To quote from one of the dust-jacket blurbs, this wonderfully insightful study shows "how the largely self-taught composer set himself on a clear path to attain musical perfection." In tracing Bach's compositional odyssey, Wolff emphasizes works of "exemplary status, unique features, and innovative character," in other words, compositional "benchmarks" (p. xv). He offers numerous remarks on the organ works, including the collection of forty-five chorale settings known as the *Orgelbüchlein*. Masterpieces *en miniature*, the *Orgelbüchlein* chorales are among the shortest works in the Bach catalogue, lasting no longer than two minutes

The Afterlife of Bach's Organ Works. Russell Stinson, Oxford University Press. © Oxford University Press 2024.
DOI: 10.1093/oso/9780197680438.003.0002

on average, and they are at the same time among the most profound. As the nineteenth-century Bach biographer Philipp Spitta stated, specifically in reference to the *Orgelbüchlein*, "the narrower the circle in which Bach had to turn, the deeper he went."[1] Writing about twenty-five years earlier (1847), in a review of one of the first editions of the *Orgelbüchlein*, the organist and composer Louis Kindscher expressed outright amazement that a composer of Bach's stature could have authored works of such modest dimensions.[2] Kindscher also praised the "endless diversity" of musical techniques found in the collection, just as Bach inscribed on the title page of the autograph manuscript that the main purpose of the *Orgelbüchlein* is to show budding organists "how to set a chorale *in all kinds of ways.*"

What has survived of the *Orgelbüchlein* is a mere fragment of what Bach originally conceived. The original plan was a collection of 164 chorales, arranged according to the liturgical year. Early on in his discussion (p. 36), Wolff writes that

> in preparing the manuscript and before setting down a single note, Bach spaced the headings of the 164 hymns throughout the manuscript in such a way that the compact form of each single piece was actually predetermined by the length of the chorale tune. For the vast majority of the chorale preludes he allowed a single page ruled with six staves. Only sixteen longer melodies were spread over two pages: one that varied in all three strophes [the setting of "Christ ist erstanden," BWV 627] received three pages, and a single very short melody was confined to two-thirds of a page, leaving extra room for the following longer chorale tune.

Two accompanying photographs in Wolff's book reveal this "very short melody" to be "Christus, der ist mein Leben," which contains only four phrases, and the "following longer chorale tune" to be "Herzlich lieb hab ich dich, o Herr" (a melody so exquisitely set by Bach to end the St. John Passion), which contains no fewer than ten phrases.

Wolff also mentions "sixteen longer melodies" for which Bach reserved two pages but most of which he never set. One that he did set is "O Mensch, bewein dein Sünde groß," whose composition resulted in the celebrated work catalogued as BWV 622. Consisting of nine phrases, this tune was too long to fit onto a single page but not long enough to take up two full pages. With this extra space at his disposal, Bach proceeded, quite unusually, to write a varied repeat of the Stollen (here, the first three phrases) rather than penning a set of repeat marks to indicate a note-for-note restatement.

Among the longer melodies never set is one titled in the autograph *Wir gläuben all' an einen Gott.* According to Peter Williams, it is unclear whether Bach meant the famous Dorian-mode tune "Wir glauben all an einen Gott" or the decidedly more obscure major-mode melody "Wir glauben all an einen Gott, Vater."[3] Bach must have meant the former, however, for this tune is eleven phrases long, as opposed to the four phrases of the latter. Furthermore, Bach is not known ever to have set the major-mode tune. The popular double-pedal arrangement of that melody catalogued as BWV 740 is today rightly attributed to Bach's pupil Johann Ludwig Krebs.

Eventually, Wolff narrows his gaze onto a handful of settings that appear at or near the beginning of the autograph manuscript. One is the Advent chorale "Herr Christ, der ein'ge Gottessohn," BWV 601, a work in which Bach, remarkably, repeats the Abgesang as well as the Stollen of the hymn tune, thereby approximating the binary form (AABB) of a movement from a Baroque dance suite. Wolff concludes that this entry is a fair copy rather than a composing score, a circumstance that suggests to him, quite logically, that the piece existed before the *Orgelbüchlein* was begun (p. 39). Yet nowhere does he state that a different, unquestionably earlier version of this work is also extant, namely, the version of "Herr Christ" found in the so-called Neumeister Collection of organ chorales from the Bach circle. This is a baffling omission on Wolff's part, since it was he who discovered and authenticated the Neumeister chorales in the first place. By comparing the two versions, one sees that Bach's original concept was shorter (no repeat of the Abgesang) and simpler (no passing tones added to the chorale melody in measures 2 and 9).[4]

Wolff's comments on the famous New Year's chorale "Das alte Jahr vergangen ist" ("The old year has passed"), BWV 614, also give pause. This exceedingly chromatic and poignant work, in which the hymn tune appears profusely ornamented in the soprano voice, was a favorite of such early romantics as Felix Mendelssohn and Robert Schumann, and it was transcribed for piano by Franz Liszt's pupil Carl Tausig. Writing around 1840, in a passage from his *Kompositionslehre*, the theorist Adolph Bernhard Marx claimed that the soprano line gives the impression less of a cantus firmus than as a kind of rhapsody to be appreciated on its own terms.[5] In 1831, the conductor Johann Nepomuk Schelble published a four-hand piano arrangement of the piece in a collection titled *VI VARIERTE CHORÄLE für die Orgel von J. S. Bach für das Pianoforte zu vier Händen eingerichtet.*[6] Nowhere in the print itself is Schelble named as the transcriber, but he is so named in the thematic catalogue of Bach's oeuvre prepared by the nineteenth-century baritone Franz Hauser, who worked on that massive tome for over fifty years of his long life.[7] Corroborating evidence is provided by a review I very recently came across of Henri Bertini's four-hand arrangement of Bach's Well-Tempered Clavier. Published in 1843 and authored by the composer Bertold Damcke, the review claims that Schelble's four-hand arrangements of "several chorale preludes" by Bach were the first such arrangements of Bach's keyboard works ever undertaken.[8] It bears mentioning that Marx, Schelble, and Hauser all belonged to Mendelssohn's inner circle.

According to Wolff (p. 42)—and this is more to the point—Bach "modifies the quatrain structure" of the chorale text in the *Orgelbüchlein* setting of "Das alte Jahr" by restating its first and last lines, "thus lengthening the song and its setting." But what Wolff really means—because there is no sung chorale text—is that Bach writes six rather than the expected four musical phrases by immediately repeating the first phrase, in a significantly varied guise, and by adding a phrase at the very end, resulting in the musical form of AABCDE. Wolff reasons that Bach adopted this procedure to (1) "fill the page in the autograph manuscript" and (2) emphasize the third line of the first stanza, with its mention of the "great danger" of the old year, even if the text's overall message is gratitude to Christ for deliverance from that danger.

Both of these points beg to be qualified. To begin with the latter, by claiming that the restatements of the first and fourth lines of the implied text actually emphasize the *third* line, Wolff must be alluding to the chromatic eighth-note motive that accompanies or embellishes every one of the six phrases of the hymn tune, and that obviously serves as a metaphor for danger. Making the piece longer simply allows for more statements of the motive. As to Wolff's former point, he seems to suggest that Bach's other reason for expanding the work from four to six phrases was to use all the available space on that page of the autograph, as if Bach would normally have set the melody with only four phrases. In actuality, though, all four of Bach's settings of this hymn, which include the four-part harmonizations BWV 288 and 289 and the Neumeister chorale BWV 1091, follow this same six-phrase scheme. This is also how the melody was sung in churches throughout Thuringia, according to contemporary hymnals.[9] Bach, therefore, knew and arranged this most unusual chorale—another anomaly is the modal switch from Dorian to Phrygian between the last two phrases—as containing six musical phrases, with the first and last lines of each verse repeated.[10]

With all due respect, I must also take issue with Wolff's contention, quoted earlier, that Bach entered the titles of all 164 chorales into the autograph manuscript before inscribing a single note of music. In the case of the Christmas chorale "Puer natus in Bethlehem," BWV 603, whose last two bars spilled onto the top of the facing page in the autograph, this is almost certainly incorrect.[11] Bach's practice in this section of the manuscript was to begin the chorale titles in the upper left corner of the page. But the title that was entered on the facing page here, "Lob sei Gott in des Himmels Thron," is conspicuously centered, thus avoiding any overlap with the two measures of "Puer natus." One can only conclude that the complete musical text of "Puer natus" had already been entered.

||

The second book I will refer to is *Bach's Feet: The Organ Pedals in European Culture*. Authored by David Yearsley and published in 2012 by Cambridge University Press, this provocative and elegantly written study adds new dimensions to our understanding of a wide range of organ compositions by J. S. Bach. Take, for instance, the six Trio Sonatas, BWV 525–530, a collection that might be thought of, using Yearsley's terminology, as conceived for three voices but for four limbs. In a chapter titled "Inventing the organist's feet," Yearsley illuminates the "virtuosic independence of hands and feet" in these sublime masterpieces, choosing as a case study the last movement of the first sonata (E-flat major). Its music strikes him as "a flamboyant exercise in see-sawing between ever-decreasing intervals" (p. 65), since the main theme begins with leaps, successively, of an octave, a seventh, a sixth, a fifth, a fourth, and a third. Yearsley also detects something of Bach's sense of humor in how the two halves of this binary form conclude (p. 67):

> The relaxation of the cadence is one of physical relief and musical contrast: the intervallic closeness and technical ease come in humorous contrast to the bawdy back and forth so prevalent up to this point. The rustic stomping at either end of the pedalboard has given way to the refinements of polite conversation, as if to say it could have all been made this easy, but, of course, was not. Not even the typical octave leap is asked for in the pedal when the actual cadence finally comes: all is contained and controlled, knees together, grin suppressed.

Earlier in this chapter (p. 62), Yearsley quotes and paraphrases what Bach's son Carl Philipp Emanuel had to say about these pieces, and then provides some trenchant thoughts of his own:

> Other Bach devotees praised the timeless modernity of the trios; Carl Philipp Emanuel wrote that they "are written in such *galant* style that they still sound very good, and never grow old, but on the contrary will outlive all revolutions of fashion in music." He also cites the collection as the crowning illustration of the importance of the pedals in organ playing and Bach's mastery of them: the trios are stylistically timeless, and so technically ambitious that their difficulty will not

be surpassed even by flashier "modern" pieces. But for all their conversational refinement and gallant finesse, the relentlessness of the pitfalls is unmatched, the slightest hitch is noticed, the disturbance of the flow marked by the player's body and the listener's ear. Things can go wrong immediately and irrevocably as in no other genre: it is impossible to fake your way through a trio sonata movement.

As far as the technical difficulty of Bach's trio sonatas is concerned, these sentiments were shared wholeheartedly by the nineteenth-century Leipzig organist Hermann Schellenberg. In a review of the first two volumes of the Peters edition of Bach's complete organ works, Schellenberg offered the following remarks, referring to the early Bach biographer Johann Nikolaus Forkel and to an edition of the trio sonatas by Hans Georg Nägeli that had appeared in 1827 under the title *Praktische Orgelschule*:

> The first volume contains the six sonatas for two manuals and pedals, the famous Passacaille [BWV 582], and a Pastorale [BWV 590]. According to Forkel, Bach wrote the sonatas for his eldest son Friedemann, to prepare him to become a great organist, which later on he did become. The Nägeli edition is titled *Orgelschule*. These works do constitute their own school, but in no way for the education of the beginner, as many still erroneously believe, for the music is not suitable for that purpose. Rather, the sonatas are intended for advanced organists, to raise their proficiency to even greater levels, because there is nothing more difficult on the organ, or that requires more skill, than trio playing. Thus, Bach's trio sonatas constitute a school for *master* organists.[12]

Schellenberg's comments had been anticipated in more specific terms by the composer Heinrich Birnbach, who, in a review of the *Praktische Orgelschule* published in 1828, ventured that

> because Sebastian Bach treats not only both manuals but also the pedals in the same elaborate manner, which makes [the sonatas]

Studies and Discoveries

very difficult to perform, they can be recommended only to those organists who have already achieved a significant level of proficiency and who, in order to tread in the footsteps of this great master, are striving for perfection.[13]

By writing that "it is impossible to fake your way through a trio sonata movement," Yearsley knows of what he speaks, for he is not just the most gifted prosaist in Bach scholarship today but also a virtuoso organist who has recorded all six of Bach's trio sonatas.[14] He has followed up these discs with one containing his own transcription of the second movement of the trio sonata from Bach's Musical Offering, BWV 1079, an adaptation described in the liner notes as both "limb-stretching" and "mind-bending."[15] Organists have for centuries been performing (and recording) the six-voice ricercar from this collection,[16] but Yearsley's recording affords a rare opportunity to hear a movement of this trio sonata played on the organ.

Before continuing with Yearsley's book, I would like to briefly consider a more historical matter involving the reception of the trio sonata from the Musical Offering. The matter came to light in 2003 while I was doing some research in Vienna on Johannes Brahms's Bach reception. I discovered there, in the archives of the Gesellschaft für Musikfreunde, a most interesting musical example inscribed by Brahms into his copy of Philipp Spitta's Bach biography (*Nachlass* Brahms, 3037/203).[17] At issue was Spitta's claim, found on page 675 of volume 2 of his study, that the main theme of the Musical Offering—a melody famously conceived by King Frederick the Great—was essentially absent from the opening "Largo" movement of the trio sonata, except for how all three parts (flute, violin, and continuo) emphasize the "characteristic" interval of the descending seventh: "Das Largo beschäftigt sich mit dem Thema noch nicht ernstlich, sondern praeludirt gleichsam nur über den charakteristischen Septimenschritt desselben (s. Takt 4 im Continuo, T. 13 und 14 in Flöte und Violine u. s. w.)." Brahms demurred by crossing out the second clause of this sentence, entering at the bottom of the page the first four measures of the continuo line, and marking with an "x" the first note of measure 1, the first note of measure 2,

Example 1.1. Trio sonata from the Musical Offering, BWV 1079, first movement, continuo part, measures 1–4, as annotated by Johannes Brahms

the third note of measure 3, and the first and third notes of measure 4 (see Example 1.1). These notes are the same as the first five pitches of the royal theme, which shows that the entire first phrase of the melody is present, however embellished.

Brahms had acquired an edition of the Musical Offering decades earlier, in his early twenties, and in that source he similarly annotated the outlining of the royal theme that takes place in the concluding perpetual canon (*Canone perpetuo*).[18] To judge from a letter he wrote to Clara Schumann at the end of 1855, Brahms's perusal of this score also reminded him of the third movement of Robert Schumann's Second Symphony, where Schumann alludes to the flute and violin theme (not to be confused with the "royal" theme) of the first movement of the trio sonata from the Musical Offering.[19] In that missive, after telling Clara that no other movement from any of her husband's four symphonies so enthralled him—and positing that only a German could have written such an Adagio—Brahms pointed out to her the "reminiscence" of Bach's theme within it, wondering if she too was aware of the connection.

To return to Yearsley's book, in a chapter that likens organ pedaling to walking ("Walking towards perfection: pedal solos and cycles"), he discusses in some detail the great Passacaglia in C Minor, BWV 582. This work is unquestionably the pinnacle of ostinato-bass composition for keyboard instruments in the Baroque era. One sees already in its opening bars two features that distinguish it from the organ passacaglias and chaconnes of Bach's German predecessors: the *pedaliter* ostinato bass is eight bars rather than four bars long, and it is stated at the outset entirely on its own.[20] Moreover, the piece ends, like no other ostinato bass by an earlier composer, with a full-fledged fugue on the first half of the ostinato theme. According to Yearsley (pp. 143–45), the way in which the pedal line

Studies and Discoveries

evolves is to be understood as Bach's transformation of the passacaglia as a musical genre: the feet initially seem to accept their supporting role as a harmonic basis for manual variation, but the fugue "turns the piece into a manifesto of pedal independence." While the listener may appreciate the "genre-busting intelligence, the contrapuntal acumen, the endless capacity for variation and invention above an ostinato pattern," the performer experiences the work as a "long crescendo of the body, pursuing greater rates of speed and higher levels of physical activity."

Yearsley considers Bach one of the most famous walkers in history, primarily, but by no means exclusively, because of the latter's legendary hike (two hundred miles each way) from Arnstadt to Lübeck and back in the fall and winter of 1705–1706. Twenty years old at the time, Bach seems to have made the journey both to study under the venerable Dietrich Buxtehude and to attend the Advent *Abendmusiken* performances at Buxtehude's church.[21] Having "comprehended one thing and another about his art" during his three months in Lübeck—and no doubt having improved his pedal technique under Buxtehude's tutelage—Bach trudged back to Arnstadt during some of the darkest, coldest, and snowiest days of the year.[22] Did he, as Yearsley wants us to imagine, walk pedal passages along the way, "his feet improvising solos and chaconnes as they carried him across the countryside"? After all, Felix Mendelssohn "walked nothing but pedal passages" in the streets of Leipzig over a century later as he feverishly practiced there for an all-Bach recital, one that included, coincidentally enough, Bach's C-minor passacaglia.[23] No one who has written a passacaglia since Bach has escaped the influence of this early masterpiece. This goes for Mendelssohn himself, in the case of his own youthful Passacaglia in C Minor for organ, and for Mendelssohn's friend A. B. Marx, whose *Kompositionslehre* contains a fragmentary, untitled example of the genre, also in C minor.[24]

Bach must have brought back with him from Lübeck some newly prepared music manuscripts of organ compositions by Buxtehude, and there is scarcely no better candidate for such a work than Buxtehude's Passacaglia in D Minor. At any rate, this piece has long and correctly been regarded as one of the models for Bach's C-minor passacaglia. Both

Brahms and Spitta hailed it as one of Buxtehude's finest works in any genre or for any medium, instrumental or vocal.[25] A slightly earlier devotee of Buxtehude's passacaglia was the Leipzig organist and bibliophile Carl Ferdinand Becker. Becker also owned the only manuscript of the work known to have survived, a source penned by Bach's older brother Johann Christoph and found in the anthology known as the Andreas Bach Book. In an essay published in 1840, he described the music in these terms:

> As was normally the case, the ostinato theme consists of four measures, and it is stated twenty-eight times, but in the most manifold of ways. The ostinato is, like the uppermost voice, also very singable, and it is maintained by the composer through the entire work.
>
> It certainly would have been easy for the composer to state all these variations in the same key—D minor—but he stays in this key for only the first seven variations before modulating to the relative major—F major—and proceeding with seven more variations in that key. Then he once again switches to a new key—A minor—in which he varies the theme seven more times. Following that, the master returns to the tonic key with, just as in the previous sections, seven more variations, finally bringing the piece to an end.[26]

Had Becker been somewhat more inclined toward numerology, he might have stated that the four-bar ostinato contains exactly seven notes and that four times seven equals the total number of variations.

Speaking of Johannes Brahms, no other great composer in music history so cherished the music of the past. Brahms frequently modeled his compositions after such Baroque masters as Bach (the composer he most revered) and Heinrich Schütz, and even after such Renaissance composers as Palestrina. With regard to Buxtehude, as Raymond Knapp has convincingly shown, one of the exemplars for the passacaglia-finale of Brahms's Fourth Symphony is Buxtehude's Chaconne in E Minor for organ.[27] I would propose that Brahms likewise appropriated Buxtehude's Passacaglia in D Minor as a compositional model for the passacaglia-finale of his Variations on a Theme by Haydn, Op. 56. The evidence has

Studies and Discoveries

to do with how each composer, in dramatic fashion, employs thick chords set to an iambic rhythm for exactly two successive statements of his ostinato theme. Buxtehude does so in measures 63–69 (the opening bars of the A-minor section of his passacaglia), and Brahms does so in measures 21–30. A closer comparison between the two works might suggest further borrowings.[28]

To return once again to Yearsley's monograph, in a chapter titled "The pedal in the cosmopolitan age of travel," the author makes a compelling case for the Fugue in C Major, BWV 547/2, as a "magisterial polyphonic oration" (p. 183), one that, in contrast to the cheap tricks practiced by such charlatan performers as "Abt" Vogler, revealed to music lovers of the eighteenth century the "true sublimity" of the organ. Evidently one of Bach's last organ fugues to survive, this fugue is also one of his most complex, with the subject appearing roughly fifty times in various polyphonic guises.[29] Remarkably, the pedals are not utilized until about two-thirds of the way through, and their appearance is prefaced by a virtual, *manualiter* pedal point (mm. 47–48). Yearsley's account of how Bach transforms the fugue at this critical juncture from *manualiter* to *pedaliter* (pp. 183–86) is worth quoting in full:

> The drawn-out, two-bar pedal point (without the feet!) under broken chords that follows the combination of the subject with its melodic inversion would normally portend the end of a fugue. But for the lack of a pedal entrance, the harmonic intensity and contrapuntal density would have been sufficient to close out the fugue without loss of honor to the composer or disappointment to learned listeners. Indeed, if one were to truncate BWV 547/2 and come to a cadence after this pedal point and before the eventual entrance of the pedal itself, the fugue could already have taken its place among the most erudite examples from *The Well-Tempered Clavier*. But the epic silence of the pedal seems to get louder and louder as the artifice unfolds at great length in the hands.
>
> Rather than a counterintuitive *manualiter* conclusion, the pedalless pedal point promises something far more dramatic than what

has been heard so far in this already eventful fugue. A flurry of *stretto* at the close of the pedal point in the manuals in bar 48 at last ushers in the momentous pedal entrance, which, when it comes, does so in augmentation, with the hands above treating the subject in *rectus* and *inversus*. The pedal announces itself with a depth and regal pace that only the organ, with its gravity and unlimited sustaining power, can attain: this fifth voice is not music for the little finger, but for the proudest of feet. With the arrival of the pedal Bach takes the already complicated argument to a new level of sonic and contrapuntal profundity, beyond and beneath the riches of the *manualiter* fugue that precedes the thunderous entry of the previously absent bass. The theatricality of this entry derives not only from the artfully planned staging of the crux to this contrapuntal tour-de-force, but from the larger philosophical statement the fugue makes about the pedals themselves and their defining contribution to the organ's unique status. A self-sufficient manual fugue is transformed by the arrival of the pedal into a demonstration of what lies at the true foundation of organ polyphony and what gives the instrument its distinctive rhetorical and contrapuntal power.

One issue raised by this brilliant analysis is Bach's predilection for writing longer preludes and fugues for the organ than for other keyboard instruments. For example, the Fugue in C Major, as Yearsley implies, lasts about four minutes, while a fugue from the Well-Tempered Clavier typically lasts (according to my own tally) between two and three minutes. When the preludes to these fugues are factored into the equation, the same pattern obtains: the prelude to the C-major organ fugue (BWV 547/1), like the fugue, lasts about four minutes, while the preludes to the fugues from the Well-Tempered Clavier, like the fugues from that collection, typically last between two and three minutes. In this context, it bears pointing out that the C-major prelude and fugue was first published in 1812 as part of a collection—assembled almost certainly not by Bach himself but by his pupil J. P. Kirnberger—known as the Six "Great" Preludes and Fugues for organ, BWV 543–548.[30] The moniker surely refers to the large size of these works, three of which are considerably longer even than the C major, and it probably served to distinguish these pieces specifically from the preludes and fugues of the Well-Tempered Clavier, which at the time were the best-known preludes and fugues of any kind by Bach or anyone else. Bach's tendency to write longer preludes and fugues for the organ may be seen as his attempt to match the vast dimensions of the instrument and its vast, churchly surroundings.

The Six Great were published as a set nine different times between 1812 and 1852, making them by far the most widely circulated of any of Bach's organ works during this period. They were first published in Vienna, and according to the above-mentioned review by Bertold Damcke, they had even become known a few decades later as Bach's "Viennese" preludes and fugues for organ. More importantly, Damcke mentions a four-hand piano transcription of all six works that had been undertaken by one of J. N. Schelble's pupils, prepared under Schelble's supervision, and published in Frankfurt, as a kind of companion to Schelble's four-hand transcriptions of organ chorales by Bach.[31] It is important to realize in this connection that Schelble died in 1837. Damcke does not cite the pupil by name, but the only real candidate is Carl Voigt (1808–1879), who studied with Schelble in the 1830s and who in 1834 published his four-hand transcription of the Six Great with the Frankfurt house of G. H. Hedler.[32] Voigt's print is titled *Sechs Praeludien und Fugen für die Orgel von Johann Sebastian Bach eingerichtet für das Pianoforte zu vier Händen von Carl Voigt.*

Another pupil of Schelble's who transcribed the Six Great in this manner was Franz Xaver Gleichauf (1801–1856). Gleichauf worked as a music teacher in Frankfurt and freelanced as a music copyist; indeed, he worked in the latter capacity for Felix Mendelssohn.[33] His transcriptions of the Six Great are found in the collection *Orgel-Compositionen von Johann Sebastian Bach für Pianoforte zu 4 Händen arrangirt von F. X. Gleichauf.* Issued without a date by the Leipzig house of C. F. Peters, this anthology contains nine additional free organ works by Bach arranged for four hands.[34]

I will address a number of additional issues in the list below. Since they mostly pertain to specific works as discussed by Yearsley, I will follow the order of the Bach-Werke-Verzeichnis.

THE AFTERLIFE OF BACH'S ORGAN WORKS

1. Toccata and Fugue in D Minor ("Dorian"), BWV 538. Yearsley does not actually discuss this work, but he provides a musical example (p. 253) that brings this fugue to mind. The example illustrates a rather ostentatious pedal line from a *Preludio pro Organo pleno* by Bach's pupil Johann Christian Kittel.[35] Replete with arpeggios and tremolo thirds for the feet, the passage also features a pedal trill toward the end that lasts for five bars, just as Bach includes one lasting for six bars toward the end of the "Dorian" fugue (mm. 179–84). Given the rarity of long pedal trills in organ music—for Bach, it is a unique instance—one can easily believe that Kittel was striving to emulate his teacher. Kittel is assumed to have known this fugue (and, by implication, to have studied it with Bach) on the basis of extant manuscript copies of both the fugue and toccata made by two of his pupils.[36] One of these sources bears the inscription "bey der Probe der großen Orgel in Cassel von S. Bach gespielt," documenting that Bach played the work when in 1732 he examined a newly rebuilt organ in the city of Kassel.[37] This was as far westward as Bach ever ventured.

2. Toccata in F Major, BWV 540/1. When, in 1844, the German virtuoso Adolph Friedrich Hesse played this work in Paris for the dedication of the new Daublaine-Callinet organ at St. Eustache, he was lauded by such critics as Hector Berlioz as "a giant who plays with his feet that which would have put the playing of others' hands to shame" (quoted by Yearsley on p. 234). According to various eyewitness accounts, as many as eight to ten thousand listeners were present, but Yearsley is wisely skeptical of these outlandish numbers. He is mistaken, however, in claiming that Hesse's rendition of the toccata was compromised by a pedalboard whose top note was middle C. Yes, the familiar, original version of the piece frequently goes higher than this pitch in the pedals, but that version would not appear in print until 1845, in volume 3 of the Peters edition of Bach's complete organ works.[38] Hesse no doubt performed the toccata according to an earlier edition by Peters, published between 1832 and 1834, where the

Studies and Discoveries

pedal line never ascends above middle C.[39] Confusingly enough, that version of the toccata is based on a manuscript in the hand of the Bach pupil Johann Tobias Krebs, who took Bach's original version and rewrote its pedal line to fit a standard C–c′ compass. In other words, Bach's original version contained all the high pedal notes.

3. Fantasy and Fugue in G Minor, BWV 542. In this fugue, Bach makes extraordinary demands on the performer, both *pedaliter* and *manualiter*. Both movements are also unequivocal masterpieces of musical composition. The work was first published around 1833, and shortly thereafter virtuosi such as the above-mentioned A. F. Hesse began to showcase it on their recitals. As Yearsley amusingly tells the story (p. 236), Hesse, to his dismay, also witnessed in 1851 a botched performance of the fugue at London's Crystal Palace, courtesy of a local organ duo who rendered the movement in the "English" manner, with one player taking the manual voices and the other sneakily adding the pedal part with one or both of his hands. Evidently, the latter player had entered a measure early and continued to be out of sync with his partner for a full eight bars before the performance completely broke down.

Hermann Schellenberg had a rather different idea about what constitutes an organ duo, as his arrangement of the fantasy and fugue for "four hands and double pedal" attests. He and C. F. Becker (his teacher) played the arrangement on a recital given by Schellenberg in October 1845 at Leipzig's Nicolaikirche, much to the delight of the local critics.[40] Schellenberg, who is also responsible for a four-hand piano transcription of the work, must have been inspired by Becker's organ-duet arrangement of the six-voice ricercar from Bach's Musical Offering, which the two had played together a year earlier on one of Becker's recitals at the same church.[41]

Schellenberg's interest in the fantasy and fugue was doubtless piqued when he heard Hesse play it during the latter's visit to Leipzig in January 1845.[42]

4. Fugue in A Minor, BWV 543/2. Yearsley cites this fugue as "one of Bach's greatest" (p. 209) but in what sense is not entirely clear. There are many keyboard fugues by Bach, especially ones with simpler, more compact subjects (like the C-major fugue for organ discussed above), that display more contrapuntal rigor and refinement. The A-minor, however, is undeniably one of Bach's "greatest" pedal showpieces, and it is presumably this fact that Yearsley is alluding to, especially since his context is Felix Mendelssohn's use of the fugue for this very purpose.

The virtuosity of the pedal line is not limited to the flashy pedal solo at the end. Rather, it is rooted in the subject itself, a gigue-like theme in perpetual motion (à la Vivaldi) that consumes a good half of the Baroque pedalboard. Anyone who plays this fugue knows that one of the most difficult passages occurs early on, at the end of the opening exposition, where the texture has thickened from one to four voices and where the feet are finally engaged. By saving the pedal statement for last—as is also the case in the even more technically demanding G-minor fugue just discussed—Bach delays what is a moment of truth for the performer: the feet are finally required to execute the same fast, long, and wide-ranging theme as the hands, simultaneously with three different countermelodies.[43] Enhancing this sense of drama, or even theater (to borrow from Yearsley's terminology), is the potential for a marked contrast in timbre, and possibly volume as well, between the pedal part and the three manual voices, since the pedals typically govern their own division of the pipe organ. I would suggest that Bach was keenly aware of these phenomena in writing for the organ. This would help explain why (on the basis of my own findings) in roughly three-fourths of his organ fugues he reserves the pedal statement for last. Of course, there is something inherently satisfying—a certain gravitas—about any fugal exposition that concludes with the subject in the bass register, especially if the theme has descended, one voice at a time, from top to bottom. But this particular approach to fugal composition seems not as pronounced in Bach's fugues for other keyboard instruments. For example, a smaller percentage of the fugues from the Well-Tempered Clavier, roughly three-fifths, exhibit the procedure. In eight fugues from that collection (all from Book 2), Bach even *begins* with the subject in the bass, which is a tack he never takes in a proper, *pedaliter* fugue for the organ.

5. **Fugue in E-flat Major, BWV 552/2.** Yearsley contends that this fugue was the most popular Bach fugue among English organists of the early nineteenth century "perhaps because it had been the only *pedaliter* fugue published during Bach's lifetime, but more likely still because it was widely available in England after its publication in London in 1823" (pp. 201–2). Surely another reason, however, is that the main subject of the fugue—it is a double fugue with three subjects, a unique occurrence in Bach—is melodically identical to the first phrase of the hymn tune "St. Anne," which, as sung to the text "O God, Our Help in Ages Past," had by the early 1800s become one of the most beloved of all Anglican hymns. Indeed, the resemblance was pointed out quite explicitly in an English edition of 1827 containing Benjamin Jacobs's *manualiter* duet arrangement.[44] The rather long-winded title of this print reads as follows: *A Grand Fugue by John Sebastian Bach, in Three Movements and on Three Subjects, the Principal Theme being the first Four Bars of St Ann's Psalm Tune, Arranged for Two Performers on the Organ or Pianoforte . . . by B. Jacob.* English speakers have known the fugue by the nickname of "St. Anne" for almost two centuries now.

In typical fashion for Bach, the pedal statement of the main subject in the opening exposition is saved for last. In fact, the feet have the last word altogether, for the very last statement of the main subject (mm. 114–15) is also played *pedaliter.* The English organist Harvey Grace, writing around 1920, wondered if there was a better pedal entry anywhere in Bach's organ works.[45] Grace was less enthusiastic about the E-flat prelude, complaining that the second theme was overly repetitive, that the fugal treatment of the third theme was harmonically monotonous, and that the modulation at measures

174–77 from C minor to E-flat major, which takes place as the final statement of the first theme begins, was a bit jarring.

6. Passacaglia in C Minor, BWV 582. Yearsley is especially perceptive about this piece, Bach's only ostinato-bass composition for the organ. Yet he fails to mention its status as one of the longest "continuous" works of the whole Baroque era. Nor does he wonder why Bach chose to call the work a "passacaglia" rather than a "chaconne." To address the first issue, Bach's passacaglia comprises around thirteen or fourteen minutes of *continuous* music. There may be Baroque variation sets that last longer and are even more difficult to play—most notably, Bach's Goldberg Variations—but in those works the player at least has brief resting points from one variation to the next.[46] Bach's passacaglia affords no such breaks. In designating the piece as a "passacaglia," Bach may have been bowing to a tradition established by his French and German predecessors, whereby, as Peter Williams put it in reference to André Raison and Dietrich Buxtehude, "passacaglias had a simple upbeat, chaconnes not."[47] Johann Pachelbel, another huge influence on the young Bach, might also be mentioned in this connection. Pachelbel left behind five ostinato works for keyboard. All of them are designated as "chaconnes," and their themes all start on the downbeat.[48]

7. Wir glauben all an einen Gott, BWV 680. According to Yearsley (p. 107), the quasi-ostinato pedal theme of this popular work "provides one of the clearest evocations of a walker's attitude" to be found in any of Bach's pedal parts. The player quite literally walks up the top half of the pedalboard and then, going twice as fast, back down again. Yearsley, though, nowhere mentions that English speakers since around 1845 have actually known this piece by an ambulatory nickname, that being "The Giant Fugue." Once upon a time, the striding pedal theme suggested "a giant ascending the stairs, who, having arrived at the top, tumbles and bumps his way down to the bottom every time."[49] Fanciful nonsense, to be sure.

Studies and Discoveries

III

I will now turn my attention to a unique source that sheds light on the reception of Bach's organ music in nineteenth-century Germany. It is housed today at the Riemenschneider Bach Institute (Baldwin Wallace University) in Berea, Ohio.[50] The source consists of two early editions of Bach's free organ works owned by the organist and editor Wilhelm Rust. Rust chose to bind the two editions together to form a miscellany, which he titled "Orgelcompositionen von J. S. Bach." The contents are, in the order of their appearance, A. B. Marx's edition of the first movement of the Pastorale in F Major, BWV 590, published in 1825 as a supplement to the *Berliner Allgemeine Musikalische Zeitung*; and the three volumes of *Johann Sebastian Bach's noch wenig bekannte Orgelcompositionen*, a collection of eight Bach works edited by Marx and Felix Mendelssohn and published in 1833 by Breitkopf & Härtel.[51] Rust also provided a table of contents in which he listed the individual compositions as follows: *Pastorella in f dur* [BWV 590/1], *Praeludium in a moll* [BWV 569], *Praeludium und Fuge in e dur* [BWV 566], *Praeludium und Fuge in d moll* [BWV 539], *Fantasia in g moll* [BWV 542/1], *Praeludium und Fuge in g dur* [BWV 550], *Praeludium und Fuge in d dur* [BWV 532], *Praeludium und Fuge in e moll* [BWV 533], *Fuge in g moll* [BWV 542/2], and *Fantasia in d moll* [BWV 565]. The last page of the source contains Rust's handwritten organ registrations for various sacred vocal works that he must have accompanied, including oratorios by Handel (*Samson, Joshua*, and *Messiah*) and Mendelssohn (*Elijah*) as well as unspecified compositions by Rossini and Cherubini.

Born in Dessau in 1822, Rust began his career in Hungary, where he served as a music tutor to a noble family.[52] From 1849 to 1878 he worked in Berlin, becoming organist at the Lukaskirche in 1861 and directing the city's Bach-Verein from 1862 to 1875. In 1878, he was appointed organist of the Thomaskirche in Leipzig, and in 1880 he became the cantor of the church—the same position held by Bach over a century earlier—remaining in that post until his death in Leipzig in 1892. In addition to his activities as a performer, conductor, and teacher, Rust was a driving force behind the Bachgesellschaft edition of Bach's complete works (hereafter cited as BG), the first truly complete edition of the composer's oeuvre ever attempted. He edited twenty-six of the forty-five volumes—many more than anyone else—and in 1858 became editor-in-chief. One of the volumes of the BG edited by Rust is volume 15 (*Orgelwerke. Band 1*), published in 1867, which contains twenty-seven of Bach's free organ works, including all of those in the Marx-Mendelssohn edition except BWV 550 and 569. As numerous references in his critical notes evince, Rust relied heavily on the Marx-Mendelssohn edition in preparing BG 15.

The Riemenschneider miscellany contains literally hundreds of markings in Rust's hand. By far the most common of these are instructions to change manuals or use two different manuals simultaneously. For example, the movement from the *Pastorella*, more commonly known as the Pastorale in F Major (BWV 590), is prescribed for three manuals, with the hands jumping from one manual to the next and split virtually the entire time. Rust was extremely fond of both of these techniques, however inauthentic. Rust also entered a smattering of registration indications and a few fingerings as well, and he corrected certain typographical errors.[53] In addition, he altered the triplet figuration in measures 8–9 of the Toccata in D Minor, BWV 565 (designated by Rust in his table of contents as a "Fantasia"), by transposing the third note of every triplet up an octave. Presumably, he reasoned that Bach would have written the passage this way if his manual compass had extended up to e′′′. No such alteration is to be found in BG 15, but Rust's rewriting here is a reminder of his occasionally unscrupulous editorial practices.[54] I will focus my discussion on a series of extraordinary markings entered by Rust into the scores of the Prelude in D Minor, BWV 539/1, and the Fantasy in G Minor, BWV 542/1. In the former instance, Rust added his own rudimentary pedal part; in the latter, he made numerous annotations that reveal the source to be a conceptual draft for his orchestral transcription of the work.[55] Rust prepared his orchestration in 1867, the same year that BG 15 appeared.

While the Prelude in D Minor is for manuals only, the fugue with which it is paired (a transcription from the Sonata in G Minor for Solo Violin, BWV 1001) is a *pedaliter* movement. Rust may therefore have composed his own pedal part for the prelude because of this discrepancy. Surely,

Studies and Discoveries

though, like certain contemporaries of his, Rust also found the prelude somewhat deficient because it lacks a pedal part. Indeed, of the twenty-eight free organ preludes listed in the Bach-Werke-Verzeichnis, this is the only pedal-less specimen. In editing the prelude for BG 15, Rust voiced no such concerns—the movement is printed there in the standard version for manuals only—but the Leipzig organists C. F. Becker and Hermann Schellenberg certainly did so in their reviews of volume 3 of the Peters edition of Bach's complete organ works, published, respectively, in 1845 and 1846.[56] Becker maintained that no organist would have prefaced a *pedaliter* fugue with a *manualiter* prelude and that no connoisseur of the organ would have voluntarily dispensed with a pedal part in composing for the instrument. Echoing his teacher Becker but speaking more directly to the issues, Schellenberg opined that the prelude was without a doubt written for harpsichord and that Bach would never have completely bypassed the use of pedal in writing an organ work.

The page from the Riemenschneider score containing the D-minor prelude is reproduced in Figure 1.1. In addition to inserting his own pedal part, Rust prescribed the use of two manuals, indicated by the Roman numerals "I" and "II."[57] He prescribed frequent manual changes as well. Only the primary manual is accompanied by the pedals, which suggests that it is to be played with a relatively full registration. Musical common sense leads to the same conclusion, especially considering that the primary manual is used for the two ritornello statements at the beginning (mm. 1–6) and end (mm. 34–39). Whereas the former statement involves a change to the secondary manual three bars in, at the harmonic shift toward the subdominant, the latter statement does not, probably by accident. Consequently, the pedal part there lasts about a bar longer. The pedal part on the whole consists either of pedal points or, starting in measure 17, pairs of quarter notes. These quarter notes may lend rhythmic vitality, but they also create parallel octaves with the tenor voice (E–F) between measures 16 and 17 and parallel fifths with the alto (D/A and E/B) between measures 21 and 22. More curious than infelicitous, and prefaced by a deceptive cadence on the VI chord, the final cadence is to be rendered, rather like an echo, on the secondary manual (and, therefore, without pedal).

Figure 1.1. Prelude in D Minor, BWV 539/1, as arranged by Wilhelm Rust (Riemenschneider Bach Institute, Baldwin Wallace University)

Despite its quirks and shortcomings, Rust's adaptation makes for an interesting alternative to the original. Those interested in playing it are referred to Example 1.2, which presents my own performing edition. For obvious musical reasons, I have extended the pedal part in two passages (see mm. 22–24 and 41–42), and I have taken certain liberties to facilitate the manual changes at measures 7 and 15. I have also freely altered measures 42–43 for a more convincing conclusion.

The score of the Fantasy in G Minor begins five pages later in the Marx-Mendelssohn edition. Its three pages, as they appear in the Riemenschneider volume, are reproduced in Figure 1.2a–c. Here, Rust entered three different sets of markings, two aimed at organ performance and a third involving his orchestration of the work. No doubt he was drawn to the G-minor fantasy because of the piece's bold and innovative style. Massive chords—fortified in the first three bars with notes added by Rust himself—alternate with bravura passagework, and nowhere else in Bach's

Studies and Discoveries

Prelude in D Minor, BWV 539/1

Example 1.2. Performing edition (by the author) of Rust's arrangement of the Prelude in D Minor, BWV 539/1

Example 1.2 Continued

Studies and Discoveries

Example 1.2 Continued

Figure 1.2a Fantasy in G Minor, BWV 542/1, measures 1–14, as annotated by Wilhelm Rust (Riemenschneider Bach Institute, Baldwin Wallace University)

output—not even in the so-called Chromatic Fantasy, BWV 903/1—does the composer reach such a threshold of dissonance and chromaticism.

Rust must have played the G-minor fantasy on the organ years before he decided to orchestrate it. We can therefore assume that his first, original set of markings was one of the two made for the sake of organ performance. In one of these sets, the manual divisions of the organ are indicated by the letters "H," "O," and "U," which stand for Hauptwerk, Oberwerk, and, in one instance (top of measure 18), Unterwerk; in the other set, the Roman numerals "I," "II," and "III" are used for the same purpose. To judge from Rust's jottings in measure 25 (= Figure 1.2b, the second page of the Marx-Mendelssohn edition, third system, second bar), where the two "O" markings are positioned directly below or beside the manual voices at the start of the imitative section there, and where the Roman numerals, consequently, look very much like later additions, the original set was the one with the three letters.

Studies and Discoveries 33

Figure 1.2b Fantasy in G Minor, BWV 542/1, measures 15–34, as annotated by Wilhelm Rust (Riemenschneider Bach Institute, Baldwin Wallace University)

These markings clearly exemplify Rust's predilection for changing manuals and playing on two manuals at the same time. They also involve the addition or subtraction of the Hauptwerk-Pedal coupler, as may be seen in measure 20 ("Coppel"), 24 ("weg!"), and 33 ("Coppel"). Observe, too, that in measures 20 and 24 the coupler is engaged or canceled, quite conveniently, where the feet are inactive. In measure 33, however, the device is to be re-engaged in the midst of continuous eighth notes in the pedal line, between the first and second beats of the bar. To facilitate this tricky registration change, Rust altered the second beat in the left hand from a quarter note to an eighth rest followed by an eighth note. Thus, the left hand draws the coupler on the beat and switches to the Hauptwerk on the second half of the beat. At some later point, and perhaps for a different instrument, Rust decided to re-annotate the score by using Roman numerals in place of letters. He probably chose not to add the Roman numerals in measures

Figure 1.2c Fantasy in G Minor, BWV 542/1, measures 35–49, as annotated by Wilhelm Rust (Riemenschneider Bach Institute, Baldwin Wallace University)

4, 6, and 7 to avoid any confusion with the numerous markings that were already in place. The only real musical difference posed by the Roman numerals is the use of two manuals in measures 31–32.

Rust entered a flurry of markings in measures 31–36 (= the last four bars of the second page of the Marx-Mendelssohn edition, in Figure 1.2b, plus the first two bars of the third page, in Figure 1.2c), and they show that he used various manual and registration changes to achieve a lengthy crescendo for this astonishing passage, one in which Bach modulates, via the circle of fifths, from D major all the way to D-flat major. (There is no indication that the swell box is to be employed.) Rust started with the Unterwerk and Oberwerk; then, on the second beat of measure 33, switched the left hand to the Hauptwerk, with the Hauptwerk-Pedal coupler now engaged; then, on the downbeat of measure 35, concluded with both hands on the Hautpwerk, with the Hauptwerk-Pedal coupler still engaged. Bach makes his own crescendo in these six bars as well, by gradually thickening the texture from three to six voices. Rust might be accused of ruining this effect with his addition of quarter notes (both on d′) at the very beginning of the passage, that is, on the second and third beats of measure 31.

The third set of markings made by Rust into the score of the G-minor fantasy shows that he worked off this score in conceiving his orchestration of the work. Rust never published this arrangement, but it survives in a beautifully penned autograph score and an equally beautiful set of (mostly) autograph performing parts. Both sources are housed today at the Bach-Archiv in Leipzig as part of the extensive Sammlung Manfred Gorke.[58] The score is dated December 1867. Ostensibly, therefore, Rust originally intended the orchestration for a performance by the Berlin Bach-Verein, since he was directing that ensemble at the time. Rust chose ⁶⁄₈ as the time signature for his orchestration, versus Bach's use of common time. Thus, the orchestration has roughly twice as many measures.[59]

The first such marking occurs in measures 4–5, where Rust added his own countermelody in the middle staff. Its first half equates roughly to how the cello part reads in measures 7–8 of the orchestration. The tied notes on a′′ added by Rust above the top staff of measure 7 equate to how the flute and oboe parts read in measure 13 of the orchestration.

Rust added a different type of countermelody within the two fugato sections of the fantasy, inscribing it into and above the staff in measures 10–14 and 25–27. It consists mainly of syncopated tied notes and corresponds to how the first and second horn parts read in measures 20–27 and 50–54 of the orchestration. Within the second fugato, Rust made some additional markings. They include (1) the inscription "Viol" found above the top staff of measure 29, on the second half of beat one, exactly where in measure 57 of the orchestration those two sixteenths and the three notes that follow are found in the first violin part;[60] and (2) an added eighth note on g′′ above the top staff at the end of measure 29, on the second half of beat four, that is slurred to the second, third, and fourth sixteenth notes in the alto voice on the next beat, thus forming a four-note motive that corresponds to how the first oboe part reads in measures 58–59, even though the sixteenths there are transposed up an octave and found in the second clarinet part as well.

Additional markings that connect specifically to Rust's orchestration are found in measures 31–43. For the above-mentioned circle-of-fifths passage at measures 31–35, Rust added a descending, stepwise (d′–c′–b♭–a) countermelody above the bottom staff, set to the rhythm of a half note followed by two quarter notes, that equates to how various parts, especially the upper strings, read in measures 61–68 of the orchestration. The countermelody ends with an embellished variant of this rhythm (two tied notes on the pitch a, set as a quarter and an eighth note, followed by an eighth note on the same pitch and four sixteenths in the order d′–f′–a′–d′′) that equates to how the first violin, second violin, and viola parts read in measures 67–68.

The next such markings appear in measures 35–36 (= the first bar of the third page of the Marx-Mendelssohn edition), a passage that anticipates nineteenth-century practice in its use of enharmonic modulation. On the second and third beats of measure 35, Rust made two inscriptions. The upper one, inserted between the bottom two staves, reads "Blech," meaning "Blechblasinstrumente" (or brass instruments); the lower one, entered below the bottom staff, reads "Fag 8," meaning the "Fagott" (or bassoon) playing an octave higher or lower than the pitches notated. Precisely at this juncture in the orchestration (mm. 69–70), the sound is reduced from full orchestra to the brass and woodwinds, with the bassoons playing the pedal line from the organ version an octave higher than notated. Rust made a further inscription on the first beat of the next bar (m. 36), writing "Viol in 8" above the middle staff. Precisely here in the orchestration (m. 71), the upper strings take the thirty-second-note motive assigned to the left hand, with the violas playing an octave lower than the violins. Two beats later in the Riemenschneider score, Rust added three eighth notes of his own composition, two in the top staff on b′ and e′ and one in the middle staff (second half of the beat) on g.[61] In the orchestration (m. 72), these added notes are played, respectively, by the trumpets and all the strings except the contrabass.

Rust's markings in measures 39–43 of the Riemenschneider score also connect to his orchestration. For example, on beats two and three of measure 39, he added two tied notes on d′′′, along with the inscriptions

"Fl" (above the top staff) and "Fag" (between the top two staves). Sure enough, in the orchestration (m. 77) these same tied notes are found in the first flute and first bassoon parts. Observe, too, that the inscription "col Clar" follows the second tied note and that the left-hand quarter note on beat four is marked "Horn." These indications agree with measure 78 of the orchestration. There, the first clarinet part contains the same sixteenths found in the first flute and first bassoon parts, and the third horn part contains, in a passage extending to the downbeat of measure 80, the same material played by the left hand in the organ version.[62]

This "material" is in fact a distinct motive consisting of seven sixteenths, starting off the beat and prefaced by tied notes. Bach treats the motive as a point of imitation between the two hands, and Rust's inscriptions betray an intent to highlight the motive by passing it from one instrument to another. This intent is fully realized in the actual orchestration, where in measures 77–79 the motive is passed from the woodwinds to the third horn and in measures 80–81 from the first violins to the cellos. Both of the statements by the strings correspond to markings made by Rust in measure 40 of the Riemenschneider score, as attested to by the inscriptions "Viol" on beat two (above the top staff) and "Cello" on beat four (below the middle staff).[63]

Rust's markings in measure 41 of the Riemenschneider score feature a stratospheric countermelody written above the top staff on the first three beats. It consists of four eighth notes on d''', $f\sharp''$, g'', and $e\flat'''$, followed by a quarter note on $e\flat'''$, which itself is followed by the inscription "es" (German for the pitch e-flat). The countermelody was never fully realized in the orchestration, but the high e-flats agree with how the top voice of the organ version is duplicated at the upper octave in the first flute part (m. 82). Furthermore, Rust inscribed "unis" below the top staff on beat three, which agrees with how, in the orchestration, the violins and cellos play this passage in unison with the first flute.

Rust made five additional markings in measures 42–43 of the Riemenschneider score. On beat four of measure 42, between the top two staves, he wrote "Pos," and he made the same inscription on beat one of measure 43, between the bottom two staves.[64] The latter marking is followed by a horizontal line extending to beat two, which itself is followed by a quarter rest. "Pos" obviously refers to "Posaune" (or trombone), but the material found here in the alto and tenor voices hardly corresponds to how the trombone parts read in measures 84–85 of the orchestration. Three further markings appear on the second half of beat two of measure 43, in conjunction with the secondary leading-tone diminished-seventh on c-sharp found there: above the top staff Rust inscribed "Viol 1 u[nd] Fl," even though the right-hand flourish here equates only to how the first violin, and not either of the flute parts, reads in measures 85–86 of the orchestration; above the middle staff he wrote "Corno," signifying a passage (for the left hand) that equates to how the third horn reads; and above the bottom staff he inscribed "Fag solo," signifying a passage (for the feet) that equates to how the two bassoon parts read.

To consider a further aspect of Rust's orchestration, the Riemenschneider score reveals that Rust orchestrated the fantasy in a couple of places similar to the free and flamboyant style in which he played the work on the organ. For example, where in measure 4 he changed manuals every beat for the series of thirty-second notes there, in the orchestration he shifted the material, one beat at a time, from one string part to the next. And where in measures 31–35 he created a long crescendo for the circle-of-fifths passage by changing manuals and engaging the Hauptwerk-Pedal coupler, in the orchestration he began pianissimo, minus any upper woodwinds or trombones (but with a pianississimo timpani roll for the first three beats), and then gradually added those instruments while also ramping up the dynamics in general.

Having examined Rust's markings in the Riemenschneider score of the G-minor fantasy, let us consider how his transcription relates to Johannes Brahms. Brahms lurks in the shadows here not just because his personal copy of Rust's BG edition shows that he meticulously studied Bach's use of invertible counterpoint within the two fugato sections of the G-minor fantasy.[65] Rather, the main reason has to do with the fact that, after turning down the job of cantor at the Leipzig Thomaskirche in 1879, following the death of Ernst Friedrich Richter, Brahms recommended his colleague Rust for the post.[66] Rust earned a fine reputation for his work in that exalted position, but not all the residents of the city were happy with him. Certainly not Brahms's dear friend and former pupil Elisabet von Herzogenberg, who, along with her husband, Heinrich, was an ardent champion of Bach's music. Writing to Brahms in the spring of 1881, Elisabet teasingly reported that Rust was causing nothing but vexation with what she considered his tasteless transcriptions of Bach's organ works, including an orchestration of the "G-minor organ fugue" and arrangements for four voices of certain chorale settings: "We are always having fresh trouble and disappointments here. For one thing, Rust is having the G-minor organ fugue, arranged for orchestra, played at St. Thomas's on Palm Sunday. He has also set some chorale preludes for four voices, with the chorale text underlaid throughout. And *you* recommended him to us!!"[67]

As to the identity of these works, we know next to nothing about which organ chorales Rust set; the autograph of his choral arrangement of the organ chorale "Durch Adams Fall ist ganz verderbt," BWV 705, dates from around 1885, which would seem to exclude that piece from consideration.[68] But the "fugue" mentioned by Herzogenberg is undoubtedly the same G-minor *fantasy* currently under discussion. This is made clear by a notice in the *Musikalisches Wochenblatt* for the city of Leipzig that the music performed at the Thomaskirche on Palm Sunday (10 April) in 1881 included an "organ fantasy in G minor by J. S. Bach, orchestrated by W. Rust."[69] It matters not that Herzogenberg referred to the piece as a fugue. The word "fugue," especially in reference to Bach, was commonly used during the nineteenth century for any organ work, as we know, for example, from the letters of Felix Mendelssohn.[70] The genre was simply that common for that instrument. The complete listing from the *Musikalisches Wochenblatt* of the music performed that Palm Sunday at the Thomaskirche reads as follows: "Leipzig. Thomaskirche: 10. April. 'Am See Tiberias,' geistlicher Gesang f. Soli, Chor u. Orch. v. W. Rust. Orgelphantasie in G moll v. J. S. Bach, orchestrirt v. W. Rust. Missa brevis (A dur) f. Orgel v. J. S. Bach." Thus, the selections included, in addition to Rust's orchestration, his oratorio *Am See Tiberias* ("By the Sea of Galilee") and Bach's Mass in A Major, BWV 234. The curious reference to the use of organ for the Bach mass might mean that only organ accompaniment was used; surely it cannot mean that the entire work was rendered as an organ solo. Rust would have conducted professional soloists, the Thomanerchor, members of the Leipzig Gewandhaus orchestra, and Thomasorganist Carl Piutti, who had succeeded Rust at that post in 1880.[71]

Brahms may not have heard Rust's orchestration of the G-minor fantasy that Sunday, or at any time in his life, but at least twice he heard an orchestration of the *fugue* with which the fantasy is often paired. I mean, of course, the Fugue in G Minor, BWV 542/2, and the orchestration of that fugue by the composer and conductor Johann Joseph Abert (father of the Mozart biographer Hermann Abert). Abert's orchestration of the fugue comprises the third movement of his *Präludium und Fuge von Joh. Seb. Bach und Choral von Abert für Orchester eingerichtet*, published in 1871, a compilation that begins with the Prelude in C-sharp Minor from Book 1 of the Well-Tempered Clavier (transposed to D minor), continues with a chorale-like movement in G minor composed by Abert himself, and concludes with the G-minor fugue.[72] Brahms may have first heard this montage in 1874, coincidentally enough, in Leipzig, when he appeared as a guest conductor and pianist on a program at the Gewandhaus.[73] On that occasion, Brahms conducted the orchestra in three of his own compositions and served as piano accompanist for another, while the Gewandhaus conductor Carl Reinecke led the ensemble in Abert's orchestration. Ten years later, in Berlin, on a program in which Brahms conducted three more of his orchestral works, he heard Ludwig von Brenner and the Berlin Philharmonic perform Abert's arrangement.

The one orchestration of a Bach organ work known to have been conducted by Brahms himself is that by Bernhard Scholz of the Prelude in E-flat Major, BWV 552/1.[74] That performance took place in 1875 at a concert in Vienna featuring the Brahms *Requiem*. The venue was the Großer Musikvereins-Saal of the Gesellschaft für Musikfreunde, an organization that boasted Brahms both as its principal conductor and artistic director. Scholz was an old friend, not to mention a fellow signatory of the infamous "Manifesto" against the so-called New German School of composition (a document at least cowritten by Brahms), and he had hosted Brahms as a guest performer and conductor in Breslau only a few weeks before the

Studies and Discoveries

concert in Vienna. Perhaps, therefore, the decision to perform Scholz's orchestration was made during that visit.

As is well known, Brahms also enjoyed playing Bach organ works at the piano throughout his career.[75] He especially favored the Toccata in F Major and the Fantasy in G Major, BWV 572, but he also played the Fugue in A Minor, BWV 543/2; the Prelude in B Minor, BWV 544/1; and the Pastorale in F Major, BWV 590. Numerous private as well as public performances are documented, including about twenty for the F-major toccata and fourteen for the G-major fantasy. A recently unearthed review from a recital in Vienna testifies to how Brahms captured the sound of the organ in his rendition of the fantasy:

> The *Fantasie* begins in the Bach style with a short Prelude (Presto), followed by a pure organ movement. With the aid of the damper pedal, Mr. Brahms simulated the effect of organ playing, and even the full organ, most ingeniously, and finally even let us hear the organ pedal and the 32-foot pipes with his left hand. The effect of this manner of playing was extremely powerful and grand.[76]

Over the years, Bach's organ works have meant different things to different people. To the Bach biographer Forkel, writing at the turn of the nineteenth century, the music suggested a deeply spiritual, even cosmic force to be reckoned with: "Even in his secular compositions [Bach] disdained everything common, but in his compositions for the organ he kept himself infinitely more distant from it; so that here, it seems to me, he does not appear like a man, but as a true disembodied spirit, who soars above everything mortal."[77] To Carl Friedrich Zelter, director of the Berlin Singakademie and the teacher of one Felix Mendelssohn-Bartholdy, Bach's organ works represented a kind of inner sanctum wherein the composer forged his own, transcendent style. Writing in 1827 to his friend (and fellow Bach fanatic) Johann Wolfgang von Goethe, Zelter waxed more than a little poetic on the subject: "The organ is Bach's peculiar soul, into which he breathes immediately the living breath. His theme is the feeling just born, which, like the spark from the stone, invariably springs forth, from the first chance pressure of the foot upon the pedals. Thus by degrees he warms to his subject, till he has isolated himself, and feels alone, and then an inexhaustible stream passes out into the infinite ocean."[78] Writing in 1839, in a review of various editions of keyboard music by Scarlatti and Bach, including an edition of Bach's Six Great Preludes and Fugues for organ, Robert Schumann made basically the same claim as Zelter, but in his own words: "It is only at his organ that Bach appears to be at his most sublime, most audacious, in his own element. Here he knows neither limits nor goal and works for centuries to come."[79]

The sentiments expressed by these three writers were echoed years later, albeit in less metaphysical terms, by the English organist Harvey Grace. Grace may be an unknown quantity outside the organ world, but he knew and understood Bach's organ works better than anyone of his time. His classic study *The Organ Works of Bach*, published in 1922, concludes with these lines, which still ring true today:

Varied as were Bach's activities, he no doubt had his favourite sphere. Bearing in mind the obstacles he met with in the performance of his more difficult concerted works, choral and instrumental, we may be sure that he was happiest, when, as performer and composer combined, he depended upon himself alone. The organ, with its ample resources, must have given him a sense of power and freedom he found nowhere else. Forkel tells us he would improvise organ music for two hours at a time—a long string of movements on a single theme. In the organ loft, then, he won his greatest triumphs and expressed his deepest feelings, and we may well believe that, given his choice, it is there, above all, he would have his memory kept green.[80]

2

On the Reception of Bach's Organ Works in Nineteenth-Century Leipzig

Rochlitz, Becker, Schellenberg, and Their

Reviews of Two Early Editions

The signal importance of J. S. Bach's organ music in the lives and activities of nineteenth-century musicians is a phenomenon documented as far east as St. Petersburg and as far west as Chicago. I have written exten- sively on how several of the greatest composers of the nineteenth century (Mendelssohn, Schumann, Liszt, Wagner, Franck, Brahms, and Elgar) responded to the model of Bach's organ music. Here, I will focus on three lesser-known figures from that era. I was inspired to pursue this line of inquiry by the publication in 2007 of volume 6 of the *Bach-Dokumente* series. Titled *Ausgewählte Dokumente zum Nachwirken Johann Sebastian Bachs 1801–1850*, this 815-page tome richly chronicles the rediscovery of Bach's oeuvre during the first half of the nineteenth century. Accordingly, I have chosen three individuals who during those fifty years reviewed early editions of Bach's organ works. All three spent their entire lives in the "Sebastianstadt" of Leipzig, which is also where both of the editions in question were published.

The Afterlife of Bach's Organ Works. Russell Stinson, Oxford University Press. © Oxford University Press 2024.
DOI: 10.1093/oso/9780197680438.003.0003

FRIEDRICH ROCHLITZ AND HIS REVIEW OF *J. S. BACH'S CHORAL-VORSPIELE FÜR DIE ORGEL MIT EINEM UND ZWEY KLAVIEREN UND PEDAL*

Friedrich Rochlitz (1769–1842) was a chorister at the Leipzig Thomasschule, where he studied composition and counterpoint with the Thomaskantor (and Bach pupil) Johann Friedrich Doles.[1] Rochlitz composed various works in his youth, but he chose the career of a writer. At the age of twenty-nine, he was selected by the Leipzig house of Breitkopf & Härtel as the editor of a new weekly periodical, the *Allgemeine Musikalische Zeitung* (hereafter, AMZ). He edited that publication from its inaugural issue in 1798 until 1818, when he voluntarily resigned. Rochlitz holds a special place within the annals of Bach reception, for he witnessed two seminal events in the history of that phenomenon, events separated by fifty years. He was present at the Leipzig Thomaskirche in 1789 when Mozart was treated to a performance of the double-choir motet "Singet dem Herrn ein neues Lied," BWV 225, and he was also at the church in 1840 when Mendelssohn played his legendary all-Bach organ recital to raise funds for a Bach monument there.

During Rochlitz's two decades as editor, the AMZ vigorously promoted the music of Bach. This is not to imply, though, that Rochlitz was a life-long Bach fanatic. As a young man, he struggled in vain to grasp Bach's intricate polyphony. He had been intimidated by the technically difficult Bach cantatas and motets he sang under Doles, and he had not had time to fully understand those compositions.[2] After Mozart's visit, he made for himself a collection of works by Bach, but was still mystified by their elaborate style. When he took the reins of the AMZ, he resolved finally to comprehend Bach's music in all its complexity. He began by analyzing the four-part chorales and then moved on to the Well-Tempered Clavier, undergoing a kind of epiphany in the process.

The 9 October 1805 issue of the AMZ included an anonymous review of an edition of Bach's organ chorales by Johann Gottfried Schicht, who at the time was the conductor of the Gewandhaus concerts in Leipzig, music director of the city's Neukirche, and director of the Leipzig Singakademie (he would later become Thomaskantor).[3] We can only assume that it was Rochlitz himself who authored this review,[4] despite no evidence that he played the organ or previously knew any of the works contained in Schicht's edition. The edition was published in four volumes from 1803 to 1806. For the next four decades, it would constitute the most comprehensive collection of Bach's organ chorales on the market. Titled *J. S. Bach's Choral-Vorspiele für die Orgel mit einem und zwey Klavieren und Pedal*, the print contains roughly forty pieces: the six Schübler Chorales, BWV 645–650, given out of order; the Canonic Variations on "Vom Himmel hoch, da komm ich her," BWV 769a; ten chorale settings from Part 3 of the *Clavierübung*; three works from the *Orgelbüchlein*; one work from the Great Eighteen Chorales; one work from the *Clavierbüchlein vor Wilhelm Friedemann Bach*; and a host of miscellaneous works, both authentic and spurious.[5] Schicht's edition represents a milestone in the publication history of Bach's organ chorales, for the Schübler Chorales, Canonic Variations, and chorales from Part 3 of the *Clavierübung* had been out of print for over fifty years, and the other works had never been published.

Rochlitz reviewed only the first two volumes of Schicht's edition, both of which appeared in 1803. He began with some general (and rather verbose) remarks on the music, followed by a pithy statement or two on each of the twenty-four works:

It is a laudable effort by the publisher to circulate these bequeathments to the art of organ playing by J. S. Bach, a composer completely deserving of his exalted position in the realm of classical music. Musical taste has rather changed since Bach's time . . . but as far as the treatment of this royal instrument is concerned, Bach's works will remain the model for all times. Any organist who has enough respect and feeling for art to want to raise himself above the usual empty, mechanical style of playing through his careful attention to these works will truly be rewarded. Admittedly, this is possible only with (1) an accomplished performer who has been initiated in Bach's style, (2) a good instrument, and (3) and artistically inclined listeners . . . In the history of music, with regard to the genre of the chorale prelude, these works should be considered monuments of their time. With regard to the treatment of the organ and to Bach's unique mastery of melody and harmony, these works will long remain artistic models. Furthermore, they will constitute a most instructive school for those wishing to become consummate organists . . . All the preludes are written in imitative style, some more strictly so than others.[6]

1. Wachet auf, ruft uns die Stimme, BWV 645 (Schübler Chorales)
The chorale *Wachet auf, ruft uns die Stimme* is set in the tenor. It is like the admonishing voice of a friend. There is in the upper voice a lovely, simple, and motivically constructed part set in the alto register.[7]

2. Meine Seele erhebt den Herren, BWV 648 (Schübler Chorales)
A small, intricate fabric woven from three parts, upon which the chorale *Meine Seele erhebt den Herren* enters as a fourth part in the soprano voice.[8]

3. Wo soll ich fliehen hin, BWV 646 (Schübler Chorales)
A duet in imitative style. The upper voice, played on an eight-foot stop, and the lower voice, played on a sixteen-foot stop, have a theme lasting only a single bar, but they state the theme in tandem for thirty-two bars. Meanwhile, the chorale *Wo soll ich fliehen hin* enters on a four-foot stop in the pedals, one phrase at a time. The anxious search for peace is masterfully painted, and the effect is completely wonderful and unique.[9]

4. Wer nur den lieben Gott lässt walten, BWV 647 (Schübler Chorales)
A *manualiter* trio on the chorale *Wer nur den lieben Gott lässt walten*, with the chorale tune proper played on the pedals. Once again, masterfully handled! The individual phrases of the chorale melody provide the material for the manifold points of imitation between the two upper voices.[10]

5. Ach bleib bei uns, Herr Jesu Christ, BWV 649 (Schübler Chorales)

With the chorale melody *Ach bleib bei uns, Herr Jesu Christ* sounding in the upper voice, the simple tenor part offers many instructive passages and is a good exercise piece [for the left hand], despite its length.[11]

6. Kommst du nun, Jesu, vom Himmel herunter, BWV 650 (Schübler Chorales)

In this work, the chorale *Kommst du nun Jesu vom Himmel* etc. sounds in the alto voice, in ¾ time. An experienced performer is required because the upper voice and bass move in ⅞ time. However entertaining and instructive, the piece is a bit long.[12]

7. Allein Gott in der Höh sei Ehr, BWV 675 (setting in F major from Part 3 of the *Clavierübung*)

The melody *Allein Gott in der Höh' sey Ehr* appears between two masterfully conceived free voices. In listening to this beautiful, imitatively textured work, one forgets how long it is. However, this reviewer feels that the chorale tune stands too much in the background.[13]

8. Allein Gott in der Höh sei Ehr, BWV 676 (setting in G major from Part 3 of the *Clavierübung*)

A magnificent, 124-bar-long trio on the same chorale, in which the two upper voices alternate between the chorale tune proper and a brilliant free theme based on the chorale melody. A rigorous exercise piece![14]

9. Allein Gott in der Höh sei Ehr, BWV 677 (setting in A major from Part 3 of the *Clavierübung*)

A pretty fughetta on the same chorale, derived at the beginning from the first phrase of the melody, then from the second phrase.[15]

10. Wir glauben all an einen Gott, BWV 680 (*pedaliter* setting from Part 3 of the *Clavierübung*)

A masterpiece of art for full organ on the old melody *Wir glauben all an einen Gott*. The theme, taken from the melody, passes through the three upper voices in the manner of a fugue, to which the pedals add a countertheme. In one instance, the countertheme is appropriated by the tenor.[16]

11. Wir glauben all an einen Gott, BWV 681 (*manualiter* setting from Part 3 of the *Clavierübung*)

A kind of fughetta on the same chorale, in the so-called French style.[17]

12. Lob sei dem allmächtigen Gott, BWV 704

A pretty, three-voice fughetta on the melody *Lob sey dem allmächtigen Gott*.[18]

13. Ach Gott und Herr, BWV 692

Here, three *manualiter* voices are employed. The melody *Ach Gott und Herr* is stated in manifold ways.[19]

14. Ach Gott und Herr, BWV 693

A setting of the same chorale, which appears as a cantus firmus in the uppermost voice and is stated by the lower voices in diminution. Throughout the work, one hears nothing but the individual phrases of the chorale melody.[20]

15. Wer nur den lieben Gott lässt walten (*Clavierbüchlein vor Wilhelm Friedemann Bach*), BWV 691

A small, ornamental setting of *Wer nur den lieben Gott* etc.[21]

16. Durch Adams Fall ist ganz verderbt, BWV 705

The whole chorale *Durch Adams Fall ist* etc. is set for four voices in imitative texture, in the style of the church [im Stilo alla capella].[22]

17. Schmücke dich, o liebe Seele, BWV 759

A friendly rendition of the chorale *Schmücke dich, o liebe Seele*.[23]

18. Liebster Jesu, wir sind hier, BWV 706, 634 (*Orgelbüchlein*), and 633 (*Orgelbüchlein*)

Four different ways of arranging the melody *Liebster Jesu wir sind hier*. In the last two settings, which are in five voices, the chorale is presented in the two upper voices as a canon at the fifth. Some small, insignificant discrepancies between these two works may be seen in the two middle voices.[24]

19. Allein Gott in der Höh sei Ehr, BWV 711

The chorale *Allein Gott in der Höh* etc. is set with a simple, third-rate countermelody beneath. The work is somewhat stiff and, because of its length, tiresome.[25]

20. Allein Gott in der Höh sei Ehr, BWV 664b (trio in A major from the Great Eighteen Chorales)

A splendid, instructive trio on the same melody. One happily overlooks its length, considering how artfully the material is handled.[26]

21. Ich hab mein Sach Gott heimgestellt, BWV 708a and 708, and

22. Ich hab mein Sach Gott heimgestellt, BWV 707, followed by a four-part harmonization of the chorale

Three different harmonizations of *Ich hab mein Sach Gott* etc., along with a prelude [BWV 707] lasting 140 bars in which this chorale is set in imitative texture. The melody appears in augmentation in the uppermost voice and can be played by a different instrument. But the figuration beneath is rather dry.[27]

23. Wir Christenleut, BWV 710

Another splendid work, with imitative figuration between the two upper voices and with the cantus firmus played on the pedals.[28]

24. Gelobet seist du, Jesu Christ, BWV 697

A pretty fughetta on the chorale *Gelobet seyst du Jesu Christ*.[29]

We may ignore Rochlitz's remarks on Nos. 13, 14, and 17, since all three works are clearly inauthentic: the first two were composed by Bach's cousin Johann Gottfried Walther, the third by Bach's pupil Gottfried August Homilius.[30] On the whole, however, Rochlitz's commentaries are sufficiently interesting to deserve some discussion here. To begin with the Schübler Chorales, it may not be coincidental that the two settings most admired by Rochlitz, Nos. 3 and 4, are also the shortest of the six, for he criticized the two longest works in the set, Nos. 5 and 6, specifically because of their length. What Rochlitz may really have been objecting to, though, is how both works are dominated by a long and ostensibly "free" ritornello (in other words, a ritornello seemingly unrelated to the chorale melody) that is presented in its entirety at the end as well as the beginning of the piece in addition to being stated between all the phrases of the chorale. Compared to other organ chorales by Bach, these aria-like compositions are quite progressive, foreshadowing the organ chorales of such later composers as Doles, Homilius, and Johann Ludwig Krebs.[31] Both works are, in fact, as all the Schübler Chorales presumably are, transcriptions of arias from Bach's sacred cantatas, something Rochlitz was almost certainly unaware of. Rochlitz did concede, however, that the busy and wide-ranging ritornello of No. 5 made for "a good exercise piece," obviously for the left hand.[32] With regard to No. 6, he was concerned that the combination of $\frac{3}{4}$ time for the middle voice and $\frac{6}{8}$ for the two outer voices posed an obstacle in performing the work, but this problem is easily overcome by reading all three voices in $\frac{6}{8}$.

The five works from Part 3 of the *Clavierübung* commented on by Rochlitz include two trios, two fughettas, and one full-fledged fugue, and he seems to have recognized these works for the mature masterpieces they truly are. This statement applies particularly to No. 8, the G-major trio on "Allein Gott in der Höh sei Ehr," which may represent nothing less than a summation of Bach's chorale-trios for the organ.[33] This work, too, incorporates a ritornello, but one much shorter than those in Nos. 5 and 6. Furthermore, the ritornello of the "Allein Gott" trio is unquestionably derived from the chorale melody, as Rochlitz realized. He was also correct about how the top two voices trade off between the ritornello and the chorale tune proper: phrases 1–2 are stated first by the middle voice (mm. 12–33), then, in a stunning example of the Stollen of the chorale being varied with the help of invertible counterpoint, by the upper voice (mm. 45–66), phrase 3 is stated by the upper voice (mm. 78–82) and phrase 4 by the lower (mm. 87–91), and phrase 5, which becomes the subject of its own fugal exposition, is stated first by the lower voice (mm. 99–103), then, transposed up a fifth, by the upper voice (mm. 105–9); and finally, transposed back down a fifth to the home key, again by the upper voice (mm. 118–22).[34] In designating the work as "a rigorous exercise piece," Rochlitz was acknowledging its virtuosic nature: all three voices move quickly and range widely, with the hands frequently crossed, and the player has to cope with these technical demands for roughly five minutes. Rochlitz was happy to overlook the length of the piece in view of its artistic merits, just as he did with No. 20, the A-major trio on "Allein Gott" from the Great Eighteen Chorales.

Another admirer of the G-major trio on "Allein Gott" was Rochlitz's English contemporary Samuel Wesley (1766–1837), the de facto leader of the British "Sebastian Squad" of the early nineteenth century. Wesley likewise owned this piece in Schicht's edition—he owned only the first two volumes—and when in 1809 he wrote about this publication to the organist William Crotch, who owned at least the first two volumes himself, Wesley particularly recommended to Crotch's attention Nos. 8, 10, 15, 18, 19, and 20. These works include three of the five settings of "Allein Gott" edited by Schicht. In addition, Wesley offered his colleague some comments on the two volumes as a whole: "You are (I presume) aware that the German Titles to the several Pieces are the first Words of certain Lutheran hymns to which Sebastian added all that florid Counterpoint in Fugue & Canon which you meet with & which I need not tell you produces on the Organ the most magnificent Effect."[35] Wesley also thought highly of No. 17 from Schicht's edition, a trio on "Schmücke dich, o liebe Seele" now known, as mentioned earlier, to have been composed by G. A. Homilius. (Rochlitz, too, had a favorable opinion of this piece.) Writing in 1810 to his brother and fellow organist Charles Wesley junior, and using a common English moniker for Bach at the time, Wesley pronounced this work "a divine scrap of 'the old Wig.' "[36] What is more, Wesley made various annotations in his personal copy of Schicht's edition, housed today at the Royal College of Music, London.[37] They include his own translations of all the work titles; a set of fingerings for No. 19; and a footnote to the "Schmücke dich" trio that reads "N. B. This choral I heard a Congregation sing at the Lutheran church in the Savoy—it was all but 11 in the Day." This footnote, in turn, connects to Wesley's letter to his brother, which describes in greater detail his activities that morning: he visited various London churches in the span of a few hours, hearing "Schmücke dich" sung as a communion hymn at the Lutheran Chapel at the Savoy, in the Strand.

Rochlitz also admired, if more discriminately, Nos. 7 and 9, the other two settings of "Allein Gott" from Part 3 of the *Clavierübung*. What so impressed him about No. 7 was the exquisitely wrought two-part invention comprised by the outer voices. In that work, the unadorned chorale melody appears as a middle voice and is to be played on the same manual as the outer voices, a design that, according to Rochlitz, has the unfortunate effect of obscuring the cantus firmus. None other than Robert

Schumann, a slightly later owner of Schicht's edition, must have agreed with Rochlitz on this point, for Schumann in his personal copy of the print designated the middle voice as a pedal line, an alteration that in performance serves to clarify the polyphonic texture.[38] Rochlitz had less to say about No. 9, except that it was a "fughetta" (Bach's own term) not just on the first phrase of the chorale melody, which is usually the case with such works, but on the second phrase as well. The format is actually that of a double fugue, with separate expositions for the two subjects (mm. 1–7 and 7–16), followed by a final exposition in which the subjects are combined (mm. 16–20).

As for the two settings of "Wir glauben," Rochlitz hailed No. 10 as "a masterpiece of art."[39] He correctly observed that in No. 10 a three-voice fugue on the first phrase of the chorale takes place in the hands, while the feet stamp out their own countermelody. His claim, however, that the countermelody only once migrates to the hands is somewhat misleading, for the passage in question (mm. 76–82 of the tenor voice) features three consecutive statements of the first eight notes of the theme. With regard to No. 11, Rochlitz was astute enough to detect French-overture style without the benefit of any such heading.

Of the remaining works in Schicht's edition commented on by Rochlitz, I will take into account three, starting with No. 16, "Durch Adams Fall" (BWV 705). The form of this rather severe opus is that of the chorale ricercar or chorale motet, whose modus operandi is for each phrase of the chorale to be set as a point of imitation, along the lines of the Renaissance vocal motet. No other such work is to be found in any of the four volumes of Schicht's print, whose heading for the piece reads *Fuga sopra il Canto fermo, a Cappella, ed a quattro voci*. No doubt the designation of *a Cappella* was what prompted such nineteenth- and twentieth-century musicians as Wilhelm Rust, Bernhard Friedrich Richter, and Diethard Hellmann to transcribe the work for four-part choir.[40] Rochlitz's description of the work is merely a loose translation of Schicht's heading.

To continue with No. 19, a miscellaneous, *manualiter* setting of "Allein Gott" (BWV 711), Rochlitz criticized no other work in such harsh terms. Scored for just two voices, this is the only example of a chorale bicinium in the two volumes reviewed by Rochlitz. He seems to have been particularly annoyed by the left-hand theme, which, as it bounces along its merry way, functions as a ritornello. (The piece sounds rather like one of the Schübler Chorales shorn of its pedal part.) But rather than speculate about why this theme so offended Rochlitz, let us consider how the eminent theorist Adolph Bernhard Marx explained this same work a few decades later. Marx rightly extolled the piece for its rhythmic vitality and organic unity:

> Writing in ⅜ time, Bach ornaments the cantus firmus here and there, but only moderately. He introduces his accompanimental voice in a graceful and supple manner. At the entrance of the cantus firmus, the accompaniment becomes more active, shaking back and forth, so to speak; it then returns to the original theme. Through these meager means, Bach produces a chorale arrangement lasting sixty-three bars (not counting the repeat). The work achieves unity and clarity by how the accompaniment regularly returns to its original theme and how the cadential notes of each phrase of the cantus firmus are sustained. The modulations are, as always with Bach, simple and strong, always to a closely related key and always leading further.
>
> Quite delightfully, the accompanimental voice itself is derived from the cantus firmus . . . but with significant alterations. Bach fortifies the accompanimental theme by inserting an eighth-note motive between two groups of sixteenths, and in such a way that the rhythms in bar 3 are the same as those in bars 1–2, but reversed . . . With the entrance of the chorale tune proper, the accompanimental voice assumes its supporting role, but in a rich and lively manner.[41]

Apropos of Marx's statement that "the accompanimental voice is derived from the cantus firmus," it bears mentioning that Johannes Brahms also appreciated this aspect of the work, to judge from how he annotated his personal copy of the piece.[42] What is more, Brahms seems to have based the opening bars of his organ chorale "Herzlich tut mich erfreuen," Op. 122, No. 4, on the ritornello of Bach's bicinium.

54   THE AFTERLIFE OF BACH'S ORGAN WORKS

The third work is No. 22, a setting of "Ich hab mein Sach Gott
heimgestellt" that is catalogued as BWV 707. Nos. 21–22 of Schicht's edition actually encompass four different settings of this hymn, three of
which (BWV 708, BWV 708a, and the four-part chorale that follows BWV
707) are merely harmonizations. With regard to BWV 707, which may
be one of Bach's earliest surviving compositions altogether, Rochlitz correctly perceived a certain monotony in how each phrase of the chorale is
so laboriously "pre-imitated" in the three lower voices.[43] His description of
the piece as a whole ("ein Vorspiel, worin dieser Choral, fugirt, 140 Takte
so durchgeführt wird, dass auch diese Melodie in der Oberstimme per
augmentationem erscheint") corresponds closely to the Italian heading
provided by Schicht (*Qui si trova il Canto fermo fugato, come ancora
separatamente nella Parte superiore aumentato*). Rochlitz, however, also
recommended for the augmented version of the chorale melody found in
the soprano voice to be played by a different instrument, obviously to enhance the audibility of the part. His suggestion recalls chorale settings by
G. F. Kauffmann (1679–1735) and J. L. Krebs scored for organ and a solo
wind instrument.

Rochlitz's review ends with a similar, albeit more radical recommenda-
tion about the performance of works in imitative texture. His caution here
against approaching Bach's more complex creations without some knowledge of music theory resonates with how, as a young chorister, he had
been intimidated and mystified by the master's compositions:

The reviewer will now allow himself, following this all-too-brief critique, to make some additional statements for those who wish to
study works by Bach in this genre and be educated by them. One dares
not approach works by Bach without having some level of musical
accomplishment and some understanding of harmony. Otherwise,
one runs the risk of making mistakes in performance or of being
scared off by the severity of the accompanimental voices. One learns
from these original products of artistic genius how the raw materials
get so elegantly refined . . . One needs to realize particularly that a
piece in imitative texture makes the best effect when it is performed

on various instruments, as opposed to being played on the organ or piano. If not, such passages as when the individual voices jump over one another, intersect with one another, lead to unfavorable cross relations, or dissonantly grind against one another—such passages cannot be properly heard and become merely music for the eyes.[44]

To Rochlitz, therefore, a piece like "Durch Adams Fall" (BWV 705) would ideally have been rendered with a different instrument for each of the four voices, a disposition that would have imparted to each voice its own timbre and illuminated the entire polyphonic structure. For Bach's organ chorales, virtually no such transcriptions from the late eighteenth or early nineteenth century survive. But many similar ones do survive for the composer's "free" keyboard fugues, especially those from the Well-Tempered Clavier.[45] These transcriptions represent the work not just of anonymous arrangers but also of such luminaries as Mozart and Beethoven. Surely they both would have been sympathetic to Rochlitz's viewpoint, however impractical it might have been.

CARL FERDINAND BECKER, HERMANN SCHELLENBERG, AND THEIR REVIEWS OF *JOH. SEB. BACH'S COMPOSITIONEN FÜR DIE ORGEL*, VOLUME 3

Carl Ferdinand Becker (1804–1877) and his pupil Hermann Schellenberg (1816–1862) were both prominent Leipzig organists. Becker received instruction in keyboard playing, harmony, and composition from J. G. Schicht.[46] Thereafter, he studied the organ with Johann Andreas Dröbs, organist at the Peterskirche and a student of the Bach pupil Johann Christian Kittel. Becker held two important organist posts, first at the Peterskirche (1825–1837) and then at the Nicolaikirche (1837–1854). From 1846 to 1854, he taught organ and music history at the newly opened Leipzig Conservatory. He was renowned as an antiquarian, scholar, and critic. He was also a founding member of the Bachgesellschaft.

Less is known about Schellenberg.[47] He served as organist of the Johanniskirche from 1846 to 1854 and succeeded Becker as organist of the Nicolaikirche in 1854, remaining in that position until his death. He was also responsible for the Nicolaikirche's acquisition of the magnificent Ladegast organ that still adorns its rear gallery. In addition to his organ playing, Schellenberg was active as a pianist, composer, and critic. Furthermore, he freelanced as a music proofreader, most notably on the editions of Bach's organ chorales by Felix Mendelssohn published in 1845–1846 by Breitkopf & Härtel.[48] Like Becker, Schellenberg played public organ recitals in Leipzig throughout his career. Of particular interest is a program he gave at the Nicolaikirche on 17 October 1845 featuring his own arrangement of the Fantasy and Fugue in G Minor, BWV 542, for four hands and "double pedal," with Becker assisting.[49] Schellenberg's surviving piano transcriptions include a four-hand arrangement of this same fantasy and fugue and an arrangement for two pianos, eight hands, of the opening chorus of Bach's St. Matthew Passion.[50]

A review of the October 1845 recital appeared the following month in the *Neue Zeitschrift für Musik*. Its author had nothing but praise for all seven works on the program, which began with the Prelude and Fugue in F Minor, BWV 534, an "Adagio" by Becker, and a chorale setting by J. L. Krebs, and which ended with three of Schellenberg's own compositions.[51] The centerpiece was Schellenberg's arrangement of the G-minor fantasy and fugue, described by the reviewer in these terms:

The next work on the program was the remarkably provocative and poignant Fantasy and Fugue in G Minor by J. S. Bach, arranged by Mr. Schellenberg for four hands and double pedal. We know of no other composition for the organ that matches the splendor and strength of this piece, which has just been published in this arrangement by Breitkopf & Härtel, and we recommend this work to any organist who makes a claim to virtuosity. The performance, in which Mr. Schellenberg was assisted by Mr. Becker, was worthy of the work.[52]

Writing in the fall of 1845, Schellenberg described the G-minor fantasy and fugue as one of Bach's most magnificent and exquisite works for the organ.[53] He had heard a most unusual performance of the piece in Leipzig earlier that year by Adolph Friedrich Hesse (1803–1869), arguably the leading organist in all of Europe at the time. As we know from a report by Schellenberg in the 18 January 1845 issue of the *Neue Zeitschrift für Musik*, Hesse, who was based in Breslau, had come to Leipzig in early January 1845 to conduct his latest symphony. According to a letter written by Hesse on 10 January to the composer Louis Spohr, the symphony (Hesse's sixth) had been performed to great acclaim the previous evening at the Leipzig Gewandhaus: "Last evening here at the Gewandhaus, I conducted my sixth symphony. It was an excellent performance and received lively applause after each movement."[54] It so happens that on the afternoon of 10 January, Hesse performed on the organs of the Nicolaikirche and Thomaskirche for a small group of admirers. In Schellenberg's words,

Mr. Adolph Hesse, the music director from Breslau and the famous, celebrated organ virtuoso, spent a few days in our city last week in order to lead a performance of his newest symphony (the sixth). He used the last day of his sojourn to delight our organ devotees by playing for them on that great instrument. A select circle of artists and patrons had gathered on the afternoon of Friday the 10th at our magnificent Nicolaikirche, and those who had never heard Hesse play were excited to hear how he would handle the splendid organ there. Hesse played some of his own larger works as well as a beautiful trio of his own composition. He also gave us the opportunity to marvel at his use of double pedal. After playing these original compositions, Hesse wished to perform some of Bach's creations, but, oh, how unfortunate, one of the pedals of this otherwise so solidly built organ failed to function. A tracker had broken, which may usually be a minor matter, but because the tracker could not be fixed on the spur of the moment, this rare treat suddenly ended in the most merciless way. The master's suggestion that he continue by playing on the organ at the Thomaskirche was met with favor, so the whole group, including the organ blowers, moved to the Thomaskirche. Playing full organ on that instrument makes a great effect, but for the player it is doubly difficult. The layout of the stops is hopelessly confused, with the Untersatz and other pedal stops situated between the manual stops, and with the various stops for the three manuals scattered here and there. This makes a quick overview of the stops impossible. In addition, the key action is so monstrously heavy that it requires the player's full strength. At this time of year, ciphers are to be expected even in the best of organs. They occurred here as well, to the chagrin of all. Considering these adverse circumstances, one cannot say enough about how Mr. Hesse, through sheer force of will but also with great poise, was able to negotiate one of Bach's most magnificent organ works, the great Fantasy and Fugue in G Minor (No. 4 in volume 2 of the new Peters edition) as well as some of his own larger compositions. Although the frequent ciphers on several different keys forced him to stop numerous times, Mr. Hesse played until the onset of darkness. These interruptions meant that we could not enjoy the works in one sitting, but all of us who heard Mr. Hesse thank him most sincerely.[55]

The issues raised by this charming vignette go well beyond the problems encountered by Hesse in playing on these two organs.[56] For one thing, Hesse was by this date a well-known guest artist in Leipzig, having regularly given organ recitals there since 1828, when he was only twenty years old.[57] Moreover, Bach's G-minor fantasy and fugue, which only a few months earlier had been published in volume 2 of the Peters edition of Bach's complete organ works, had long been one of Hesse's signature pieces.[58] He must have reveled in the rhapsodic style of the fantasy, while he surely used the fugue, which features one of Bach's most demanding pedal parts, as a pedal showpiece of sorts. Hesse was renowned for his pedal playing, and one of his favorite pedal techniques was to play in fast octaves.[59] This may very well be what Schellenberg means here by Hesse's "use of double pedal." As for Hesse's audience that afternoon, it presumably included C. F. Becker, who was then the organist of the Nicolaikirche.

Felix Mendelssohn, to cite another Leipzig-based organist of that era, could not have been present, because he had temporarily relocated to Frankfurt.[60]

To focus now on Becker and Schellenberg in their capacity as music critics, they both published reviews of the first three volumes of *Joh. Seb. Bach's Compositionen für die Orgel*, an eight-volume edition of Bach's organ music issued from 1844 to 1852 by the Leipzig house of C. F. Peters. Edited by Friedrich Conrad Griepenkerl and Ferdinand Roitzsch, this publication was the first complete edition of Bach's organ works ever brought to fruition. Still widely used today, it represents one of the first text-critical editions in the field of musicology.

Becker and Schellenberg each wrote two different reviews of these three volumes, one covering volumes 1 and 2 and another devoted to volume 3. Becker's reviews begin, memorably, with the proclamation that "the organ is the queen of instruments and Bach's works are its jewelry."[61] They were published first, in the *Neue Zeitschrift für Musik*, with Schellenberg's following a few months later in the *Allgemeine Musikalische Zeitung*.[62] To judge from the strong similarity in format, content, and wording, Schellenberg modeled his reviews after those by his teacher. Of particular interest, because of their detailed nature, are the reviews by Becker and Schellenberg of volume 3 of the Peters edition, edited by Griepenkerl. Whereas their reviews of volumes 1–2 deal primarily with Bach's organ music as a whole, those of volume 3 consist of brief commentaries on each of the ten works included. Becker's review appeared on 28 October 1845, only months after the publication of volume 3 (whose preface is dated May 1845), with Schellenberg's following on 28 January 1846.

For each work, and for purposes of comparison, I will provide the commentaries of both Becker and Schellenberg, followed by my own remarks. Because Schellenberg discussed Nos. 9 and 10 as a pair, I have likewise paired these works on Becker's behalf. I will also take into account the concluding remarks of both critics, followed by my own comments. It is not surprising that, as professional organists, Becker and Schellenberg had strong feelings about Bach's organ works. They doubtless saw themselves as guardians of the great legacy that is Bach's organ music. As such, they were loath to add to that legacy any work they suspected to have been written by another composer or to have been written by Bach for the harpsichord rather than the organ.

1. Prelude and Fugue in E-flat Major, BWV 552

BECKER: Prelude and Fugue in E-flat Major, in five voices and with a threefold change of meter. Magnificent and ingenious, but probably well known to all Bach devotees from its inclusion in Part 3 of the *Clavierübung*.
SCHELLENBERG: Prelude and Fugue in E-flat Major, taken from the *Clavierübung*. The fugue in particular is undeniably delightful. The prelude, despite its somewhat old-fashioned cadences, also contains many valuable elements. The particular style of the prelude requires a wise, experienced player.[63]

Becker included this fugue on his all-Bach recital at the Neukirche in Leipzig on 24 October 1847.[64] His commentary touches on two of the fugue's more salient features, namely, the presence of five rather than four voices and, as the movement progresses from section to section, the use of three different time signatures. Schellenberg clearly ranked the fugue above the prelude. The "somewhat old-fashioned cadences" that he detected in the prelude are presumably the ones within the French-overture-like ritornello, such as those on the downbeats of measures 2, 4, 20, and 32, that are delayed by appoggiaturas, whether from below or above the harmonic tone.

2. Toccata and Fugue in F Major, BWV 540

BECKER: Toccata and Fugue in F Major. Already published in an earlier edition by Peters but edited here according to various manuscript copies. One must recognize the fugue, with its peaceful, stepwise motion, as an example of true organ style. Even though many of us would regard the toccata as less significant, we greatly appreciate the diligence shown by Bach in writing the two-part canon that begins the movement.

SCHELLENBERG: Toccata and Fugue in F Major (already published in an earlier edition by Peters). A magnificent work. Once the player gets beyond the two long pedal points and the two pedal solos at the beginning of the toccata, it must be a joy to perform.[65]

Both Becker and Schellenberg seem to have prized the fugue of this work over the toccata. Their colleague Felix Mendelssohn, conversely, seems to have championed the toccata to the exclusion of the fugue.[66] In referring to the piece's prior publication by C. F. Peters, they meant that firm's "Bureau de Musique" edition of various free organ works by Bach, issued between 1832 and 1834 and containing three additional works from volume 3 of *Joh. Seb. Bach's Compositionen für die Orgel*: the Toccata and Fugue in D Minor ("Dorian"), BWV 538; the Prelude and Fugue in G Minor, BWV 535; and the Prelude and Fugue in A Minor, BWV 551.[67] For Becker, the first subject of the fugue—the movement is in fact a double fugue—with its slow rhythms and mostly stepwise motion, epitomized idiomatic writing for the organ. Schellenberg, for his part, took a dim view of the two pedal solos at the beginning of the toccata, even though both passages would have allowed him to demonstrate his (dubious) trademark of raising his hands above his head when executing a pedal solo. As Gotthold Frotscher described this practice, in reference to Schellenberg's own compositions, "[Schellenberg] liked to thrust his hands high in the air during pedal solos to show the astonished audience that he really was playing with his feet."[68]

3. Toccata and Fugue in D Minor ("Dorian"), BWV 538

BECKER: Toccata and Fugue in D minor. Like the previous work, already published by Peters but edited here according to various manuscript copies. In the preface to Griepenkerl's edition, this piece is designated as "Dorian." However, one searches in vain here for the Dorian mode. The matter merely involves the defective key signatures found in older manuscripts. In works from the eighteenth century written in minor keys requiring flats, the sixth degree of the scale is rarely flatted, because the pitch occurs just as often as a major sixth above the tonic as a minor sixth. For this reason, one finds in older music the key of D minor notated without a key signature, the key of G minor notated with one flat, and the key of C minor notated with two flats. We make this point so that an ignorant user of the edition will not be confused, so that he will not think he has in front of him a true "Dorian" composition, that is, a work in one of the church modes or even one of the ancient Greek modes. Nothing could be any more far removed from Sebastian Bach.

SCHELLENBERG: Toccata and Fugue in D minor, Dorian? (already known, thanks to the earlier Peters edition). To enhance the wonderful effect made by the toccata, organ virtuosos normally dispense with the fugue, as it creates rather the opposite effect.[69]

This work was cited by Griepenkerl as "Toccata et Fuga aus D moll (Dorisch)." Becker disapproved of the nickname, and Schellenberg seems not to have known it. As Becker pointed out in his commentary, the only aspect of the work suggestive of the Dorian mode is how the key of D minor is notated without any flats in the key signature, in accordance with most of the older manuscripts of the piece as well as the earliest print.[70] As an expert on early keyboard music, Becker also explained that Baroque composers commonly used such notation when writing in the minor mode in keys requiring flats because of how often the sixth degree of the scale is raised a half step, as when moving to the dominant chord or key. In other words, the last flat in the key signature (or, in the case of D minor, the only flat) is canceled, alleviating the need to "naturalize" all the instances of the raised sixth degree. Bach regularly used "Dorian" notation until around 1717, his last year in Weimar.[71]

Of the many free organ works by Bach transmitted in Dorian notation—and included in this list is BWV 565, the only other organ toccata and fugue in D minor attributed to Bach—only BWV 538 has acquired the nickname of "Dorian." How the nickname originated is unclear, but the preface to Griepenkerl's edition, contrary to what has been assumed, did not mark the first time that the moniker had been cited in print. That distinction would seem to belong to the earliest edition of the piece, the above-mentioned "Bureau de Musique" edition issued by C. F. Peters between 1832 and 1834. There, the word "Dorico" is embedded within the score at the very beginning of the first measure.[72] Griepenkerl, therefore, in adopting the nickname of "Dorisch," seems merely to have been following the only edition of the work then in existence.

That the nickname was gaining in popularity by 1840 is suggested by the December 1842 issue of the periodical *Euterpe*, which contains a review of a "Gesangfest" that had taken place over two years earlier (on 2 September 1840) in the Lower Silesian village of Züllichau (today, Sulechów, Poland). Authored by the cantor and organist Friedrich August Leberecht Jakob, one of the editors of *Euterpe*, the review lists the final work on the program as "Toccata und Fuge für Orgel—dorisch—von Sebastian Bach." In addition, Jakob offered the following encomium, complete with a coy mention of the third-century saint and martyr who may be thought of as Bach's namesake: "The program concluded with a work by the great, profound, and incomparable Sebastian. It was truly Sebastian-like, which is to say it was worth revering."[73]

The "Dorian" toccata has always enjoyed great popularity. With its motoric rhythms, circle-of-fifths sequences, and frequent manual changes within the context of ritornello form, the toccata is as compelling and attractive as a fast movement from one of Vivaldi's violin concertos. Indeed, the toccata should be regarded as a simulation of Vivaldi's concerto style. But the "Dorian" fugue, one of the longest and most complex fugues that Bach wrote for any medium, has suffered a different fate. According to Schellenberg, the leading organists of his day (he and Becker included?) preferred to dispense with the movement entirely. That this situation was essentially unchanged a hundred years later is suggested by a passage from Hermann Keller's *Die Orgelwerke Bachs*: "This magnificent fugue, set to one of the most magnificent themes ever conceived, is a favorite neither of listeners nor players."[74]

4. Prelude and Fugue in D Minor, BWV 539

BECKER: Prelude and Fugue in D Minor. Edited according to a manuscript copy. Neither the fugue nor the short prelude can be accepted as an authentic organ work. . . . The prelude seems not to belong with this fugue and could hardly have been appended by Bach or any other organ player, because no connoisseur of the organ would voluntarily dispense with the pedals in writing for the instrument.

SCHELLENBERG: Prelude and Fugue in D Minor. The editor [Griepenkerl] says of this work: "It is remarkable that the fugue was also arranged by Bach himself for the violin. The fugue, transposed to G minor, is found in this version in the first of the well-known sonatas for violin [BWV 1001], because it could not be played on the violin in D minor." . . . But did Bach really intend this fugue for the organ? No, there is no trace of Sebastian's organ style to be found in it. The prelude was undoubtedly conceived for the harpsichord. Would Bach—apart from the fact that the prelude is a very insignificant piece of music—have completely bypassed the use of pedal in one of his organ compositions, like here? No![75]

Contrary to what Becker's commentary implies, this work, too, had previously been published, in an edition by A. B. Marx and Felix Mendelssohn titled *Johann Sebastian Bach's noch wenig bekannte Orgelcompositionen*. Issued in 1833, this anthology contains two additional works from the volume of *Joh. Seb. Bach's Compositionen für die Orgel* currently under consideration: the Prelude and Fugue in C Major, BWV 566 (first two movements only); and the Prelude and Fugue in E Minor, BWV 533.[76]

Becker and Schellenberg voiced decidedly negative opinions of the D-minor prelude and fugue, bristling at the notion that Bach originally intended either movement for the organ. With regard to the fugue, they were both correct, for, contrary to what Griepenkerl implies, this movement was doubtless transcribed from the unquestionably authentic version in

G minor for solo violin. (Griepenkerl believed that Bach transposed the fugue up a fourth to avoid pitches lower than g, the lowest possible pitch on the violin.) Whether Bach himself did the transcribing, however, is unclear, and whether he even composed the prelude is a matter of debate.[77] At all events, this is one of the oddest prelude-fugue couplings found anywhere in the Bach catalogue: the fugue is over twice as long as the prelude, and the prelude has no pedal part, suggesting that it was written for the harpsichord.

5. Prelude and Fugue in G Minor, BWV 535

BECKER: Prelude and Fugue in G Minor. Edited according to the earlier edition by Peters and some manuscript copies. The player is thankful for such a beautiful fugue as this. He will have less of a taste for the prelude, with its massive amount of sequential, harpsichord-like figuration.
SCHELLENBERG: Prelude and Fugue in G Minor (already published by Peters). The prelude consists mostly of running figuration and contains nothing special. The fugue, conversely, is unequivocally in the style of Bach.[78]

As in the case of the F-major toccata and fugue (No. 2), both Becker and Schellenberg preferred the fugue of this work to the prelude. Perhaps they specifically admired the contour of the fugue's subject, with its emphasis on the sixth degree of the scale, and the manner in which the theme accelerates from quarter notes to eighths and finally to sixteenths. What they objected to in the prelude was the long series of arpeggiated seventh chords in measures 19–32. With the texture here reduced essentially to one voice, minus pedal, Becker found the passage more suited to the harpsichord than the organ. The only texture that he and Schellenberg really seem to have regarded as appropriate for the organ was the standard disposition of four voices, with the bass voice played on the pedals.

6. Fantasy and Fugue in C Minor, BWV 537

BECKER: Fantasy and Fugue in C Minor. Published here for the first time and certainly to the joy of all Bach devotees, and according to a manuscript copy whose authority can hardly be doubted.
SCHELLENBERG: Fantasy and Fugue in C Minor. Published here for the first time, and according to a manuscript from Krebs's estate. The editor counts this work among Bach's most splendid. However, this may be said only of the fugue.[79]

Contrary to the statements of Becker and Schellenberg, and contrary to what Griepenkerl himself believed, the Peters edition may not represent the initial publication of this work, as it also appeared in 1845 in an edition by the Erfurt-based music publisher and organist Gotthilf Wilhelm Körner.[80] At that time, the only known manuscript was a copy thought to be entirely in the hand of J. L. Krebs, but which has since been shown to be primarily by Krebs's father, Johann Tobias, also a Bach pupil. J. T. Krebs copied through measure 89 of the fugue, with J. L. Krebs adding the last forty-one bars. J. L. Krebs's portion of the manuscript, which includes a note-for-note restatement of measures 5–22, may well represent his own completion of what was a fragmentary Bach work.[81]

According to Griepenkerl's preface, the piece ranks as one of Bach's best. While Becker likewise esteemed the work as a whole, Schellenberg could muster enthusiasm only for the fugue. This reveals a serious lapse of taste on his part, for the fantasy is a unique and unequivocal masterpiece. The true spirit of the movement was captured a few years later in a review of Körner's edition by the organist and composer Louis Kindscher. Kindscher was enthralled by the "grandiosity" of the opening pedal point and, more importantly, the seemingly inexhaustible means by which Bach develops the two main themes.[82]

7. Prelude and Fugue in C Major (originally E Major), BWV 566

BECKER: Prelude and Fugue in C Major. The subject of the first fugue is so thoroughly dry and opposed to Bach's spirit that one must doubt whether he could ever have conceived it, despite the many manuscript copies naming him as the composer. The subject of the second fugue, which comes after a harpsichord-like middle movement, is slighter still, and neither subject is developed in a way that is at all exemplary. The prelude is too short and lacking in ideas to merit any interest.

SCHELLENBERG: Prelude and Fugue in C Major. Published here for the first time, and according to various manuscript copies. The prelude, although containing some Bachian traits, is very insignificant. There are two fugue subjects, the first of which may have been written when the composer was in a peculiar mood. The second, which comes after an interlude, is evidence enough that Bach cannot have written this piece for the organ. The editor claims that the work will provide organ virtuosi with a legitimate opportunity to display the brilliance of their instrument by means of manual changes and changes of registration. This is a claim we cannot accept.[83]

Prior to the Peters edition, only the first two movements of this four-movement work had ever been published, in the above-mentioned edition by Marx and Mendelssohn. To judge from its heavy indebtedness to the multisectional *praeludia pedaliter* of Dietrich Buxtehude, the work originated during Bach's studies with Buxtehude in the winter of 1705/6. This would make it one of the earliest free organ compositions by Bach to have survived.

The four movements may be thought of as a prelude (mm. 1–33), a fugue (mm. 34–122), a toccata-like interlude (mm. 123 33), and a second fugue (mm. 134–229). One can easily imagine why Becker and Schellenberg reacted so violently against the two fugue subjects, especially if they had no idea of the early composition date. The first subject, with its many pedantic sequences, is one of Bach's most tedious, while the second consists of little more than repeated notes. Both commentators were more charitable toward the prelude, but they probably felt, as seems to have also been the case with the Prelude in D Minor (No. 4), that the movement was effectively dwarfed by the fugue that follows it. The sparing use of pedal in the third movement—minus the last few bars—must have suggested to Becker that the music was inherently "harpsichord-like." Similarly, it must have been all the repeated notes in the subject of the second fugue that Schellenberg found opposed to idiomatic writing for the organ (but that, presumably, he found well suited to the harpsichord). Griepenkerl, obviously, took a different view of things.

8. Toccata, Adagio, and Fugue in C Major, BWV 564

BECKER: Toccata and Fugue in C Major. Edited according to two manuscript copies. The toccata is not without its peculiarities, but it is greatly overshadowed in this respect by the fugue, which features a hunting-horn-like subject and many unrefined passages that are completely foreign to Bach's style, for example [at this point, Becker illustrates measures 93–94 of the fugue, showing the parallel fifths there]. Would Bach, if he really did compose the fugue, have concluded without any pedal? Has he done this anywhere else in one of his organ fugues?

SCHELLENBERG: Toccata and Fugue in C Major. (Edited according to manuscript copies.) The same accusation can be made against this work as the previous one: neither the harpsichord-like toccata nor the fugue, with its trumpet-like subject, can be regarded as an organ composition by Bach.[84]

Example 2.1. Fugue, measures 93–94, from the Toccata, Adagio, and Fugue in C Major, BWV 564

Despite the objections of Becker and Schellenberg, this is another unquestionably authentic organ composition by Bach. Unbeknownst to either critic, the work had already been published several months earlier as volume 21 of G. W. Körner's *Der Orgel-Virtuos*.[85] The piece is strikingly original, if not, to quote Becker, "peculiar." Griepenkerl described it as "little-known and yet very interesting." Schellenberg's mention of the toccata's "harpsichord-like" style probably has to do with the virtual absence of pedal in the opening twelve bars. Curiously, none of the three even mentioned the beautiful "Adagio" movement that stands between the toccata and fugue. In stark contrast to how Becker and Schellenberg denounced the work, the music pedagogue Ernst Julius Hentschel, writing in 1845, praised it as "a composition that by itself would give sufficient testimony to Bach's gigantic genius, even if no other note by this lofty master had survived."[86]

Most noteworthy are Becker's criticisms of the fugue. He was absolutely indignant (as later commentators have been) about how the pedals drop out for the last three bars, reasoning that someone other than Bach must have been responsible. Concerning the subject itself, Becker found the fanfare-like figure used for the first three phrases more evocative of the hunting horn than the organ. In his concluding remarks, he described the tune, as did Schellenberg in his commentary, as a "Trompetenthema." The passage that he illustrated as evidence of the fugue's "unrefined" style (mm. 93–94) contains a whole series of parallel fifths between the top two voices (see Example 2.1).[87] Remarkably, the same passage was cited about twenty years later by Johannes Brahms, in his famous collection *Octaven und Quinten*, and by Wilhelm Rust, in the preface to volume 15 of the Bachgesellschaft edition of Bach's complete works (p. xxxiv), published in 1867, and then about a century later by Hermann Keller, in his monograph on Bach's organ works.[88] Brahms tolerated these fifths because they alternate between a diminished and a perfect fifth, while Rust changed the first note of the lower voice in measure 94 from f♯″ to e″. Keller maintained that only a musical philistine would object.

9 and 10. Prelude and Fugue in A Minor, BWV 551, and Prelude and Fugue in E Minor, BWV 533

BECKER: Prelude and Fugue in A Minor. Published in an earlier edition by Peters and edited here according to a manuscript copy. A small work indeed, but not an unworthy one.

Prelude and Fugue in E Minor. Edited according to some manuscript copies. The two movements are of slight importance and absolutely do not whet the organist's appetite.

SCHELLENBERG: Prelude and Fugue in A Minor. Prelude and Fugue in E Minor. We cannot find anything worthy of praise in these two works, the first of which is already known from an old Peters edition, except that they are allegedly by Bach. If this is the case, they probably have no place in the volume under review.[89]

Neither Becker nor Schellenberg managed to shed any light on either of these pieces. Schellenberg questioned Bach's authorship, just as he doubted that either work could have been composed for the organ. In fact, both compositions are undoubtedly genuine, if early, organ works by Bach. Circumstantial evidence suggests that Becker taught the A-minor prelude and fugue to his esteemed colleague Robert Schumann, who saw fit in his personal copy of the "Bureau de Musique" edition to enter various registration markings.[90]

THEIR CONCLUDING REMARKS

BECKER: Having considered the individual contents of this volume, we have no recourse but to urge the editor, as he prepares the hopefully soon-to-appear fourth volume of this series, to select only those works from Bach's oeuvre that this hero of music actually intended for the organ, that is, the church organ. Not every fugue with pedal was conceived for the church organ. Many of Bach's pedal fugues, in our opinion, are appropriate only for use in the home.

Divorced from this context, they completely lose their purpose. It is not improbable that a few of the works in the present volume were merely sketched out and performed in the heat of the moment at the composer's home. After all, every keyboard instrument at the time had its own pedalboard. The triviality and capriciousness of some of these fugue subjects make them inappropriate for use in the church. Consider the scurrilous subject of the fugue from No. 10 [BWV 533]; or the long-drawn-out subject from that of No. 7 [BWV 566], a theme that reminds one of the pigtails and periwigs of the Seven Years' War; or the horn-like, trumpet-like subject from that of No. 8 [BWV 564]. For merrymaking in the home, however, such melodies are completely appropriate . . . We believe that it is absolutely necessary to carefully consider a work's character before assuming that it was intended for the church organ, especially when dealing with a work from the eighteenth century, which was an era when household instruments such as the harpsichord, positiv, and portativ came equipped with a pedalboard. Without such careful consideration, one does a disservice to the old masters. Who would want to sin in such a tasteless way against Bach, who knew so well the difference between music for the church and music for the home?

SCHELLENBERG: We urge the editor to carefully consider his choice of music in future volumes of this series. The Bach that we know and revere is seen only in No. 1 [BWV 552], No. 2 [BWV 540], No. 3 [BWV 538], the fugue of No. 5 [BWV 535], and the fugue of No. 6 [BWV 537]. No one would want to accuse him of such aberrations as No. 7 [BWV 566], No. 8 [BWV 564], No. 9 [BWV 551], or No. 10 [BWV 533]. Forkel speaks of this himself, how this master of music for the church and the home, of music for the organ and the harpsichord, knew so well to separate the two spheres and to treat the two instruments unlike the other. How can we assume that pieces like the latter named ones were intended by Bach for the organ?[91]

Happily, Becker's and Schellenberg's concluding remarks allow for a somewhat better understanding of their commentaries on the individual works contained in Griepenkerl's edition. To start with the works deemed by them as "harpsichord-like," they both evidently believed those pieces to have been composed not for the large church organ, but for *household* instruments fitted with a pedalboard, such as the harpsichord, clavichord, positiv organ, and portativ organ.[92] Schellenberg cited Johann Nikolaus Forkel as an authority in these matters, surely in reference to the following passage from Forkel's Bach biography, published in 1802:

> When we compare Bach's harpsichord compositions with those for the organ, we perceive that the melody and harmony in the two are of an entirely different kind. Hence, we may infer that, to play properly on the organ, the character of the ideas which the organist employs must be of primary import. This character is determined by the nature of the instrument, by the place in which it stands, and, lastly, by the object proposed. The full tone of the organ is, in its nature, not adapted to rapid passages: it requires time to die away in the large and free space of a church. If it is not allowed this time, the tones become confounded, and the performance indistinct and unintelligible. The movements suited to the organ and to the place must therefore be solemnly slow.[93]

Forkel, therefore, would probably have agreed with Becker that the slow, largely stepwise subject of the Fugue in F Major (No. 2) represented a kind of organ ideal, and that the excessively busy subject of the first fugue from the C-major prelude and fugue (No. 7) and the choppy, gigue-like fugue subject of the Toccata in C Major (No. 8) were the antithesis of that ideal. Still, the nineteenth-century notion that the organ is inherently incompatible with fast figuration is an arbitrary one, and one that is refuted time and again by Bach's compositions for the instrument.[94]

To continue with Becker's remarks on two of the fugue subjects, he must have found the subject of the E-minor fugue (No. 10) to be "scurrilous" because of the repeated notes at the outset and the note-for-note repetition of the four-note motive that follows.[95] Both traits, however, merely betray the influence of the North German organ school on the young

Bach. Repeated notes also factor prominently in the subject of the first fugue from the C-major prelude and fugue (No. 7), but the theme is truly "long-drawn-out" because of all the sequential material in its last three bars. Again, both traits characterize the music of such North German composers as Buxtehude and Georg Böhm. Curiously, this fugue subject suggested to Becker the music of the post-Bach generation—the Seven Years' War took place from 1756 to 1763—when in fact it was inspired by the works of Bach's predecessors. Becker must have associated its repeated notes and sequences with the frilliness of Rococo style.

In closing, it is my hope that the material presented here not only enhances our understanding of musical life and thought in the city of Leipzig during the first half of the nineteenth century but also allows us to imagine what it must have been like to encounter a new work by Johann Sebastian Bach at this point in history, when the so-called Bach revival was still in its infancy. At the very least, by studying how these three individuals reacted to the music, we see these timeless masterpieces in a new and interesting light.

3

Karl Gottlieb Freudenberg's *Erinnerungen aus dem Leben eines alten Organisten* and Bach Reception in the Nineteenth Century

In this essay, I hope to demonstrate that the memoirs of the organist Karl Gottlieb Freudenberg constitute an important but largely neglected source of information on the reception of the music of Johann Sebastian Bach in the nineteenth century. They shed light on the reception of various works by Bach, including some of the composer's most beloved organ compositions and his monumental St. Matthew Passion. In addition, these memoirs offer, quite surprisingly, a couple of anecdotes about Franz Liszt that seem to have gone completely unnoticed in the musicological literature. They also make for an entertaining read, thanks to Freudenberg's wit and sense of humor.

Freudenberg was born in 1797 in the Silesian village of Sipta. After serving in a huntsmen corps during the last two years of the Napoleonic Wars (1814–1815), he vowed to become a professional musician. He studied

The Afterlife of Bach's Organ Works. Russell Stinson, Oxford University Press. © Oxford University Press 2024.
DOI: 10.1093/oso/9780197680438.003.0004

first in Schmiedeberg with Christian Benjamin Klein, then in Breslau (today, the Polish city of Wrocław) with Friedrich Wilhelm Berner and Joseph Ignaz Schnabel. In the fall of 1822, he matriculated at the newly opened Institute for Church Music (Königliches Institut für Kirchenmusik) in Berlin, studying the organ with August Wilhelm Bach (no relation to Johann Sebastian), singing with Bernhard Joseph Klein, and theory with Carl Friedrich Zelter. The following year, Freudenberg returned to Breslau, offering musical instruction himself according to the methodology of Johann Bernhard Logier. In June 1825, Freudenberg began a pilgrimage to Italy, stopping en route in Vienna to meet Beethoven and spending nine months in Rome. While in Rome, he made the acquaintance of Giuseppe Baini, general administrator of the choir of the Sistine Chapel and the author of an influential book on Palestrina. Freudenberg greatly appreciated the choir's singing but thought little of Baini's organ playing, as these lines from the *Erinnerungen* illustrate: "Baini had no clue about the high art of playing Bach's organ works in the German manner [that is, with obbligato pedal]. His ideal was the Roman organist Frescobaldi, who was a dwarf in comparison to Bach's gigantic spirit."[1]

Freudenberg returned to Breslau in August 1826 and resumed his activities as a music instructor. Three years later, he was appointed Oberorganist at the Magdalenenkirche there, a position he retained until his death in 1869. Freudenberg's memoirs, titled *Erinnerungen aus dem Leben eines alten Organisten*, were published in 1870 by the Breslau house of F. E. C. Leuckart.[2] They are known primarily for the hour-long conversation Freudenberg had with Beethoven, in which the master assessed various composers past and present, and for an incident involving the young Felix Mendelssohn-Bartholdy.

To begin with the former, it is commonly and erroneously believed that Freudenberg's transcript of his meeting with Beethoven represents the earliest source for Beethoven's famous pun on "Bach," a word that in the German language means "brook." The passage in question reads as follows: "Beethoven held Bach in the highest esteem. 'His name should not be *Brook* but *Ocean*,' Beethoven said, 'because of his infinite and inexhaustible wealth of melodies and harmonies.'"[3] In fact, there are at least three earlier citations of Beethoven's wordplay in nineteenth-century sources, not to mention a document in Beethoven's own hand from 1801 in which he used the Bach/brook pun in reference to Bach's daughter Regina Susanna.

The earliest of these citations was made by the Leipzig organist, critic, and music professor Carl Ferdinand Becker, who in 1840 published in the Leipzig-based *Neue Zeitschrift für Musik* an article on the history of "Hausmusik." In discussing the evolution of theme-and-variations form, Becker stated that even Beethoven was eclipsed by Bach as a titan of this genre:

Proficient masters of our own time stand closer to Bach in this realm than do Bach's predecessors, and they have created splendid works of this type. But have they surpassed Bach? Certainly not. Even if Beethoven, the composer of such a great work as the Diabelli Variations, Op. 120, had been honored in his lifetime for all his compositions in theme-and-variations form, he would merely have passed on those laurels to Bach, who, Beethoven said, should not be called *Brook* but *Ocean*.[4]

Ten years later, in the summer of 1850, and in conjunction with an event in Leipzig commemorating the centennial of Bach's death, the Leipzig singer (and Mendelssohn biographer) Wilhelm Adolf Lampadius authored an eleven-stanza poem in praise of Bach that incorporates Beethoven's pun.[5] This encomium was recited by Lampadius himself to begin the gathering and was then published, less than two weeks later, in the *Neue Zeitschrift*. In stanza five, Lampadius likens Bach's music to an ocean of rising waves. He then concludes the stanza with these lines: "Und wunderbar ist uns das Wort enthüllt / des edelsten von deines Geistes Söhnen: / 'Er war kein Bach, er war ein Meer des Schönen.'" A translation would go something like this: "And how wonderful are these words by that most noble son of your spirit: 'He was no *brook*, he was an *ocean* of beauty.'" Lampadius added a footnote to the last line that reads "Beethoven sagte so" ("Beethoven said so").

Almost exactly two years later, in late July 1852, we find the same pun mentioned by the composer and conductor Woldemar Bargiel in his personal diary.[6] Known unofficially as Bargiel's "Rhineland" diary, this was the journal kept by the young artist during the summer of 1852, while a guest at the home of Robert and Clara Schumann in Düsseldorf. As Clara's half-brother and an acquaintance of Robert's since 1839, Bargiel was well connected to both Schumanns. Robert also seems to have primed Bargiel to become as formidable a Bach connoisseur as he was himself. After going on a walk with Robert one day and discussing various matters related to Bach and his oeuvre, Bargiel wrote the following lines about their conversation: "When I said that Beethoven had said about Bach that he was no *brook* but an *ocean*, Schumann contended that Beethoven could not properly perceive Bach, because he was too preoccupied with his own compositions and because during Beethoven's time only the Well-Tempered Clavier and a few motets were known."[7]

The common denominator for these three citations of Beethoven's pun is the city of Leipzig, where, of course, Bach spent most of his career. Becker and Lampadius spent their entire lives there, and Bargiel was a student at the Leipzig Conservatory from 1846 to 1850, during which time he was one of Becker's organ students.[8] One can only conclude that by 1850 the pun had become common knowledge among musicians in Leipzig and that it had been transmitted there orally, either directly or indirectly, by one or more of Beethoven's personal acquaintances. (Robert Schumann, too, was undoubtedly aware of Beethoven's pun. Schumann lived in Leipzig from around 1830 to 1844, and he was the editor of the *Neue Zeitschrift* at the time Becker published his "Hausmusik" article.)

I would propose as prominent links in this line of transmission two different individuals. One is the critic and editor Friedrich Rochlitz (1769–1842), who was probably the original link in the whole process. Rochlitz spent virtually his whole life in Leipzig, but in 1822 he made a trip to Vienna, where he claimed to have met Beethoven. At that time, he could have heard the pun from Beethoven himself or from one of Beethoven's Viennese acquaintances. As an ardent proponent of the music of both Bach and Beethoven, Rochlitz undoubtedly would have enjoyed sharing

Beethoven's brilliant bit of wordplay with any number of *his* acquaintances upon returning to Leipzig. The other individual is the pianist Ignaz Moscheles (1794–1870). Before moving to Leipzig in 1846—he remained there for the rest of his days—Moscheles had for many years been one of Beethoven's closest confidants. Like Rochlitz, he was also a Bach champion in his own right. Furthermore, like Becker, he was one of Bargiel's professors at the Leipzig Conservatory.[9]

All of which leads to Beethoven's above-mentioned use of the Bach/brook pun in reference to Regina Susanna Bach (1742–1809), J. S. Bach's twentieth and last child. In 1800, none other than Friedrich Rochlitz had made an appeal to the readers of the *Allgemeine Musikalische Zeitung* for donations on behalf of this Bach daughter, who was evidently living in abject poverty. A year later, Beethoven learned of the meager amount of those donations and expressed his outrage in a letter to his publisher, Breitkopf & Härtel. More importantly, he proposed that the proceeds of one of his future compositions be contributed to the cause. Nothing came of Beethoven's plans, despite his magnanimity:

> A good friend whom I recently visited showed me the account of what had been collected for the daughter of the Immortal God of Harmony. I was astonished by the negligible sum that Germany, *your* Germany, has dedicated to this person whom I so revere because of her father. This brings me to a thought: how would it be if I brought out something for her benefit on a subscription basis? Write me quickly how this would best be accomplished, so that it may happen before *this Bach* dies, that is, before *this brook* dries up, and we can no longer water it. It goes without saying that you must be the publisher.[10]

As for the "Mendelssohn incident" referred to above, the Staatsbibliothek zu Berlin today owns a manuscript copy in Mendelssohn's hand of J. S. Bach's Prelude and Fugue in E Minor for organ, BWV 533. The manuscript bears the inscription "Von Freudenberg auf der Akademie erhalten und abgeschrieben, d. 9. Dez. 1822" ("received from Freudenberg at the Academy and copied on 9 December 1822").[11] In this context, the word "Akademie" can mean only the famous Berlin Singakademie, as Mendelssohn was then singing in the choir of this ensemble and Freudenberg was known to attend its rehearsals. Therefore, it is reasonable to assume that in conjunction with a rehearsal of the Singakademie on 9 December 1822, Mendelssohn copied the work from a manuscript in Freudenberg's hand. Freudenberg's manuscript has not survived, but he no doubt prepared it from a still extant manuscript then owned by August Wilhelm Bach, Freudenberg's organ professor at the Institute for Church Music in Berlin.[12] The work was not published until 1833, in the edition by Mendelssohn and Adolph Bernhard Marx titled *Johann Sebastian Bach's noch wenig bekannte Orgelcompositionen*.[13]

Although only thirteen years old at the time, Mendelssohn had been a private organ student of A. W. Bach's since the fall of 1820. This Bach, however, seems only to have resented his star pupil, both because of his superior musicianship and his ethnicity, as the following story from Freudenberg's *Erinnerungen* illustrates:

[A. W.] Bach taught organ playing. He was an efficient composer of fugues and a talented organist, although he did not possess the insights into chorale playing that my teacher in Schmiedeberg, Herr Klein, did. He was normally quite pleasant. but little Felix's ever-growing prominence made him suspicious and envious. Mendelssohn wanted to make a copy of an unpublished [J. S.] Bach fugue from his copy, but he would not allow it. He said to me, because I had already copied out the fugue for myself, "Why does that Jew-boy have to have everything? He has enough as it is; don't let him copy that fugue." I did, however, unhesitatingly allow dear Felix to copy that holy relic. He was delighted. He shook my hand and told me, "Freudenberg, for this gift I will never forget you!"[14]

Felix Mendelssohn, of course, would go on to become one of the leading musical talents of his generation. It is a little-known fact that shortly after Mendelssohn's tragically early death in November 1847, Freudenberg organized for the citizens of Breslau a memorial service in honor of the great man. The venue was presumably the Magdalenenkirche, where Freudenberg was Oberorganist. According to the periodical *Urania*, Freudenberg played two of Mendelssohn's organ sonatas, two chorale settings by J. S. Bach, and another chorale setting of his own composition.[15] Perhaps he also played the Bach prelude and fugue that Mendelssohn had copied from him decades earlier.

To return to the academic year of 1822/23 at the Institute for Church Music, Freudenberg at some point was required to undergo the equivalent of an organ "jury," or, as he referred to it, an "öffentliche Prüfung im Orgelspiel."[16] In attendance were his three main professors (A. W. Bach, B. J. Klein, and C. F. Zelter), plus the eminent hymnologist Carl von Winterfeld, various other "musical celebrities," and even the Prussian education minister Karl vom Stein zum Altenstein. Freudenberg played his own prelude on "Ein feste Burg ist unser Gott" as well as "a difficult fugue in G minor by Sebastian Bach." The Bach work was presumably the Fugue in G Minor, BWV 542/2, which is not only one of the composer's most technically challenging organ works but one closely associated with A. W. Bach, since he was the first to publish the piece.[17] Freudenberg played well, but he insulted his distinguished audience by exiting the hall without even looking in their direction. They were "horrified," and Zelter was appalled by the young man's "unsurpassed rudeness."

Freudenberg tackled a different fugue by J. S. Bach when in 1829 he successfully auditioned for the post of Oberorganist at the Magdalenenkirche in Breslau. The only other contestant was a man by the name of "Voigt," who, like Freudenberg, had studied in Schmiedeberg with Christian Benjamin Klein. Freudenberg described his audition in these terms:

> The requirements for this audition were more difficult and involved than usual. First, you had to improvise a trio on a chorale tune, using two manuals and pedal and observing the rules of counterpoint. Then you had to improvise preludes to two different congregational chorales. One was to be a hymn of mourning, while the other was to be more joyous in nature. Then you had to sight-read a prelude and

play another one that had been prepared ahead of time in which not only "hand and foot" but also "heart and mind" were engaged. For the latter prelude, I chose from the masterworks of Sebastian Bach. It was a piece of the highest order: a long, five-voice fugue consisting of a "Largo" with broad, serious, and majestic chords; a lively "Fugato" on a long-winded subject; and a "Presto Finale" with all manner of contrapuntal chicanery. It was a mighty composition that, owing to its diverse contents and sheer poetry, I played to my heart's content.[18]

There can be little question about which Bach fugue was offered by Freudenberg on this occasion. To begin with, keyboard fugues of any kind by Bach in five voices are quite rare. Only one such fugue by him, however, at all matches the particular tripartite structure described by Freudenberg, and it is the sublime Fugue in E-flat Major (BWV 552/2) that closes Part 3 of the *Clavierübung*. Bach may not actually have marked the first part of this fugue (mm. 1–37) to be played "largo," yet the absence of any rhythm faster than a quarter note implies a relatively slow tempo. Moreover, the texture is unusually homorhythmic for a fugue, an aspect of the music that does sometimes suggest a series of chords. In the second part of the movement (mm. 37–82), following a change in meter from common time to $\frac{6}{4}$ time, Bach introduces a livelier second subject, whose twenty-three eighth notes, versus the seven notes in the first subject, do indeed make for a comparatively "long-winded" theme. The third part of the fugue (mm. 82–117) bears no tempo marking such as "presto," but its gigue-like time signature of $\frac{12}{8}$ and its fast rhythms imply a sprightly tempo. What Freudenberg means by "contrapuntal chicanery" is how the new subject here is ingeniously combined with the original one. Bach employs the same technique in the second part of the fugue.

Freudenberg's supervisor at his new position in Breslau was the elderly Johann Wilhelm Fischer (1762–1850), a native of Breslau who had been at the church for twenty years. Fischer was appointed Pfarrer there in 1809, Konsistorialrat in 1810, and Superintendent in 1815.[19] In 1831, he became the "inspector" of the Protestant churches and schools in the city as well as the "Pastor primarius" at the Magdalenenkirche. It is clear from Freudenberg's

Erinnerungen in general and from the following vignette in particular that the two men did not always see eye to eye on liturgical issues. In this instance, they argued on one of the happiest days of the church year, Jubilate Sunday, the fourth Sunday in the Easter season and one named after the introit for that day, "Jubilate Deo, omnis terra" ("Make a joyful noise unto God, all ye lands"). An unspecified prelude by Bach figures in the story, but the main topic from a musical perspective, was whether the final note of the German Credo, Luther's "Wir glauben all an einen Gott," should be harmonized with a major or minor chord, that is, with or without a Picardy third. As Freudenberg related the incident,

once, the querulous Herr Fischer came up into the organ loft during an afternoon worship service just as I was joyously playing a magnificent prelude by Sebastian Bach; I was playing well technically, and it was a rousing performance altogether. After I finished, I was expecting from the man a cheerful "Bravissimo" for my performance of this beautiful piece. Instead, I had to hear him say, "My God, how can you conclude the Credo on a major chord?" I was dumbfounded that the Bach prelude could be mistaken for the Credo, and I explained to Herr Fischer the difference between the two. "No," he said, "I'm talking about the service we had this morning." I responded, "Oh, I see. Well, a major chord works well to conclude a tune in the Dorian mode and ending the Credo on a minor chord would make Jubilate Sunday feel more like one of the Rogation days."[20] Fischer responded, "My God, you and your innovations!" To which I said, "My God, why do you worry so much about my organ playing when you understand nothing about it? The pulpit is your realm, the organ is mine. Otherwise, I would dictate to you the content of your sermons, and I would have to put up with your ignorant objections to my organ playing." To which Fischer responded, "This is outrageous! In its five hundred years, the Magdalenenkirche has never had such a rude organist!" To which I responded, "And the church has never seen within its walls such a musical ignoramus as you. God must have made you church inspector in a fit of rage." Meanwhile, our conversation had attracted various unwanted spectators and listeners into the organ loft, but I quickly got rid of them. Herr Fischer then asked, "Should I leave too?" "Naturally," I answered, "no one has any business up here except me." He went and I stayed. All my anger gradually subsided, and I was able to conclude the service in peace.[21]

Whereas Freudenberg may merely have tolerated J. W. Fischer, he sincerely admired other residents of Breslau, and none more so than Johann Theodor Mosewius (1788–1858).[22] One of the staunchest Bachians of the day, Mosewius in 1825 founded the Breslau Singakademie, an ensemble that he would conduct over the next thirty-three years in numerous choral works by Bach, including several of the composer's cantatas and motets as well as portions of the B Minor Mass and Christmas Oratorio.[23] But no Bach work was performed more often by Mosewius's Singakademie than the St. Matthew Passion, which the group presented nine different times from 1830 to 1847. Such was Mosewius's interest in the work that in 1852 he published a seventy-nine-page analysis of it. Titled *Johann Sebastian Bach's Matthäus-Passion*, this study introduced Bach's masterpiece to legions of music lovers across Europe.[24]

In discussing Mosewius's character and personality, Freudenberg recalled how a certain movement from the St. Matthew Passion had lifted his friend's spirits on even such a sad occasion as the burial of one of his children: as the child's coffin was borne through the church, Freudenberg played on the organ the four-part chorale "Was mein Gott will, das g'scheh allzeit" ("What my God wants, may it always happen") from Part 1 of the Passion, utterly transforming Mosewius's demeanor. According to Freudenberg, that chorale harmonization was Mosewius's favorite of the twelve contained in the work:

In his domestic life, Mosewius had to endure much sorrow, anxiety, and pain. But by taking walks to experience the beauty of nature and by spending time with fellow artists and scholars, he was able to pull himself out of his depression and once again have the strength and courage to continue his artistic endeavors. Take, for example, the burial service of his beloved young son. As the boy's coffin was carried through the church, I played to Mosewius on the organ his favorite chorale from the St. Matthew Passion, "Was mein Gott will, das g'scheh allzeit, sein Will der ist der beste" ["What my God wants, may it always happen; His will is always best"], and exactly as Bach wrote it, without adding or subtracting a single note. I saw Mosewius's mood change from despair to absolute confidence in the will of God.[25]

A biography of Mosewius by Anna Kempe, published the year after his death, further illuminates the man's sorrowful domestic situation. We learn from this source that a few years before the death of his son, Mosewius's wife had unexpectedly died, leaving behind five young children without a mother. Also, according to Kempe, the son who died had been in poor health for some time, and Mosewius had regularly and lovingly attended to him during his long illness. The boy's death haunted Mosewius for the rest of his life:

A few years after the death of his wife, a sweet, charming boy of his died after a long, debilitating illness. His love of the child was such that Mosewius would rush to the boy's sickbed whenever he could find a free hour in his work schedule, but the boy's illness was also deeply painful to him. He carried the loss of his son in his thoughts for many years thereafter, and it caused him to shed many a tear.[26]

Turning more to musical matters, Mosewius's vivid account of the harmonization of "Was mein Gott will" in his monograph on the St. Matthew Passion deserves to be quoted at length, for in writing that the main message of the chorale was "steadfast trust in God . . . even in times of *sorrow and adversity*" ("festes Vertrauen auf Gott . . . *in Leid und Ungemach*"), he was surely thinking of his son's death, which had occurred decades earlier. As for the "splendidly expressive" voice leading mentioned in the penultimate sentence of this passage, Mosewius no doubt had in mind the rising

Example 3.1. Harmonization of "Was mein Gott will, das g'scheh allzeit" from the St. Matthew Passion, BWV 244, measures 4–12

scalar figures in the middle voices with which the final phrase begins (see Example 3.1). Their upward motion suggests a positive affect, and the way the voices overlap suggests a canon at the fifth:

> In this instance, Bach sets the first stanza of the chorale text, which in general speaks about a steadfast trust in God ... even in times of sorrow and adversity. Already, the strong, positive conclusion of the first line ["What my God wants, may it always happen"] makes a strong impact, and the conclusion of the fifth line, with the text "fromme Gott" ["er hilft aus Not, der fromme Gott" / "He helps us in times of need, this faithful God"], does as well. In setting the text "und züchtiget mit Massen" ["and punishes us in good measure"], Bach begins in the tenor voice with a downward series of sigh motives and concludes with a beautiful triadic figure, thereby exuding a sense of gentle resignation. Then, with the text "Wer Gott vertraut, fest auf ihn gebaut" ["He who trusts in God builds firmly upon Him"], the message becomes more positive again. For the powerful conclusion, set to the text "den wird er nicht lassen" ["God will not abandon him"], the voice leading of the alto and tenor is splendidly expressive.

Again, we are left with a great masterpiece that deeply expresses its poetry.[27]

Not to dwell too long on Mosewius, but one other passage from his monograph on the St. Matthew Passion needs to be considered. It is the very next paragraph in his book, and it implies that he in fact may not have been entirely satisfied with Freudenberg's rendition of this chorale, despite Freudenberg's good intentions (and his strict adherence to Bach's score). Mosewius may be stating the obvious here, but the negative tone of his remarks is seriously at odds with Freudenberg's report on the matter:

It cannot be restated enough that such chorale harmonizations, if played on an instrument, can never express themselves as well as when they are sung. Anyone who knows the chorales in their heart and mind realizes that they do reveal something of their essence when played rather than sung. But without their texts, their true content remains locked. Otherwise, Bach becomes less a musical poet than a mere technician, even if he is the grandest and most meticulous of all musical architects.[28]

Over a decade after the funeral of Mosewius's son, Freudenberg performed at the Magdalenenkirche under much happier circumstances. The occasion was a visit to Breslau in December 1841 by the music theorist and composer Adolph Bernhard Marx. Marx had come to town to oversee the premiere of his oratorio *Moses*, which was being performed by the Breslau Singakademie under Mosewius's baton.[29] Mosewius was one of Marx's closest friends, and Freudenberg had presumably at least gotten to know Marx during his year at the Institute for Church Music in Berlin: Marx was also living in Berlin at that time, and both he and Freudenberg belonged to the social and artistic circle of the Mendelssohn family.[30] Freudenberg is also known to have relied on Marx's *Die Lehre von der musikalischen Komposition*, published between 1837 and 1847, in his own teaching.[31]

It cannot be said that the premiere performance of *Moses* was an unqualified success—or that the oratorio itself was ever critically acclaimed. An organ recital played by Freudenberg for Marx during his stay in the Silesian capital, however, must have delighted its honoree. The program began and ended, respectively, with chorale settings by Marx and Freudenberg (the same arrangement of "Ein feste Burg" that Freudenberg had played on his organ jury at the Institute for Church Music), and it also included the Toccata in F Major, BWV 540/1, a piece that Marx had referred to in his *Kompositionslehre* as "the *mighty* Toccata in F Major by Sebastian Bach."[32] Freudenberg described the event as follows:

> In the year 1841, the famous theorist Adolph Bernhard Marx appeared in Breslau in order to gain some validity as a practical musician through a performance of his oratorio *Moses*, which took place on 2 December. . . . To honor Marx, I had planned an organ concert at the Magdalenenkirche. As he entered the church, I greeted him with his own imposing organ prelude to the chorale "Triumph, Triumph, es kommt mit Pracht," from his *Choral- und Orgelbuch*. I also played Bach's Toccata in F Major and some other pieces, and I concluded with my prelude to Luther's chorale "Ein feste Burg ist unser Gott," a work that met with Marx's full approval.[33]

The Bach toccata essayed by Freudenberg in honor of Marx is a work actually more associated with another organist who lived in Breslau at that time, Freudenberg's friend and colleague Adolph Friedrich Hesse (1809–1863). Hesse was based in Breslau his entire life, but he also regularly toured as a concert artist. In 1831, at the tender age of twenty-two, he was appointed Oberorganist at the Bernhardinkirche, a position he held until his death. Hesse may also be regarded as the single greatest organ virtuoso of the era. Something of a child prodigy, he was already concertizing in Germany as an organist and pianist at the age of nine. He is documented to have played the F-major toccata in 1838 on a concert tour of northern Germany and Denmark, but by far his most famous performance of the movement took place in 1844, when he inaugurated the

Daublaine-Callinet organ at the church of St. Eustache in Paris.[34] His huge audience on that occasion took particular pleasure in Hesse's footwork, an aspect of his organ technique that would have been on full display in the two lengthy and demanding pedal solos of Bach's toccata. Hesse, in turn, was presumably *in* the audience when Freudenberg performed the toccata in honor of Marx.

Hesse figures prominently in the next excerpt from Freudenberg's *Erinnerungen* to be discussed here, one that involves a visit to Breslau in January and February 1843 by Franz Liszt, who was then arguably the most famous musician in the world. Thirty-one years old at the time, Liszt was on a concert tour of Silesia, and he was making his debut in Breslau, where he spent about two-and-a-half weeks.[35] In addition to conducting Mozart's *Die Zauberflöte* at the local opera house, he played a total of twelve piano recitals, by all accounts dazzling his audiences. According to Freudenberg's *Erinnerungen*, Liszt also (1) had an awkward but amusing conversation with Freudenberg and Hesse about which of the two should play an organ recital in his honor and (2) was treated to such a recital by Freudenberg, whose program contained a goodly number of works by J. S. Bach. The passage in question, quoted below, is both informative and humorous, yet to my knowledge it has never been mentioned in the literature on either Liszt or Bach:

> Hesse and I met with Liszt during his visit, and, like everyone else in town, we were taken in by the amiability of the young virtuoso. Hesse offered to play a recital for Liszt at the Bernhardinkirche, but Liszt then proposed that I, as an Oberorganist, should also "ride" my organ for him! Although I was not as bold a "rider" as Hesse, I agreed to Liszt's proposal, and I hoped to survive the ordeal. Hesse, though, felt that only he should have the privilege of such opportunities, that only he should be allowed to "let his light shine" before foreign artists; my friend Hesse's cheeks got as red as a boiled crab. My organ recital, which took place at the Magdalenenkirche, was unexpectedly attended by many high-society ladies, who definitely had not come out of any passion for "learned" organ music: their eyes

were more fixed on Liszt than their ears were fixed on my playing. I performed various organ works by Bach, including a trio on the chorale "Schmücke dich, o liebe Seele." The many trills and other embellishments in this work, much to Liszt's amusement, could not be properly realized on such a sluggish instrument.[36]

This excerpt raises a whole host of issues, starting with the conversation Liszt had with these two organists. Hesse, who was a celebrated virtuoso himself, felt that the privilege of playing for Liszt was his alone. Liszt, who may have been offended by Hesse's selfishness, disagreed, proposing that Freudenberg offer a recital as well, since Freudenberg was an "Oberorganist," meaning the principal organist of his church. Unbeknownst to Liszt, however, Hesse was also an Oberorganist, only at a different church. Still, it may be said that Hesse won out in the end, for we know from another source that he played not one but two recitals in Liszt's honor, both presumably at the Bernhardinkirche. According to this source, which is a letter written by Hesse a few months later to the composer and violinist Louis Spohr, Liszt also heard in Breslau a performance of Hesse's fifth symphony, no doubt conducted by the composer. To quote from Hesse's letter, "I spent much time with Liszt. He also heard my latest symphony, and I gave two organ recitals for him."[37] When Spohr visited Breslau in 1850, Hesse played an organ recital at the Bernhardinkirche in *his* honor, causing the honoree to praise the performer's "total mastery" of his art on that "sublime instrument."[38]

Another musical luminary of the era for whom Hesse played organ works by Bach is Clara Wieck. Thanks to her newly published *Jugendtagebücher*, the diaries she kept before marrying Robert Schumann, we know that Clara first heard Hesse at the organ in the winter of 1836, while she was concertizing in Breslau. Accompanied by her father, she was only sixteen years old at the time. As she wrote in her diary, "After lunch, Hesse played for us on the organ, and with the exquisite command of his instrument for which he is known. He played many works by Bach and himself, and he improvised a free fantasy. He is indisputably the greatest of all living organists."[39] In November 1839, Clara again heard Hesse play, but this time in Berlin, where she was again concertizing (and visiting her mother) and where he was preparing for a performance of his fifth symphony. As she wrote in her diary, "Before we went to the theater, we had a completely different kind of enjoyment. We heard Hesse play the organ at the Garnisonkirche, and masterfully so, like nobody else. He played some charming variations, then fugues by Bach, then a concert piece, etc. The organ took on a completely indescribable, magical quality."[40]

Hesse seems always to have included the music of Bach on his organ recitals, and there is no reason why he would not have done so when he played for Liszt, who was an avid Bach enthusiast himself.[41] If Hesse's surviving programs are any indication, he selected fugues from the Well-Tempered Clavier—playing his own *pedaliter* transcriptions of these movements—and from the so-called Six Great Preludes and Fugues for organ, BWV 543–548.[42] Liszt would have approved of either collection, since as a piano recitalist he played from both of them (his transcriptions of the "Six Great" were published in 1852). Of the fugues from the Well-Tempered Clavier, one of Hesse's favorites was the Fugue in C-sharp Minor from Book 1, one of only two triple fugues in the entire collection and one whose opening subject famously inspired Beethoven in the first movement of his String Quartet in C-sharp Minor, Op. 131. This fugue by Bach also seems to have been the one from the Well-Tempered Clavier most often played by Liszt.[43] Indeed, Liszt is documented to have played this fugue (along with its prelude) on his tour of Berlin during the winter of 1841/42, that is, just a year or so before his stay in Breslau.[44] It stands to reason, therefore, that when Hesse played for Liszt in Breslau, he chose this very fugue.

The recital that Freudenberg played for Liszt took place under less than ideal circumstances. The church was bitterly cold; the organ was in need of repair; and the audience was full of grandes dames more interested in ogling Liszt than in listening to "learned" organ music.[45] According to his *Erinnerungen*, Freudenberg essayed various pieces by Bach, including an arrangement of "Schmücke dich, o liebe Seele." But which of the three organ settings of this chorale composed by or ascribed to Bach did Freudenberg mean: the famous and undoubtedly authentic setting from

Karl Gottlieb Freudenberg's *Erinnerungen*

the Great Eighteen Chorales, BWV 654; the setting catalogued as BWV 759, now known to be by Bach's pupil Gottfried August Homilius; or the setting catalogued as BWV Anh. 74, a work evidently also composed by Homilius?[46]

Disappointingly, all the evidence points to the inauthentic BWV 759. First of all, this is the only one of the three works that was then in print, at least in a version for organ, and it had been so for almost forty years, as one of about forty works contained in J. G. Schicht's four-volume edition *J. S. Bach's Choral-Vorspiele für die Orgel mit einem und zwey Klavieren und Pedal*, published between 1803 and 1806.[47] It is far more likely that Freudenberg owned this widely circulated print than a manuscript of either

Example 3.2. Gottfried August Homilius, "Schmücke dich, o liebe Seele" (BWV 759), measures 1–12

of the other two settings. More tellingly, Freudenberg described the piece that he played as "an organ trio . . . with many trills and embellishments." By organ *trio*, of course, he meant a setting in three voices. This factor eliminates from consideration the Great Eighteen chorale, which has four voices. BWV Anh. 74 *is* an organ trio, but it is relatively unembellished, containing only three rather standard cadential trills and lacking any ornamentation to the chorale tune itself. Besides, this piece is so obscure that it remains unpublished even today.[48] Freudenberg's description, however, perfectly matches BWV 759, or at least the version of the work published by Schicht.[49] In this version, identical to that published in volume 40 of the Bachgesellschaft edition of Bach's complete works, there is a profusion of ornaments already in the first phrase of the chorale tune, which is furnished with three trills, a turn, and two sets of thirty-second notes (see Example 3.2). The ornamentation continues, albeit less profusely, until the end.

The final passage from Freudenberg's *Erinnerungen* that I would like to discuss almost certainly *does* concern the setting of "Schmücke dich" from the Great Eighteen Chorales. It originated in an essay by Freudenberg on the organ and its religious connotations that was published, toward the end of his life, in the 13 May 1868 issue of the *Breslauer Zeitung*, and then republished in the *Erinnerungen*, in a series of chapters appended by the editor of the book.[50] The passage betrays an enthusiasm for Bach's oeuvre bordering on outright religiosity: "Bach's music to 'Schmücke dich, o liebe Seele' is a gospel from his musical bible. He who does not believe that is an unmusical 'doubting Thomas' and has no right to parade either his musical knowledge or his sense of musical beauty."[51]

By way of explanation, the setting of "Schmücke dich" from the Great Eighteen Chorales had appeared in four different publications by the time Freudenberg penned these lines, most notably in an edition by Felix Mendelssohn titled *15 Große Choral-Vorspiele für die Orgel von Johann Sebastian Bach*, published in 1846, and in volume 7 of the Peters edition of the complete Bach organ works, whose preface is dated 1847.[52] Therefore, the piece had been in wide circulation for over twenty years. Furthermore, both Mendelssohn and Robert Schumann—two of the most celebrated musicians of the nineteenth century—were widely known to have revered the Great Eighteen chorale, and their veneration of the work no doubt exalted its status within German musical circles.[53]

Given these circumstances, one can only assume that Freudenberg, who was both a staunch advocate for the music of Bach and a veteran Protestant organist, knew the Great Eighteen chorale at the time he wrote his essay, and that he was referring to this work. Of course, he also knew the setting of "Schmücke dich" by Homilius (BWV 759), but it seems impossible that this overtly galant and relatively insubstantial piece could have inspired such religious fervor. Conversely, the Great Eighteen chorale is a compelling work both in terms of its musical content and its spirituality. Its inherent mysticism absolutely complements the subject matter of the chorale text, which is the rite of Communion.

To sum up, Karl Gottlieb Freudenberg was a true champion of the music of J. S. Bach. No doubt he would have agreed with how his erstwhile colleague Felix Mendelssohn once assessed Bach's place within the pantheon of great composers. In Mendelssohn's words, Bach was that "immortal master who in none of his works stands beneath any other master, and who in many of his works stands above all other masters."[54]

4

Bach Goes to Hollywood

The Use of His Music in Motion Pictures

That Johann Sebastian Bach has exerted a profound and enduring influence on posterity is an incontestable fact of music history. In other words, the Bachian legacy has significantly impacted and enriched the musical world at large, whether we mean composers, performers, conductors, critics, or listeners. One vital aspect of this phenomenon has been the mass dissemination of Bach's works in the twentieth century by means of technological innovations. In addition to the multitude of advances made in the field of recorded sound, these breakthroughs include the invention of radio and the birth of the digital age.

The advent of motion pictures has also played a major role in this process, as a multitude of films from the twentieth century feature the music of Bach in some way or another. An exact tally of these productions is impossible, given all the independent filmmakers involved, but according to that magnificent website known as IMDb (the Internet Movie Database), Bach's compositions have been appropriated in no fewer than 1,731 films and television programs from 1931 to the present.[1] Here, I would like to consider three films, one from the 1970s and two from the 1990s, that treat Bach's music with particular skill and imagination. Coincidentally, each won the coveted "Best Picture" Academy Award for the year of its release. Each also happens to be adapted from a bestselling novel.

The Afterlife of Bach's Organ Works. Russell Stinson, Oxford University Press. © Oxford University Press 2024.
DOI: 10.1093/oso/9780197680438.003.0005

Bach Goes to Hollywood

To begin with a picture from 1972, the climactic, five-minute-long baptism scene toward the end of Francis Ford Coppola's *The Godfather* incorporates two of Bach's organ works as well as some organ music written by Nino Rota, the composer of the film's score.[2] In reference to this scene, which is virtually absent from the Mario Puzo novel, the film-music scholar Royal Brown has contended that "no [other] film has used music so literally . . . to link megalomaniacal villains to their godlike aspirations."[3] In terms of Bach reception in the twentieth century, I would maintain that there is no more effective use of the composer's organ music to be found anywhere in the genre of cinema. To quote at some length from Brown's discourse,

Coppola mixes flamboyant crosscutting with almost imperceptible metamorphoses on the music track to suggest the final transformation of Michael Corleone (Al Pacino) into the new godfather. The sequence begins with a long shot of the interior of a cathedral in which Michael's nephew (also named Michael) is being baptized, with Michael standing as godfather. On the (apparently diegetic) music track, a solo organ modulates athematically through a series of major-mode chords. Some twenty-four seconds later, following a close-up of the baby Michael, the sequence cuts away for the first time to the preparations for what will become a series of five rubouts. But although we see the arms and hands of a killer preparing his weapon, we still hear the voice of the priest reciting the baptismal ceremony. And we still hear the organ music, although the tone has become slightly more ominous through the modulation to a minor-mode chord. This carefully choreographed pattern will continue: throughout the sequence, the crosscutting between the baptism and the executions moves along its ironic course, accelerating as the moments of the actual shootings approach. Never leaving the solo organ, on the other hand, the music seems to emanate solely from the church, although it backs both the baptism and the killings. A careful listening, however, reveals that if the timbres of the music belong to the church, the harmonies, form, and, ultimately, genre belong increasingly to the rubouts. Once the camera returns to the church following the first cutaway . . . , for instance, the music begins to suggest the passacaglia from Johann Sebastian Bach's famous Passacaglia and Fugue in C Minor, a morose work decidedly unsuitable for a baptism. During the third cutaway, which begins with Albert Neri (Richard Bright) taking a gun and a policeman's badge out of a bag, the passacaglia solidly establishes its identity. The music has moved into its second phase.

But the musical metamorphoses do not stop here, even though *The Godfather*'s end titles attribute the music for the "baptism sequence" simply to "J. S. Bach." In the next (fourth) cutaway, which begins with Barzini (Richard Conte) walking toward the screen, the music enters a third phase by actually switching genres into what might be called "silent-film doom-and-gloom," which begins to swell in the lower registers of the organ. In the next baptism shots the diegetic sound of baby Michael's crying adds an additional note of tension as the organ continues to crescendo. Then, preceding the first and second rubouts (the sixth and seventh cutaways), the organ, in classic silent-film fashion, crescendos to a sustained chord that acts as a prelude for each of the murders, which also, for the first time, include diegetic sound (gunshots, screams). By the end of the fifth rubout (Barzini's), the organ music metamorphoses back into its second phase, moving to the end of Bach's passacaglia. A sustained seventh chord accompanies the final cutaway (a series of three corpse shots) and then a shot of Michael with a candle in the foreground. A cut to the exterior of the cathedral, with its bell tolling, signals the end of this virtuoso sequence in which even diegetic sound—the baby's crying (all shots of the infant show an entirely placid, sleeping child), the church bells—tends, as a kind of musique concrète, to slip away from the diegesis.[4]

Trenchant commentary, to be sure, although one might argue that the "moroseness" of Bach's passacaglia is mitigated by the lively figuration that tends to accompany the ostinato.[5] I would also point out that what Brown hears in the fourth phase of his analysis as "classic silent-film" music actually comes from another organ work by Bach, the otherwise buoyant Prelude in D Major, BWV 532/1.[6] Bach's diminished-seventh chords here, especially the high-pitched one at the outset, more than faintly recall the infamous Toccata in D Minor, BWV 565, which is the piece that may have originated "scary" organ music as a cinematic trope in the first place, with Rouben Mamoulian's 1931 film *Dr. Jekyll and Mr. Hyde.*[7] Considering all the films from the next four decades that would exploit the toccata for this effect, the appearance of the D-major prelude in this scene comes as a pleasant surprise.

The protagonist of our second film is a man of great refinement who happens also to be a cannibal. I refer, of course, to Jonathan Demme's 1991 film *The Silence of the Lambs*, starring Anthony Hopkins as Dr. Hannibal Lecter. The Apollonian in Dr. Lecter loves the arts, and in one pivotal scene where he frees himself from two of his captors, killing them both, he is found listening to Bach's Goldberg Variations, as played by pianist Glenn Gould. As the movie begins, Lecter is serving multiple life sentences for a series of cannibalistic killings. He is first held in a hospital for the criminally insane, but by the time of this scene, and in compensation for assisting the FBI in its hunt for another serial killer, he has been promised a transfer to a prison with such amenities as a view of the woods and increased access to books. Before being moved to this new facility, Lecter is temporarily housed at a different location, where he is confined to what is essentially a steel cage. There he is provided with, among other luxuries, a cassette tape player for listening to music, having requested "Glenn Gould, the *Goldberg Variations*" as his listening selection.[8] The authorities have presumably supplied Gould's recording from 1981, and not that from 1955, since only the later recording was ever issued on cassette. In actuality, though, and to save money on royalties, the film used a recording made just for it by pianist Jerry Zimmerman.

The "Goldbergs," as I will refer to the work, have proven to be one of Bach's most popular pieces in either motion pictures or television probably because of the inherent gracefulness of the theme, an exquisitely ornamented, major-mode melody that exemplifies the Baroque dance type known as the sarabande and that is lyrical enough for Bach to have called it an "aria." At any rate, it is the Aria itself rather than any of the variations that is most often employed in these productions. Obviously, its gentle beauty makes for great irony within this extremely violent scene. The complex, even mathematically exact design of the Goldbergs as a whole, however, also symbolizes the calculating mind of this exceedingly cerebral criminal. For example, the Aria itself, which appears at the very beginning and end of the composition, comprises thirty-two measures, just as the work as a whole comprises thirty-two movements; the total number of variations is thirty, which is a multiple of three; and, in a unique tour de force of counterpoint, every third variation is wrought as a canon, starting at the unison and progressing all the way up to the ninth, in mathematical terms, 3×3. Furthermore, as the pop culturist Thomas Fahy has observed, Dr. Lecter carries out the killings in a remarkably meticulous, even artistic manner, all the while reveling in one of Bach's most meticulous creations.[9]

The use of classical music to denote culture may have become a cinematic commonplace,[10] but Fahy contends that cinematic aesthete-killers like Hannibal Lecter invert the idea of culture as a civilizing and humanizing force.[11] In other words, Lecter's actions in this scene, which is the only time in the movie when the audience witnesses physical violence by him, seem to shatter any assumptions about a connection between culture and civility. Surrounded by the trappings of high culture, represented here not only by classical music but also by tasteful reading material (copies of *Poetry* and *Bon Appétit* magazines), original artwork, and a gourmet meal, Lecter becomes a monstrous killer. The Thomas Harris novel introduces this scene as follows:

> Dr. Lecter toyed with his food while he wrote and drew and doodled on his pad with a felt-tipped pen. He flipped over the cassette in the tape player chained to the table leg and punched the play button. Glenn Gould playing Bach's Goldberg Variations on the piano. The music, beautiful beyond plight and time, filled the bright cage and the room where the warders sat.[12]

Bach Goes to Hollywood

With material from Howard Shore's film score inserted between two excerpts from the Goldbergs, the musical structure of this scene suggests a lopsided ABA form. Having already listened to the entire cassette at least once, Lecter flips it over, guaranteeing that the tape will replay from the beginning. And yet the first music we hear is cued in from measure 10 of the first movement, where the Aria itself is presented for the first time. This excerpt, which incorporates a repeat of the second half of the theme, continues for roughly two-and-a-half minutes until the end of the movement, but a terrifying chord from Howard Shore's orchestral score drowns out the final note, just as Dr. Lecter begins to break free. In the words of musicologist Carlo Cenciarelli,

> the timing of the attack is deliberately cut against the Aria's final cadence: just as the music's final appoggiatura is about to resolve on the closing tonic triad, Shore's underscore replaces the diegetic sound, eliding the resolution of the Aria with a downbeat of low brass, strings and timpani. The music is weighed down by clusters. Timpani and cymbals mark the downbeat of a slow binary tempo. In time with the dense, blasting low register, the high strings play non-legato segments which resonate with the film's stark, minor-mode main theme. The switch from Bach to the horror underscore produces a reduction of aesthetic distance that is crucial to the film's violence, designed to leave the viewer feeling shocked and violated.[13]

Following the attack, which lasts only about fifty seconds and which is accompanied only by Howard Shore's underscore, we hear a segment lasting about this long from Variation 7 of the Goldbergs. This movement was intended by Bach to suggest a gigue, as we know from a jotting made by him (al Tempo di Giga) in his personal copy of the original print of the Goldbergs.[14] The variation here seems to serve as Lecter's victory dance. To quote again from Cenciarelli's analysis,

> as the camera tracks along the lifeless body of one warden, the orchestra evaporates and the 'Goldberg' returns, the alternation of

diegetic music and underscore thus reinforcing the sequence's ternary structure. A gigue, Variation 7, is now playing, cued in from the middle of the first phrase. The tracking movement revisits details singled out at the start of the scene: Lecter's lunch, the [riot] baton, the tape player, now all spattered with blood. From the tape player the camera gradually pulls back to an establishing shot of the cage. Lecter stands at the centre of the frame, his face turned upwards and away from the corpse, moving his bloody fingers in time [to the music].[15]

Our third film is Steven Spielberg's haunting account of the Holocaust, *Schindler's List*. Released in 1993, this movie contains a nocturnal scene, entirely missing from the Thomas Keneally novel on which the film is based (*Schindler's Ark*), in which SS troops are about the business of liquidating the Jewish ghetto in Krakow. In hopes of finding occupants in hiding, a special SS squadron listens in with stethoscopes pressed to the ceiling above them. A young man who has been hiding inside an upright piano climbs out, stepping on the keyboard in the process. The resulting cluster of notes signals a group of soldiers, who charge upstairs and start shooting, presumably killing the young man. Next, we see a young SS officer expertly performing on the same piano, while the shooting continues. He is playing—at breakneck speed—the prelude to Bach's English Suite No. 2 in A Minor, a movement whose fast pace, disjunct figuration, and minor-mode harmonies are not inconsistent with this agitated situation.[16] Two of the officer's comrades, one a fellow officer and the other a common soldier, stop to observe the impromptu performance. As described by Andrew Ford, "It is a chilling moment, not least because it reminds us— if we needed reminding—that the Nazis were not monsters, but human beings behaving like monsters, and that some of them were accomplished and cultivated in other areas of their lives."[17] Still, the scene also smacks of the cultural ignorance and barbarity of the Nazi regime. The officer only guesses that Bach might be the composer, while the soldier is convinced that the music is by Mozart. Neither man really knows who the composer is, even though Bach was an unadulterated "Aryan" artist who only twice in his sixty-five years ventured outside the confines of modern Germany.[18] A work by Mozart, who was an Austrian and a cosmopolite, would not have made the same impact.

This scene has also been discussed by scholars of the Holocaust and the Third Reich. Consider, for instance, the following passage from Naomi Mandel's monograph *Against the Unspeakable: Complicity, the Holocaust, and Slavery in America*:

> The paradox of culture and genocide is a familiar one: how could a people who produced artists like Goethe and Beethoven act in so barbarous a manner? Like the machine-gun fire that illuminates the darkness of the ghetto at night, the "light" of German culture is explicitly sinister [in this context], and the questions posed by this paradox . . . are gestured toward but never answered. In this scene the paradox is rendered even more complex, since the soldiers are cultured enough to be arrested by the music, yet not cultured enough to know what they are hearing: they misidentify the composer . . . and their inaccurate choice of Mozart over Bach is significant since Mozart, unlike Bach, was not German.[19]

As for the piano-playing, machine-gun-wielding SS officer, the historian Michael Kater, in his book *The Twisted Muse: Musicians and Their Music in the Third Reich*, has postulated that this character was inspired by a Nazi archetype, one associated with the "organ-workshop" component of the Hitler Youth organization: "A tall, blond Youth leader in a smartly tailored brown uniform, flawlessly able to rattle off a Bach toccata on the organ, would possess all the desired social and political attributes; he would be universally admired, popular with the girls (to aid master-race procreation), a contemporary idol, the prototype of a new Führer."[20]

The chief ideologue of this workshop, as well as one of the leading musicians of the Nazi Confessionalist church, was the organist Herbert Haag.[21] Haag advocated that organ works specifically by Bach be played at Nazi gatherings for the glorification of that political regime. His activities as a Nazi organist need to be understood within the context of that party's adoption of the organ as its symbolic instrument of choice, something that occurred with the construction of a gigantic five-manual instrument, complete with loudspeakers, for the 1936 Nazi rally in Nuremberg. As Haag's colleague Josef Müller-Blattau described this phenomenon, the organ was "the total instrument of the total state," and Adolf Hitler was the state's "omnipotent organist." In other words, the most powerful musical instrument known to the world became linked to the most powerful politician in its history. Haag, for his part, opined that the organ was "the symbolic instrument of the [Nazi] community" and was ideally equipped to "serve a total Weltanschauung and the will expressed in its festivities."

Haag was a driving force behind these festivals, which were basically celebrations of Nazi doctrine and which featured organ music exclusively by "Aryan" composers. In 1939, he wrote the following:

> Most of Bach's free organ works easily lend themselves to festival planning. One thinks of the middle section of the G-major fantasy [BWV 572], the introduction of the E-flat-major prelude [BWV 552], the C-minor prelude [BWV 546], the D-major prelude [BWV 532], and many of the other large preludes, fugues, toccatas, and fantasies of the master. All these pieces have their place as an introduction to a festival or as an interlude, say, between two speakers or between a speaker and a choir, etc., and also at the end.[22]

Haag was therefore advocating those works, or just those sections of works, that are inherently powerful and that would traditionally have been played full organ to symbolize the totalitarianism of the Nazi regime. The relatively genteel-sounding trio sonatas would hardly have accomplished this purpose, nor would the opening section of the G-major fantasy or the lightly textured episodes of the E-flat prelude (for Haag was recommending that only the opening ritornello of the latter work be played).[23]

When he played the organ himself at these gatherings, Haag practiced what he preached—and dressed in his storm trooper's uniform, he looked every bit the part. Just consider the program for a Hitler Youth

Abendmusik event in 1937 that took place in one of Bach's own churches—the Thomaskirche in Leipzig—with Haag as the organ soloist. Limiting himself to the music of Bach, Haag performed the G-major fantasy, the E-flat prelude and fugue, and the Toccata and Fugue in F Major (BWV 540). Perhaps his rendering of the fantasy was met with the same acclaim as when the piece was heard in 1936 at another Nazi-sponsored concert, this one taking place at the Haus der deutschen Erziehung (House of German Education) in Bayreuth.[24] To quote one of the local critics, "Bach's Fantasy in G Major, which Karl August von Kotzebue consummately played on the organ, concluded the concert. In the powerful second section of the work, the organ sounded like a thunderstorm."[25] Predictably, that evening's entertainment ended with "Deutschland über alles," played as an organ solo by Kotzebue with all the might the instrument could muster.

The *New York Times* music critic Donal Henahan once wondered if the appropriation of classical music in motion pictures did not amount to "brutalizing" musical masterpieces for the sake of "cinematic gain."[26] Henahan was objecting in particular to the use of the slow movement from Mozart's Piano Concerto No. 21 in the relatively innocent and sentimental Swedish movie from 1967, *Elvira Madigan*, but he also had something to say about legendary Swedish filmmaker Ingmar Bergman's penchant for J. S. Bach:

> It still bothers me when certain deeply cherished pieces of music are merged with visual images in such a way that the sounds take on a filmmaker's specific meanings, thereby depriving me of my own—or at any rate trying to. In that respect, Ingmar Bergman has a lot to answer for in the next world. I can't pinpoint which of his films is to blame, but whenever I hear a recording of [Pablo] Casals playing a Bach [cello] suite, I am trapped in a dark room with a morbidly depressed woman.

Even though six of Bergman's films incorporate movements from Bach's cello suites, Henahan almost certainly had in mind the 1961 film *Through a Glass Darkly*, in which the mournful sarabande from the Cello Suite in D Minor is heard four different times.[27]

Similarly, if, whenever we hear Glenn Gould playing the Goldberg Variations, we have visions of Hannibal Lecter, we might think instead of the opening scene of *Thirty-Two Short Films about Glenn Gould*, a movie released in 1993, eleven years after Gould's death, and one obviously modeled in its entirety after Bach's composition, which was Gould's signature piece throughout his career. In that ethereal setting, where earth and sky become one, Gould is depicted trudging across the frozen tundra of his native Canada, to the strains of that ravishing Aria, as recorded by him in 1955. No irony, no gore, no violence of any kind, just blissful solitude.

5

New Data and New Insights

Ten Case Studies

In the context of the arts, the term "reception history," or its more familiar German equivalent "Rezeptionsgeschichte," might be defined as the historical study of artworks as reflected in the responses of critics, audiences, and performers. As a branch of musicology, it has always flourished, and it has chosen Johann Sebastian Bach as its subject more often than any other composer. There are obvious reasons why Bach's music has had such appeal to reception historians. After all, its rediscovery in the early nineteenth century marked the first time that a great composer, after a period of neglect, was given his rightful place by a later generation. As an early example of a new historicism within the arts, the Bach "awakening" eventually opened all periods of Western music to study and performance.

In this final chapter, I will offer new data on and, hopefully, new insights into the reception history of Bach's organ music by focusing on ten different works, or collections of works, that are of particular interest in this regard. I will limit myself to the past two hundred years or so, beginning with the "Bach revival" of the early nineteenth century. Essentially none of the material to be presented has appeared in any of the preceding chapters of this book or, for that matter, in any of my earlier writings on Bach reception. The works in question will be discussed in the order of the Bach-Werke-Verzeichnis.

The Afterlife of Bach's Organ Works. Russell Stinson, Oxford University Press. © Oxford University Press 2024.
DOI: 10.1093/oso/9780197680438.003.0006

THE PRELUDE AND FUGUE IN G MINOR, BWV 535

This work appears to have circulated widely within the Bach circle. It survives in numerous manuscripts prepared by his pupils, "grandpupils," and colleagues. According to recent research by David Schulenberg, one of the editors of the new (and indispensable) Breitkopf & Härtel edition of Bach's complete organ works, these manuscripts include one made by an anonymous pupil between roughly 1740 and 1750 that contains corrections in Bach's own hand.[1] To paraphrase Schulenberg's commentary, the piece might have been one of Bach's personal favorites, or perhaps it was especially useful for teaching purposes, for he returned to it several times over the years (and thoroughly revised it), making it available to pupils and acquaintances long after it was first composed, which was evidently around 1707.

Turning more to matters of reception, as a Bach fan and a regular listener to the BBC Radio 3 "Breakfast" program, I take special interest in the segment of the show known as "Bach before 7." The selections played vary widely according to genre and performance medium, and they often include transcriptions as well as free adaptations. I heard one morning a most effective piano arrangement of the G-minor prelude. The arrangement was by Alexander Siloti, and the performer was Nelson Freire. The recording dates from 2015 but was re-released in 2018 as part of the box set titled *Bach 333*. A box set, indeed, measuring 20 × 15 × 12 inches and weighing almost thirty pounds, and the ultimate box set (okay, *Bach's* set) for any Bach enthusiast. Issued 333 years after the composer's birth, the collection comprises exactly 222 compact discs—Bach would have appreciated the numerology—making it the largest production of its kind in the history of recorded music.[2] The contents are conveniently arranged according to genre, performance medium, and, to the extent possible, chronology. Twenty-two discs are devoted to the organ works proper, with a roster of performers ranging from Albert Schweitzer to Ton Koopman. Of special note is CD 119, a recording by Christian Schmitt of the early versions of the Great Eighteen Chorales (the first ever made?) prepared specifically for *Bach 333*.

Anyone interested in the reception of Bach's organ works will want to sample from the many transcriptions and free arrangements of those pieces included in *Bach 333*. Most are contained in the eight discs of the set collectively titled "Bach after Bach."[3] Those reworkings, as well as the few found in the supplementary sections titled "Keyboard Traditions" (five discs) and "Instrumental Traditions" (seven discs), represent only a fraction of what has survived, but they do remind us of the long, rich history of the tradition. The collection includes forty different such arrangements altogether that span 135 years, beginning with Franz Liszt's piano transcriptions of the Six "Great" Preludes and Fugues, BWV 543–548, published in 1852, and ending with a version of the Fugue in G Major, BWV 550/2, first recorded in 1987 by the recorder consort known as the Amsterdam Loecki Stardust Quartet.

The Russian pianist Alexander Siloti (1863–1945) was one of the most prolific piano transcribers in music history. No doubt he was influenced in this regard by his teacher Franz Liszt. Of his over two hundred extant transcriptions, Siloti's most popular would have to be that of the E-minor prelude from Book 1 of Bach's Well-Tempered Clavier, a transcription that is more an imaginative reworking of the original than a straight arrangement.[4] In the case of the G-minor prelude, Siloti created from Bach's organ figuration a highly expressive and fully idiomatic work for the piano.[5] The first fourteen bars, played pianissimo and marked "Adagio religioso," feature such added touches as a series of low pedal points for the left hand. This gravitas gives way in measures 14–18 to a burst of virtuosic display, with the thirty-second notes in the original played simultaneously by both hands instead of being passed from one hand to the other.[6] For the long chain of diminished-seventh chords in measures 19–31, the use of octave doublings and ramped-up volume every other bar achieves a compelling "reverse echo" effect. The conclusion could not be any more bombastic, like it or not.

THE TOCCATA AND FUGUE IN F MAJOR, BWV 540

Believe it or not, this toccata is alluded to by physicist (and prominent atheist) Sean Carroll in his best-selling book *The Big Picture: On the Origins of Life, Meaning, and the Universe Itself*. Apropos of his "transformation to naturalism," Carroll mentions two seminal events, the latter of which involves one of the most famous of all progressive-rock bands: "The second incident was when I heard a song, 'The Only Way,' from the Emerson, Lake & Palmer album *Tarkus*. In addition to some nifty pipe-organ work from Keith Emerson, the song featured something I hadn't heard: an unmistakable, in-your-face atheist message."[7] As any baby boomer reading this should know, "The Only Way" begins with Emerson at an actual pipe organ, serving up the first fifty-five bars of the F-major toccata, that is, all the music up to the first pedal solo. Emerson may have been a keyboard wizard, but he was not a renowned pedalist.[8]

It is hardly surprising that such a juggernaut of a composition has over the years earned numerous accolades within the scholarly literature. The earliest appears in the Bach biography of Carl Ludwig Hilgenfeldt, published in the Bach year of 1850: "Among the organ toccatas, it is primarily the one in F major that distinguishes itself. This splendid, brilliant work shows Bach at the height of his artistic powers."[9] Perhaps Hilgenfeldt heard in the music some of the same qualities that inspired Peter Williams, that most insightful of Bach commentators, to describe the toccata as a "gloriously massive" work that conveys the feeling of "endless song."[10] In other words, according to Williams, there is a sense of continuous melody being spun out in defiance of analytical labels.

The toccata has also attracted its fair share of transcribers, keyboard and otherwise. Fourteen different piano transcriptions are listed in Arthur Schanz's *Johann Sebastian Bach in der Klaviertranskription*, a 700-page offering from the Bach year of 2000 that lists more or less all the piano transcriptions of works by Bach published in the nineteenth or twentieth centuries.[11] Included in the tally for the F-major toccata is an arrangement for three pianos by the Australian-born Percy Grainger, who in the realm of keyboard transcription was following in the footsteps

New Data and New Insights

of his teacher Ferruccio Busoni. Such an overblown arrangement would have been dismissed by the English organist (and architect) Heathcote Statham as a "derangement," judging from the vitriol he spewed on piano transcriptions of Bach organ works by Liszt and Tausig. An organ purist, Statham regarded all piano transcriptions of Bach's organ works as an "aesthetic blunder," mainly because of the piano's inability to simulate the sustained sound of the organ, especially its sonorous pedal division.[12]

Writing around the same time as Statham, the young Albert Schweitzer espoused a more charitable attitude toward these arrangements. Schweitzer, who of course was already a famous organist himself, not to mention an expert on Bach, happily conceded that the transcriptions of Liszt and others provided the inquisitive pianist with "the advantage of learning works from which he would otherwise be banned" and "the aesthetic pleasure of finding organ effects cleverly realised on the piano."[13] Yet Schweitzer was also quick to point out the inherently unsatisfying nature of such arrangements, since "the various degrees of strength in the organ tone cannot be reproduced even on the modern pianoforte." Convinced that any real "joy" provided by such transcriptions was primarily educational, he lamented that many of the examples then in vogue exceeded the technical abilities of the average pianist. Schweitzer also harked back to an era when it was commonplace to play Bach's organ works as piano duets, straight off the printed page, with no added material of any kind: "We must not allow these artistic transcriptions, that often surpass the powers of the average player, to make us forget the old German domestic resource of playing the organ works from the original in arrangements for four hands, one player taking the manual parts, the other the pedal part in octaves." The latter was a form of *Hausmusik* enjoyed by such piano duos as Felix and Fanny Mendelssohn, Robert and Clara Schumann, and Clara Schumann and Johannes Brahms.

Two orchestrations of the F-major toccata survive. One is the handiwork of the nineteenth-century violinist and conductor Heinrich Esser, who, inexplicably, felt compelled to add a few rather banal bars of his own composition at the very end. The organist Ivor Atkins so disliked Esser's addendum that, before conducting the arrangement in 1908 at the opening service of the Three Choirs Festival, held that year at Worcester Cathedral, he enlisted his friend Edward Elgar to re-orchestrate the ending.[14] Elgar dispensed with Esser's "coda" altogether, and he added nine different instruments for the last twenty-three measures.

Another English organist who conducted Esser's orchestration at the turn of the twentieth century was Henry Wood (1869–1944), conductor of the London Proms from the inaugural concert in 1895 until his death. Wood performed Esser's arrangement four times between 1897 and 1906,[15] before deciding to orchestrate the toccata himself, with an eye to evoking a fuller orchestral palette. Wood completed and premiered his orchestration in 1913, and, as we learn from Hannah French's excellent new book on the maestro, it became the most frequently programmed orchestral arrangement of Bach at the Proms during Wood's tenure there.[16] That is saying a lot, considering that twenty-five such arrangements, by Wood and others, are involved. Wood's particular affinity for the toccata may be seen as early as the 1880s, when, as a teenage prodigy, he regularly included the work on his organ concerts. He even appears to have played the piece at his very first organ lesson.

The F-major toccata abounds in memorable, striking passages, two of which I would like to mention here. The first to be considered was described by Peter Williams as "one of the most startling interrupted cadences even in J. S. Bach's peerless repertory of them."[17] The passage occurs three times, first in D minor (mm. 204–06), then in G minor (mm. 318–21), and, finally, fifteen bars from the end, in the home key of F major (mm. 424–27). Remarkably, it incorporates secondary-dominant chords on N^6 and III, followed by their resolutions. Writing in the late 1940s, the organist Hermann Keller was so impressed with the audacity of these chords that he claimed they had never before been attempted in the whole history of music.[18] The final instance is the most jarring, since it occurs in a major key: both the root *and* the fifth of the Neapolitan 6th are chromatic pitches (as they would be, of course, in any major key), and the III chord is borrowed from the parallel minor. Indeed, these bars sounded to the young Felix Mendelssohn, when he played the toccata, "as if the whole church were about to tumble down" on him.[19] The second passage in question involves the famous discord in the penultimate measure, where a tonic triad in the hands grinds against the subdominant pitch in the feet. Mendelssohn must have savored this effect as well.

But what of the F-major fugue? Alas, it is a pity that this sublime contrapuntal specimen has always been overshadowed by its flashier partner. The movement holds a rare place within the BWV as a double fugue for organ whose two subjects are given their own expositions before being combined (but see also BWV 574 and 677). Still, to quote Keller, the fugue is cursed by the "smothering proximity of the toccata."[20]

THE PRELUDE AND FUGUE IN E-FLAT MAJOR, BWV 552

Mendelssohn also admired this magnificent piece. He played it in concert and, in the case of his six organ sonatas, appropriated it as a compositional model. The latter is also true of Mozart (Fantasy in F Minor, K. 608) and Schumann (Six Fugues on BACH, Op. 60). The work's popularity in general is attested to by the large number of transcriptions it has generated, not just for piano—Schanz lists fifteen, including four by Max Reger, one of the most ardent Bachians in music history—but also for orchestra. Of the four surviving orchestrations, the earliest is a still-unpublished arrangement of the prelude by Vincent Novello for orchestra and solo organ that was premiered at London's Hanover Square Rooms in 1812, with Novello and Samuel Wesley rendering the organ part, in the "English" manner, as a duet.[21] Novello called his adaptation an "Overture," realizing no doubt that the genre of the so-called French overture served Bach in this instance as a compositional exemplar. At some point, Novello also arranged the fugue as an organ duet, which he and Wesley played at the Foundling Hospital Chapel in 1814. For that performance, the fugue was prefaced by a roughly three-minute-long, four-hand "Introduction" authored by Wesley himself.[22] Wesley never published his duet, which toward the end incorporates the main subject of Bach's fugue. His autograph manuscript is titled *Duett for the Organ. Composed by Samuel Wesley. As an Introduction to the Grand Triple Fugue in E Flat by Sebastian Bach.*

Fast forward to 1827, and we find another member of the "Sebastian Squad," Benjamin Jacob, publishing his four-hand arrangement of the fugue, along with a rather naive explanatory note: "This magnificent fugue was originally composed for one performer with an obbligato pedal part, but as in that state the execution is very difficult and in the absence of pedals impracticable, the present arrangement as a duet has been made to bring it into general use. It is now suitable for an organ without pedals, or for the pianoforte."[23] The rather verbose title of Jacob's print, with its reference to the tune "St. Anne" (a tune commonly sung to Isaac Watts's hymn "O God, Our Help in Ages Past"), gives one good reason why this fugue was favored by British organists. It reads as follows: *A Grand Fugue by John Sebastian Bach, in Three Movements and on Three Subjects, the Principal Theme being the first Four Bars of St Ann's Psalm Tune, Arranged for Two Performers on the Organ or Pianoforte . . . by B. Jacob.* Jacob supplemented his arrangement with performance instructions of all kinds, including organ registrations, and he often reinforced the "Secondo" part by doubling the pedal line at the lower octave. More remarkable still—and virtually unprecedented in early Bach sources—are the analytical markings that appear throughout. Jacob explained them in this note: "T signifies the theme or subject, namely, the first four bars of St. Ann's tune; this pervades all three movements. (2) is a second subject, which in the first movement is a subordinate one, but in the second and third movements the subjects marked (2) are principal, and that marked T is subordinate. (Ɛ) is the second subject inverted." To clarify somewhat, what Jacob refers to as the three "movements" are in fact the three sections within this fugue (mm. 1–37, 37–82, and 82–117), which is actually not a triple fugue—despite Wesley's designation—but rather Bach's only double fugue with three subjects: the "St. Anne" theme is the sole subject of the first section and is then combined with a new subject in the second and third sections, after each of those new subjects receives its own exposition. Furthermore, the marking "(2)" within the first section denotes what would normally be thought of as merely the countersubject of that part of the fugue. The marking (Ɛ), which does indeed feature an upside-down

New Data and New Insights

"2," graphically illustrates Bach's use of inversion to state the second subject, starting in measure 47. Jacob found nine inverted statements altogether, between measures 47 and 76, though most are incomplete.

Another noteworthy aspect of Jacob's print is the inclusion of the first thirty-two bars of the E-flat prelude, arranged for four hands, as an "Introduction" to the fugue. To be exact, the "Introduction" extends through the third beat of measure 32, thus encompassing the entire first statement of the prelude's gigantic ritornello. By "ritornello," I simply mean the French-overture-like theme that is stated four different times during the movement (mm. 1–32, 51–71, 98–111, and 174–205) and that is analogous to the recurring tutti section of a late-Baroque concerto movement or da capo aria. Jacob's "Introduction" concludes with four bars of his own composition. Intended as a modulatory bridge between the prelude segment and the fugue, this insert is both superfluous and, with its hushed dynamics and rallentando indication, a musical cliché of the worst kind. But rather than disparage Jacob any further for this offense, let us consider his duet in the context of the all-Bach recital played by Felix Mendelssohn at the Leipzig Thomaskirche in 1840. Mendelssohn began that recital with the E-flat fugue, but he preceded the fugue with an "Introduction" (the printed program reads *Introduction und Fuge in Es dur*). Scholars have traditionally assumed that Mendelssohn improvised this "Introduction," just as he unquestionably ended the concert with an extemporization, cited in the program as a *Freie Phantasie*.[24] Anselm Hartinger, however, in his massive survey of Bach performances in Leipzig during the era of Mendelssohn, Schumann, and Moritz Hauptmann, suggests that this "Introduction" was instead "the opening part" of the E-flat prelude.[25] Hartinger, therefore, must also mean the first statement of the ritornello. The notion that Mendelssohn introduced the fugue in this manner is quite plausible, and it provides a welcome option for any organist today wishing to recreate the Leipzig recital. Mendelssohn might even have been inspired in this direction after seeing or acquiring Jacob's print on one of his many trips to England between 1829 and 1839.

At any rate, playing just the first thirty-two bars of the prelude can be a satisfying experience. Indeed, this segment of the movement, which constitutes the only truly complete statement of the ritornello,[26] feels like a perfectly formed miniature composition, not to mention a chunk of music that, at one-and-a-half minutes, lasts longer than many whole works by Bach (just think of the *Orgelbüchlein* chorales). In addition, it comprises a perfectly symmetrical musical unit, one divided into two halves of sixteen bars each, with the opening material restated in the dominant key to begin the second half. The theme of Bach's Goldberg Variations, composed at around the same time (ca. 1740), is analogous in both respects.

Thinking of the ritornello of the E-flat prelude as an independent, free-standing composition also brings to mind a scene from the film *Chronik der Anna Magdalena Bach*, released in 1968, in which the Dutch early-music pioneer Gustav Leonhardt, posing as a rather gaunt J. S. Bach, plays just the opening ritornello of the Prelude in B Minor, BWV 544/1. That theme is only seventeen bars long, yet it lasts longer than many of Bach's harpsichord preludes, including several from the Well-Tempered Clavier. Leonhardt could just as easily have chosen the Prelude in C Minor, BWV 546/1, whose ritornello is twenty-five bars long, or the Prelude in E Minor, BWV 548/1, whose ritornello is nineteen bars long. To reiterate a point made in Chapter 1 of the present book, Bach may have written longer preludes and fugues for the organ than the harpsichord to complement the large size of the instrument and its expansive surroundings.

THE TOCCATA IN D MINOR, BWV 565

No English-speaking Bach enthusiast can have anything but respect and gratitude for *The Bach Reader*. As the preface to the first edition states, the book is a "collection of the most significant early material on Johann Sebastian Bach," translated into English. Compiled by Hans T. David and Arthur Mendel, *The Bach Reader* is a classic within the field of Bach studies. The volume first appeared in 1945, courtesy of W. W. Norton, with a revised and expanded second edition following in 1966. A greatly revised

New Data and New Insights

and expanded third edition was issued in 1998, under the supervision of Christoph Wolff, as *The New Bach Reader*.

This brief history of the book's publication will allow for a better understanding of a mistake in the index of *The New Bach Reader* involving Beethoven and the infamous Toccata (and Fugue) in D Minor, BWV 565. Such an error would normally be too trifling to discuss, but this one concerns the most famous of all composers—Ludwig van Beethoven—and the most famous organ work ever written. At issue is a statement by Beethoven's amanuensis Anton Schindler that Beethoven, at the time of his death in 1827, owned various keyboard works by Bach, including "a toccata in D minor."[27] This information is indexed in the two editions of *The Bach Reader* under the entries of "Beethoven" and "*Toccatas*," in reference to page 362 of those editions. *The New Bach Reader*, though, contains a much more detailed index, complete with BWV numbers for individual compositions. Schindler's report there is indexed under "Beethoven" and "BWV 565: Toccata in D Minor," in reference to page 491 of that edition. The latter is doubtless a mistake, for the only toccata in D minor by Bach that Beethoven would have owned is the Toccata in D Minor, BWV 913, a work for harpsichord. He would not have owned either of Bach's organ toccatas in that key (BWV 565 and BWV 538/1, the "Dorian" toccata) for two reasons. First and foremost, neither work appeared in print until after Beethoven's death, whereas the harpsichord toccata was published in 1801.[28] Secondly, Beethoven is not known to have played the organ except in his youth, and in 1825 he confessed to the organist Karl Gottlieb Freudenberg that his "nerves could not tolerate the power of that gigantic instrument."[29] He did, however, play the piano his entire life and at one time was a celebrated piano virtuoso. Beethoven's compositions often betray Bach's influence, and it is certainly plausible that the rhapsodic style of BWV 565—especially its exploitation of the diminished-seventh chord, as in the introduction to the first movement of Beethoven's "Pathètique" piano sonata—would have appealed to him. But there is simply no evidence that Beethoven knew this work.

THE FANTASY IN G MAJOR (*PIÈCE D'ORGUE*), BWV 572

This piece was known as the "Fantasy" in G Major until 1978–1979, when Heinz Lohmann published it in the "old" Breitkopf & Härtel edition of Bach's complete organ works under the title *Pièce d'Orgue*. Lohmann did so in accordance with all the earliest manuscript sources, which, according to recent scholarship, include a copy made in 1722 by Bach's pupil Bernhard Christian Kayser.[30] When, in 1984, Dietrich Kilian followed suit with his edition of the work for the Neue Bach-Ausgabe, the French title got the ultimate stamp of authority. Consequently, organists began referring to BWV 572 as Bach's *Pièce d'Orgue*, just as they routinely do so today. The French title may be legitimate—witness also the French headings used for the three main sections—but the extent to which Gallic style pervades the music is debatable.

Under either name, the work is a stylistic jumble: the first section (mm. 1–28), with its perpetual motion, monophonic texture, and repetitive figuration, recalls various fast movements from Bach's sonatas and partitas for solo violin; the second (mm. 29–185), marked "gravement" and scored for five voices with pedal, is a contrapuntal tour de force; and the third (mm. 186–202) may be thought of as a glorified cadenza. Understandably, performers have focused on the second section—which is the most substantial in every sense—to the exclusion of the other two. Playing just the second section, with the harmony in measure 186 changed to a tonic triad, makes for a stand-alone piece lasting between five and six minutes. In the context of a church service, this scheme also makes for a compelling postlude, as the English organist Harvey Grace realized a century ago:

> Good as the [first and third] sections are, they are so dwarfed by the *Gravement* as to seem impertinent. It is a pity we do not play the great middle part alone as a voluntary. All we have to do is to substitute a tonic chord for the discord at the end. We then have a noble monologue which will arrest the departing faithful, whereas the *très vitement* opening section will merely hurry them, besides being much too light-hearted for use immediately after a service.[31]

New Data and New Insights

Only a few years after Grace penned these lines, his compatriot Arnold Bax took the same tack in transcribing the fantasy for piano, limiting himself to the "gravement" section and ending with a tonic triad. Bax offered his rather heavy-handed transcription as a Christmas present in 1927 to his muse and lover, the pianist Harriet Cohen. Five years later, in 1932, the transcription appeared in print, alongside Bach piano transcriptions by eleven other leading British musicians, in a collection commissioned by Cohen and published by Oxford University Press as *A Bach Book for Harriet Cohen*. This classic anthology has recently been reissued by the press, with sophisticated commentary by the pianist and broadcaster David Owen Norris, and it has recently been recorded in its entirety by both Antony Gray and Jonathan Plowright.[32]

Truncating the G-major fantasy in the manner practiced by Bax and advocated by Grace may make musical sense, yet it also means missing out on one of the most startling moments in all of Bach's organ music, one akin to the terrifying shout of "Bar-ra-bam" in Part 2 of the St. Matthew Passion, where the two choirs join forces on a diminished-seventh chord. I refer, of course, to the deceptive cadence at measures 184–85, where a dominant triad leads to a diminished-seventh chord on c-sharp (vii^{o7}/V). One performer who made sure not to deprive himself of this moment was William Thomas Best, the leading British organist of the late nineteenth century. Best exploited the passage by abruptly switching to full organ right on that sinister harmony.[33]

Such gimmickry would have been anathema to the leading French organist of the time, Charles-Marie Widor, a musician known for his strict adherence to the printed score. Widor would not have condoned abbreviating the fantasy in any fashion, nor did he think of the final, third section of the work (mm. 186–202) as empty, *perpetuum mobile* passage-work. Rather, as we read in John Near's latest publication on the *maître*, Widor defended those concluding bars to the point of insulting anyone who disagreed with him on the matter, writing in his edition of Bach's organ works that "whoever sees only a mechanical exercise there will do better to abandon music for a job as signalman on a local branch line."[34] Was the final section of the fantasy a model for the famous Widor toccata?

One of the greatest musicians altogether of the post-Bach era—Johannes Brahms—certainly had no compunction about playing all three sections of the fantasy. Brahms seems to have regularly played the work on his piano recitals, and there is no indication that he ever took any shortcuts. I was lucky enough back in 2006 to discover in the archives of the Riemenschneider Bach Institute (Baldwin Wallace University) a source that offers tantalizing clues about how Brahms played the piece.[35] The item in question is an early print of the work containing numerous inscriptions in Brahms's hand, most of which are found in the final section. These markings show that Brahms's basic methodology was to remove the nonharmonic tones from Bach's *manualiter* figuration in favor of pure triads and seventh chords. In addition, Brahms arpeggiated these harmonies for over two octaves with his right hand alone, in the tradition of bravura piano playing, with his left hand taking the bass line, no doubt, in octaves. Bach, conversely, divided the figuration between the hands, never exceeding the distance of an octave and a half, and with his feet playing the bass line.

More recently, the Brahms expert Valerie Goertzen has investigated the topic of Brahms and Bach's organ works, unearthing new evidence of various kinds.[36] With regard to Brahms and the G-major fantasy, she has discovered a second source containing inscriptions by Brahms for the second section of the fantasy, several of which correlate with those in the Riemenschneider score. As for Brahms's revamping of the third section, she astutely observes that "Brahms remade the arpeggios to enlarge and more evenly fill the pitch range, and omitted dissonances that would be grating when caught in the damper pedal." She has also located two hitherto unknown reviews of Brahms's performances of the work, including this panegyric by the composer Leopold Alexander Zellner:

The Organ Fantasie in G by Father Bach, which builds to enormous heights, was played with remarkable energy and technique and achieved captivating effects. Brahms brought so much mastery in conveying the full-voiced character and the obbligato pedal that we truly believed we were hearing the instrument of all instruments that sounds in a thousand voices, for which this pyramidal composition is envisioned. The difficulties are nearly insurmountable. Brahms didn't just play them, he played himself with them. With what security, power, and ease he let this godly thunderstorm loose; it is too beautiful for words.[37]

THE FUGUE IN C MINOR ON A THEME BY BONONCINI, BWV 574

The earliest source for this youthful opus happens to be a manuscript in the hand of Bach's brother Johann Christoph titled *Thema Legrenzianum. Elaboratum per Joan. Seb. Bach cum subjectum*. Accordingly, it was long thought that Bach had based the first of his fugue subjects in this instance—the work is a double fugue—on a theme by Giovanni Legrenzi (1626–1690). In an article published in the 1986 *Bach-Jahrbuch*, Robert Hill proposed that both subjects derive from Legrenzi, not from themes per se by him but from a whole complex of themes found in Legrenzi's Trio Sonata in G Minor, Op. 2, No. 11.[38] Hill's hypothesis, however, which involves some rather vague thematic resemblances between Bach and Legrenzi, was not unanimously accepted.[39] The matter now seems resolved, but not in favor of Legrenzi, for in an article published in the 2013 *Bach-Jahrbuch*, Rodolfo Zitellini demonstrated that Bach's first fugue subject is strikingly similar to a theme from the last movement of a trio sonata (significantly, also in the key of C minor) by Giovanni Maria Bononcini (1642–1678).[40] Indeed, according to Zitellini, the entire first section of Bach's fugue (mm. 1 37) is influenced by this movement from Bononcini's sonata. In light of these new findings, BWV 574 should now be known not as the "Legrenzi fugue" but the "Bononcini fugue." This is how the piece is cited in volume 3 of the new Breitkopf & Härtel edition of Bach's complete organ works, published in 2016, and the third edition of the Bach-Werke-Verzeichnis, published in 2022.

THE *ORGELBÜCHLEIN*, BWV 599–644

This collection of forty-five miniature chorale settings has inspired everyone from three of the greatest composers of the nineteenth century—Felix Mendelssohn, Robert Schumann, and Johannes Brahms—to two of the leading filmmakers of the twentieth and twenty-first centuries—Andrei Tarkovsky and Lars von Trier.[41] Of course, some works have proved more popular than others, especially the handful of ornamental chorales within the collection. In these works, the hymn tune is highly embellished and played on its own manual, whereas Bach's normal procedure in the *Orgelbüchlein* was to state the melody with little or no ornamentation, and on the same manual as the accompanimental voices. Mendelssohn and Schumann particularly favored the aria-like "Ich ruf zu dir, Herr Jesu Christ" (BWV 639) and the poignantly chromatic "Das alte Jahr vergangen ist" (BWV 614).

Another nineteenth-century devotee of those two works—and surely not just by coincidence—was the Leipzig-based organist Hermann Schellenberg. Schellenberg grew up in the same city where these two giants ruled the musical establishment, and in an essay commemorating the centennial of Bach's death in 1850, he praised both pieces for their lyricism and religiosity. He commented interestingly on several other Bach organ works as well, although in the most verbose and hyperbolic of terms:

> With respect to their content and structure, the organ works of this hero undeniably and completely outstrip those of his predecessors and contemporaries . . . A glance at the chorale preludes on "Aus tiefer Noth" [BWV 686] and "Wenn wir in höchsten Nöten sein" [BWV 668], or the large settings of the Kyrie [BWV 669–671], or the six-voice ricercar from the Musical Offering, or the Canonic Variations on the Christmas hymn "Vom Himmel hoch" certainly reveals the pinnacle of what the human spirit can accomplish in the realm of contrapuntal artifice. But just as amazing is the depth of expression found in these pieces, something that seems diametrically opposed to any labyrinth of contrapuntal weavings. We also

New Data and New Insights   121

encounter this profundity of feeling in those chorale preludes somewhat or completely lacking in complex counterpoint, for example,
"Schmücke dich, o liebe Seele" [BWV 654], "Das alte Jahr vergangen
ist" [BWV 614], "Ich ruf zu dir, Herr Jesu Christ" [BWV 639] and "O
Mensch, bewein dein Sünde groß" [BWV 622]. Due to their religious
as well as melodic content, these pieces appeal to connoisseurs and
laymen alike. . . . There is no doubt that Bach's genius outshines all
other masters. He expanded the field of organ music in all directions,
as we see in such works as the Preludes and Fugues in C Minor
[BWV 546], F Minor [BWV 534], G Minor [BWV 542], A Minor
[BWV 543], E Minor [BWV 548], and B Minor [BWV 544], which
are underscored with the greatest sense of power and solemnity.
Bach remains unsurpassed.[42]

To clarify and elaborate somewhat on Schellenberg's commentary, the
context of his remarks usually makes it obvious what composition he is
referring to. In the case of "Wenn wir in höchsten Nöten sein," he must
have meant not the *Orgelbüchlein* chorale by this title (BWV 641) but the
last of the so-called Great Eighteen Chorales, a work now catalogued as
"Vor deinen Thron tret ich hiermit" but originally published, as a supplement to Bach's *Die Kunst der Fuge*, as "Wenn wir in höchsten Nöten
sein." Known misleadingly as Bach's "deathbed chorale," this piece quickly
acquired legendary status. Schellenberg's organ teacher Carl Ferdinand
Becker listed the piece in his concert programs as "Das letzte Werk des
Meisters."[43]

Identifying the six free works mentioned by Schellenberg is a bit
trickier, except that those in F minor and B minor are obviously the only
organ preludes and fugues in those two keys composed by or attributed to
Bach, BWV 534 and 544, respectively. Two organ preludes and fugues in
C minor, BWV 546 and 549, by Bach survive, as do two in A minor, BWV
543 and 551, and two in E minor, BWV 533 and 548. Schellenberg cannot
be referring to either BWV 551 (A minor) or BWV 533 (E minor), since,
as was shown in Chapter 2 of the present book, he regarded both works
as lacking "anything worthy of praise." Nor, to judge from his negative

remarks on these two early compositions, would Schellenberg have thought very highly of BWV 549 (C minor), another somewhat flawed product of Bach's youth, whereas he regarded BWV 546 as a "magnificent" composition.[44] Therefore, Schellenberg's list of preludes and fugues includes all four minor-key works from the Six "Great" Preludes and Fugues, BWV 543–548. As for the work in G minor, Schellenberg cannot be referring to the Prelude and Fugue in G Minor, BWV 535. That piece may be Bach's only extant prelude and fugue for organ in that key, but, as was shown in Chapter 2 of the present book, Schellenberg regarded the prelude as "containing nothing special." Therefore, he must have meant the Fantasy and Fugue in G Minor, BWV 542, which, as also discussed in Chapter 2 of the present book, he regarded as one of Bach's most magnificent and exquisite organ works. He may simply have found it convenient to refer to the fantasy as a "prelude," or perhaps he used the terms "fantasy" and "prelude" interchangeably, as many others have over the years.

A larger issue raised by Schellenberg's mention of these six works is the fact that all of them are in minor keys. This predilection for the darker, more dissonant minor mode—and its association with negative affect—may typify nineteenth-century taste, but Schellenberg's choice of the F-minor prelude and fugue implies an egregious lapse of judgment on his part. Riddled with so many compositional defects that its authenticity is seriously questioned today, the F-minor is outclassed by any number of free organ works by Bach in major keys. In the domain of *preludes* and fugues, three mature masterpieces stand out: the Prelude and Fugue in G Major, BWV 541; the Prelude and Fugue in C Major ("$\frac{9}{8}$"), BWV 547; and the Prelude and Fugue in E-flat Major, BWV 552. In his review of volume 2 of the Peters edition of Bach's complete organ works, which contains the Preludes and Fugues in F Minor, G Major, and C Major, Schellenberg actually ranked the F-minor above the G-major, and he passed over the C-major in silence.[45] Schellenberg is not entirely to blame, though, as the F-minor was likewise a favorite work of his teacher C. F. Becker.

To return to the *Orgelbüchlein*, one way of measuring the popularity of certain works over others is by the number of piano transcriptions they

New Data and New Insights

have generated. According to Arthur Schanz's catalogue, published in 2000, the average number of extant transcriptions per work is around six, but the ornamental chorales have spawned on the average roughly twice that number. Most impressive are the statistics not only for "Ich ruf zu dir" (sixteen transcriptions) and "Das alte Jahr" (eighteen transcriptions) but also for "O Mensch, bewein dein Sünde groß" (sixteen transcriptions), a particularly beautiful Passiontide chorale whose melancholy text inspired some of the boldest harmonies Bach ever wrote.[46]

In this connection, it is worth quoting from the introduction written by the music critic Ernest Newman to Harvey Grace's *The Organ Works of Bach*, published in 1922. Newman, as he made clear to the reader, was no organist himself, but he was quite knowledgeable about Bach's compositions for the instrument. He doubtless had attained some of that knowledge about a dozen years earlier, when he translated both volumes of Albert Schweitzer's Bach monograph. With regard to "Das alte Jahr" and "O Mensch," Newman wrote the following:

> No doubt Bach's friends and pupils thought 'Das alte Jahr vergangen ist' and 'O Mensch, bewein' dein' Sünde gross' very fine things, but I make bold to say that they had no such idea of the wonderfulness of them as we have who have been through 'Tristan.' The developments of poetic music in the 19th century, in the opera, the symphonic poem, and the song, have sharpened our sense for the poetry of Bach.[47]

At first blush, these lines would seem to have resulted solely from Newman's encounter with Schweitzer's book, whose original title, after all, was *Jean-Sébastien Bach, le musician-poète*. From the standpoint of "poetic" imagery, moreover, these two works are surpassed by few if any of Bach's other organ chorales. But Newman, whom Grace thanked in his preface for his "vigilant scrutiny of the final proofs" (p. xiv), may also have been thinking of a remarkable passage in Grace's book in which the author advocates, quite radically, that in playing the ornamental chorales of the *Orgelbüchlein*, most of the ornaments that are indicated merely by symbols and not written out in notes should be omitted because they "belong to the clavecin rather than to the organ and add a great deal to the technical difficulty without contributing anything notable to the expressive side" (p. 137). Grace denounced these ornaments as "trivial," "showy," "obsolete," and "giving an antiquated effect to music which is still vital." Newman may likewise have had this passage in mind when he saluted Grace for his "frankness towards Bach's lapses" (p. viii) and for admitting that even Bach—especially in his organ works, because so many of them originated during the composer's youth or early adulthood—"often wrote below his best" (p. viii). By stating that Grace's book was that "of a worshipper, but not of a blind worshipper" (p. viii), Newman almost certainly was criticizing Schweitzer's book as an act of hagiography, which, of course, it is.

Because of Bach's tendency in the *Orgelbüchlein* to symbolize the chorale texts with specific accompanimental motives, Schweitzer argued in his monograph that the collection was a key to understanding Bach as a composer. And according to Charles-Marie Widor's preface to the book, Schweitzer had long been contemplating Bach's organ chorales in general from this angle. In his preface, Widor famously reported how Schweitzer, his former pupil, had opened his eyes to the expressive nature of these pieces by explaining their close relationship to the chorale texts. It is worth mentioning, therefore, the existence of a primary source in these matters that has only recently come to light. The source in question is a copy of volume 5 of the Peters edition of Bach's complete organ works—whose contents include all forty-five *Orgelbüchlein* chorales—that was once owned by Widor. Most intriguingly, this document preserves a multitude of inscriptions in Schweitzer's hand, including not only mini-commentaries in French on the meaning of the chorale texts but also the marking of the same accompanimental motives analyzed by Schweitzer in his book on Bach.

The owner today of this unique source is the French organist Daniel Roth, one of Widor's successors at Saint-Sulpice in Paris and the current *organiste titulaire* at the church. So far as I know, the only information to be found on the document comes from an interview granted by Roth for the

DVD *Hommage à Daniel Roth* (Organpromotion, 2008). Roth discusses his acquisition of the item, its overall significance, and the authentication of Schweitzer's inscriptions by the staff of the Musée Albert Schweitzer in Gunsbach, France. A few pages of the source are briefly shown as well. The following is a transcript of the pertinent section of the interview, which took place at the church:

Interviewer: You told me about a volume of organ music with hand-written comments by Widor and Schweitzer. What was that story again?
Roth: I can even show you this book. When I was appointed here, one Sunday a friend arrived with a book and said: "This is for you." I opened it, and one sees on the first page the big signature of Widor in blue pencil and some motives that Schweitzer had marked in the score, and for every chorale title, next to it in small writing, the meaning of the chorale text . . .
Interviewer: Written for Widor?
Roth: Of course. I took this to Gunsbach and showed it to the ladies there to find out if it was Schweitzer's hand, and they said yes, of course, it is. I am very proud to possess this document.
Interviewer: You still have it?
Roth: Yes, of course.

Let us hope that more information on this holy relic will be forthcoming in the not-too-distant future.

Schweitzer was also passionate about the works of Richard Wagner, and he was especially interested in the interplay of words and music that is the sine qua non of these compositions. As a young man, he often attended performances of Wagner's operas at the annual Festspiele in Bayreuth, and these visits allowed him to make the acquaintance of Wagner's widow, Cosima. Cosima herself was a highly trained musician—she was the daughter of Franz Liszt—as well as a formidable arbiter of musical taste who, like her husband, had an abiding interest in and reverence for the music of J. S. Bach. These facts provide a context for contemplating what

Schweitzer wrote about Cosima in his autobiography, for it seems that he educated her about Bach's organ chorales much as he had for Widor:

> When my finances permitted, I made the pilgrimage to Bayreuth in those years the festival took place. Cosima Wagner, whom I had met in Strasbourg while working on my book on Bach, made a deep impression on me. She became interested in my idea that Bach's music is descriptive. Once, when she visited the eminent church historian Johannes Ficker in Strasbourg, she asked me to illustrate my view by playing some of Bach's chorale preludes on the fine Merklin organ in the new church.[48]

According to Schanz's catalogue, the fourth most often transcribed *Orgelbüchlein* chorale, represented by thirteen examples, is "Alle Menschen müssen sterben" (BWV 643). This work is not an ornamental chorale, but it is traditionally played on two manuals. Because of the ubiquitous parallel thirds and sixths between the inner voices, plus the major-mode cantus firmus, the music possesses a euphony unmatched anywhere else in the *Orgelbüchlein*. This euphony, however, belies the somber chorale text, whose message is human mortality.[49] Among the more recent transcribers of this work is the Canadian pianist (and Bach specialist) Angela Hewitt. As may be heard on her disc *Bach Arrangements*, she plays the piece softly and slowly, and she wisely transposes the hymn tune down an octave on the repeat of the Stollen.[50] Her recording concludes with this transcription, similar to how she has offered it as a recital encore throughout her career as a concert pianist.

The allure of the *Orgelbüchlein* within the film and television industry has been limited to "Ich ruf zu dir," with the exception, that is, of an episode of the Netflix series *The Crown* (season 1, episode 5) in which "Das alte Jahr" is played in its entirety, and to fine effect, at the funeral of Mary of Teck, the grandmother of Elizabeth II. Andrei Tarkovsky's use of "Ich ruf zu dir" in his 1972 science-fiction film *Solaris*, where the piece is heard four different times, sometimes with electronic enhancement, has been discussed by numerous film scholars and musicologists, and it is only a matter of time before Lars von Trier's appropriation of the work in his film *Nymphomaniac*, released in 2013, will be as well. In an obvious nod to Tarkovsky, von Trier incorporates the chorale into an explicit sex scene where the film's protagonist, Joe, describes her relationships with a trio of complementary lovers. She likens these relationships to three-voice polyphony, a texture clearly exemplified by "Ich ruf zu dir." The three voices of the piece are reflected by the division of the screen into thirds, one for each lover.

This *ménage à quatre* notwithstanding, the most noteworthy recent bit of news on the reception of the *Orgelbüchlein* would have to be the launch in 2013 and the completion in 2022 of *The Orgelbüchlein Project: Completing Bach's Plan*. Curated by the English organist William Whitehead, this was an international composition project aimed at completing the 118 pieces planned by Bach for inclusion in the *Orgelbüchlein* but for which he provided only chorale titles in the autograph manuscript.[51] According to the website, these "ghostly gaps" have been filled by the "most interesting composers at work today," and the new compositions "survey a range of modern styles." The composers include not only such luminaries in the field of composition as Thea Musgrave, Roxanna Panufnik, Nico Muhly, and John Rutter, but also such prominent organists as John Butt, Peter Planyavsky, Lionel Rogg, and John Scott Whiteley. The pianist-composer Stephen Hough makes an appearance as well. All the new works, plus all the chorales actually set by Bach, were performed in late September 2022 at a series of concerts in London sponsored by The Royal College of Organists. A complete edition is in the offing.

"VOR DEINEN THRON TRET ICH HIERMIT," BWV 668

Known for centuries as Bach's "deathbed chorale," this work was almost certainly *not* dictated in its entirety by the infirm and blind composer "on the spur of the moment to the pen of a friend," as stated in the original print of *Die Kunst der Fuge* (1751). Rather, as Christoph Wolff has argued, Bach probably just dictated some revisions to the piece, which is a greatly expanded version of the *Orgelbüchlein* setting of "Wenn wir in höchsten Nöten sein" ("When we are in the greatest distress"). To quote from Wolff's discussion,

> it is actually unlikely that Bach dictated the expanded chorale on that occasion, since it already existed. Relevant details are not mentioned, but the unknown friend may well have played the expanded version on Bach's pedal harpsichord for the composer, who had lost his vision but was still in a working mood. Upon hearing it, Bach realized that the work could still benefit here and there from editorial improvements, and he may have proceeded to dictate some contrapuntal, melodic, and rhythmic adjustments. Finally, in the expectation of death, he seems to have asked the friend to change the heading to "Vor deinen Thron tret ich hiermit" ("Before your throne I now appear").[52]

"Vor deinen Thron" may be the stuff of legend, but it is also a stunningly beautiful piece of music that has inspired composers and transcribers alike. Take, for instance, Sofia Gubaidulina's *Meditation on the Bach Chorale "Vor deinen Thron tret ich hiermit" BWV 668*, a twelve-minute-long composition from 1993 for harpsichord, two violins, viola, cello, and double bass. Given her lifelong affinity for the music of Bach, plus her strong religious bent, Gubaidulina was naturally drawn to this organ chorale. The critic Paul Griffiths has described her rather ghostly rumination as follows:

> A sense of the uncanny is summoned at once, with imposing harpsichord entries, string tremolandos, and eventually a sustained tritone, before the first line of the chorale is intoned by the double bass. From this point on, much of the music refers to motivic elements in the chorale in continuing atmospheres of strangeness, with the chorale melody occasionally coming into full focus. An early phase of somewhat Bartókian polyphony, for instance, provides a foil for the chorale in violin harmonies with pizzicato viola. Later, the double

bass has another solo, tremolando and with sliding bow, from which it moves toward an implacable ostinato drawn from the chorale. Finally, the whole chorale bursts in on full strings, sounding in this setting like an old Russian hymn. The harpsichord, however, has the last word, closing with a sequence of chords whose top notes spell out B-A-C-H.[53]

The many transcriptions of "Vor deinen Thron" include a number of choral arrangements.[54] This is a most unusual circumstance for an instrumental work by Bach (the Swingle Singers notwithstanding!), even one, like this, whose basis is a sacred song. Even an organ chorale like this, whose every part can be sung as written, still poses the considerable challenge of how to set the text when material other than the hymn tune proper is being sung.[55] In 1950, the bicentennial of Bach's death, the conductor and composer Felix Oberborbeck took it upon himself to publish both choral and instrumental arrangements of the piece for use at "church-music festivals, concerts, and Bach memorial services."[56] According to Oberborbeck's preface, Ernst Friedrich Richter may have been the first to arrange the work for chorus when he did so in his capacity as Thomaskantor in Leipzig, a position Richter held from 1868 to 1879. Richter was succeeded by Wilhelm Rust, who, as mentioned in Chapter 1 of the present book, adapted various Bach organ chorales in this manner for services at the Thomaskirche. It is easy to imagine that "Vor deinen Thron" was one of these.

This tradition has continued in the "Sebastianstadt" well into the new millennium. For example, an *a cappella* version of the work was performed at the Thomaskirche in 2000 by John Eliot Gardiner and the Monteverdi Choir, as part of their Bach Cantata Pilgrimage that year. Theirs is a twofold arrangement, with the music sung initially to the text of the first stanza of the chorale and then, *sotto voce*, to the last stanza. A recording was issued in 2009, as the final track of volume 9 of the accompanying CD set. The same personnel sing this arrangement in *Bach: A Passionate Life*, Gardiner's video documentary from 2013. Toward the end of that outstanding production, there is a poignant scene with Sir John and a dozen of his singers performing the opening eleven bars (that is, the "pre-imitation" of and the actual statement of the first phrase), while standing around Bach's grave in the chancel of the church. That sacred space like-wise serves as the backdrop for a video released in 2013 in conjunction with an all-Bach recording by Ullrich Böhme, the Thomasorganist in Leipzig from 1986 to 2021. Titled *100 Jahre Menschlichkeit: Albert Schweitzer in Lambarene* (Rondeau Production), Böhme's recording commemorates the centennial of the founding of Albert Schweitzer's medical hospital in the African village of Lambaréné. The recording took place at the church of St. Thomas in Strasbourg, where the great humanitarian often preached and played the organ. In the video, the five members of the Calmus Ensemble, a group based in Leipzig, sing an *a cappella* arrangement of "Vor deinen Thron" to the words of the opening stanza. It is a happy coincidence that this ensemble comprises exactly five singers, as Bach thickens the texture from four voices to five in the last two bars.[57]

"IN DULCI JUBILO," BWV 729

Ever since the publication in 1948 of Hermann Keller's *Die Orgelwerke Bachs* and the translation of that book into English twenty years later, this piece, along with five others (BWV 715, 722, 726, 732, and 738) that have been interpreted as wildly extravagant hymn accompaniments from Bach's early adulthood, has been known as one of the composer's "Arnstadt Congregational Chorales."[58] That Bach composed the present work as early as his Arnstadt period (1703–1707), though, is doubtful, as is the hypothesis that a congregation could ever have sung to such ram-bunctious music.

The work is based on one of the most beloved of all Christmas carols, known to English speakers as "Good Christian Men, Rejoice." Ever since John Mason Neale translated the text as such in the 1850s, the carol has enjoyed great popularity in the United Kingdom, and it may only have gained in favor there in the early twentieth century when Gustav Holst chose it to begin his choral fantasy *Christmas Day*, a work from 1910. Regardless, five of the six piano transcriptions of BWV 729 listed in Schanz's catalogue are by British musicians.[59] Of particular interest are those by Lord Berners and Dorothea Salmon, both published in 1932. The transcription by Lord Berners (Gerald Tyrwhitt-Wilson), which comes from the above-mentioned *Bach Book for Harriet Cohen*, has been recorded by such piano greats as Angela Hewitt and Gordon Fergus-Thompson.[60] That by Dorothea Salmon is shrouded in mystery, as her identity cannot be ascertained. It does seem likely, however, that she is the same Dorothea Salmon (1899–1982) who in 1948 authored a pamphlet titled *Jungle Doctor* about none other than Albert Schweitzer.[61] More importantly, BWV 729 has for over eighty years been played by both British and American organists to conclude Lessons and Carols services as well as Christmas services in general.[62] That tradition dates back to 1938, when Douglas Guest, who was then Organ Scholar at the University of Cambridge, selected the work as his first voluntary at the end of the Festival of Nine Lessons and Carols at King's College. Played full organ, the piece makes for a brilliant albeit messy postlude.

THE FOUR DUETS FROM PART 3 OF THE *CLAVIERÜBUNG*, BWV 802–805

With respect to texture and figuration, these late, enigmatic masterpieces bear a strong resemblance to Bach's Two-Part Inventions, BWV 772–786. But whereas the Inventions rank among the composer's most popular works altogether, the Duets have long suffered from neglect.[63] Organists have avoided the Duets because they are for manuals alone, while pianists have ignored them because they are buried within a print containing mostly organ chorales. The Duets are even less well known to non-keyboardists, despite the existence of various transcriptions. One of these is by the Leipzig-trained cellist and composer Joachim Stutschwesky, who shortly after the Second World War transcribed the set for violin and cello.[64] Another, arranged for two violins, was issued in 1832 by the Viennese publisher Tobias Haslinger.[65] In that instance, the unknown transcriber also included the Fughetta in C Minor, BWV 961, an additional keyboard work by Bach scored for two voices, resulting in a print titled *5 Duetten für zwey Violinen von J. Seb. Bach*. Even though all four Duets are fugal in nature, the fughetta constitutes Bach's only true fugue in two voices, except, that is, for the more famous Fugue in E Minor from Book 1 of the Well-Tempered Clavier. Circumstantial evidence suggests that in 1847 the Bavarian pianist and composer Joseph Schad included the E-minor fugue on a recital he gave that year in Leipzig, playing both voices of the fugue in octaves![66] To return to the Haslinger print, a modern edition of the set would be most welcome, if only to augment the scant repertory available today for two violins *sans accompagnement*.

EPILOGUE

The revival of Bach's music during the first half of the nineteenth century manifested itself in various ways, not least of which was the publication of hundreds of works by him that had never before appeared in print. As Bach's compositions became increasingly available by means of this process, they were of course more frequently performed as well, whether at public gatherings or as *Hausmusik*. Nowhere was this more evident than in the city of Leipzig, where Bach himself spent most of his career. Not only were the two most prolific publishers of Bach's oeuvre (Breitkopf & Härtel and C. F. Peters) located there, but the city was home to two periodicals (the *Neue Zeitschrift für Musik* and the *Allgemeine Musikalische Zeitung*) with a decidedly pro-Bach bias. In addition, Leipzig boasted numerous performers who specialized in the music of Bach. The city also attracted Bach specialists from across the European continent who played recitals there. With these factors in mind, I would like to conclude with some comments on performances of Bach's organ works in and around Leipzig between 1840 and 1850, a decade in which Bach reception played a particularly vital role in the musical culture of that city. I will also consider a recital of sorts played for Robert Schumann in the city of Rotterdam in 1853 and, finally, the legacy of the B-A-C-H motive in the first half of the nineteenth century.[1]

No doubt the most important Bach specialist in Leipzig at that time was Felix Mendelssohn, and no doubt the most important public organ recital ever given there was that by Mendelssohn in August 1840 at the

Thomaskirche, the proceeds of which were used for the erection of a Bach monument in the church's courtyard. Mendelssohn played six different works by the master and, according to none other than Robert Schumann, ended with a lengthy improvisation on two different themes closely associated with Bach: the chorale melody "O Haupt voll Blut und Wunden," a tune set by Bach five times in his St. Matthew Passion; and the B-A-C-H motive. The program, therefore, was essentially an all-Bach affair, which was a great novelty at the time. Organists have for decades been recreating Mendelssohn's recital, and now that Rudolf Lutz's brilliant reconstruction of the improvisation has been published, they can continue to do so with relative ease.[2]

Another local Bach specialist who must have been in the audience that evening was Carl Ferdinand Becker, organist of the Nicolaikirche. Following Mendelssohn's lead, Becker would offer the citizens of Leipzig a summer organ recital at his church for the next four years, steadily increasing the amount of Bach as he went. When, in October 1847, he played the dedicatory recital for the new organ at the Leipzig Neukirche, Becker served up an all-Bach program himself, including some of the same pieces essayed by Mendelssohn in 1840.

Becker may not have improvised on the B-A-C-H motive at any of these recitals, but in 1841 he performed the Prelude and Fugue on BACH, BWV 898. Schumann also reviewed that event, and in so doing he argued against Bach as the composer of this work. Schumann would go on to write a series of BACH fugues himself, inspired, no doubt, by how Bach spells his name in this manner (with the pitches B-flat, A, C, and B-natural) in the final, unfinished movement of *Die Kunst der Fuge*. Mendelssohn, too, questioned the authenticity of BWV 898, even though he included it on an organ recital he gave in London in 1847. And, yes, whether or not Schumann and Mendelssohn sensed in the music a more modern style than that of J. S. Bach, both the harmonic language and pianistic idiom point to a composer from the late eighteenth if not the early nineteenth century. Still, the work was popular fare in the nineteenth century for organists and pianists alike (in the twentieth century, the piece was championed by the likes of Glenn Gould). The organist Carl Kloss, who

Epilogue

spent most of his life in Germany but was then based in the Hungarian village of Esperjes—and whom Clara Schumann amusingly dubbed "the most boring of all the bores"—concertized with the piece twice in Leipzig in the 1840s, first in 1843 at the Thomaskirche and then in 1847 at the university church. Several years later, in the mid-1850s, the fugue subject provided Franz Liszt with a compositional model for his Prelude and Fugue on BACH for organ. The work was even transcribed for brass instruments in 1837 at a music festival in the Prussian city of Königsberg.[3]

Of special interest is a recital given by the organist Robert Schaab on the outskirts of Leipzig in the summer of 1850. The locale was the village church of Schönefeld, and the event's stated purpose was to commemorate the hundredth anniversary of Bach's death (28 July 1850). Schaab spent his entire life in and around Leipzig, part of it as a student of Mendelssohn and Becker at the Leipzig Conservatory. Furthermore, Schaab had not only attended but had also "greatly enjoyed" Mendelssohn's all-Bach recital of 1840.[4] Schaab's recital opened with the Prelude and Fugue in C Minor, BWV 546, and a few undesignated organ chorales by Bach, then continued, in chronological order, with works by composers who had either studied with Bach in Leipzig (Johann Ludwig Krebs) or had actively promoted his music there during the first half of the nineteenth century (Mendelssohn and Schumann), and then concluded with a work by Schaab himself. To be specific, Schaab played a chorale arrangement by J. L. Krebs ("Ach Gott, erhöh mein Seufzen"), Mendelssohn's Fourth Organ Sonata, one of the more "difficult" of Schumann's Six Fugues on BACH, and his own Prelude and Fugue on "Meine Hoffnung steht auf Gott," Op. 68. Schaab's affinity for Schumann's BACH fugues is evinced by his transcription of the entire set for piano four hands. Coincidentally enough, the church where Schaab performed his recital was the same one in which Robert and Clara Schumann were married in 1840.

Apropos of the C-minor prelude and fugue, Schaab had (probably by happenstance) chosen a Bach work especially prized by Robert Schumann and perhaps by Clara Schumann as well. We know this in Robert's case from a review he published in 1839 of an edition of the so-called Six Great Preludes and Fugues for organ, BWV 543–548, and in which he singled out the C-minor prelude as a "wonderful" composition. In making this distinction, Schumann surely had in mind the ritornello of the prelude, which comprises twenty-five bars of some of the most compelling music that Bach ever conceived for his "royal" instrument, to use Schumann's (and Friedrich Rochlitz's) epithet. Played full organ, which must be how Schaab rendered the prelude, the passage is at once majestic and tragic. Just as Schaab selected the prelude to memorialize the great Johann Sebastian Bach, so the British royal family chose it to conclude the funeral services, in 1997, 2021, and 2022, respectively, of Princess Diana, Prince Philip, and Queen Elizabeth.

The work from the Six Great most associated with Clara Schumann is the Prelude and Fugue in A Minor, BWV 543. In fact, the A-minor was a staple of her repertory as a concert pianist. But she is also reported to have played the C-minor fugue at the piano, and at the moderate tempo of $\downarrow = 85$, when the organist and critic Eduard Krüger visited the Schumanns at their home in the summer of 1843. Krüger had traveled to Leipzig all the way from Ostfriesland to meet Robert Schumann and to perform Bach's organ works on the same instruments played by Bach himself. He succeeded on both counts, performing to critical acclaim "some of Sebastian Bach's most difficult pieces" for a private audience on the organs of the Nicolaikirche and Thomaskirche. On the topic of musical ciphers, as distinct from "organ ciphers" (!), it is surely by accident and not design that the fourth, fifth, sixth, and seventh notes of the subject of the C-minor fugue (F, A-flat, C, B-natural) spell the surname of Bach's contemporary Johann Friedrich Fasch, despite a recent argument to the contrary.[5]

Neither Felix Mendelssohn nor Robert Schumann could have attended Schaab's recital. Mendelssohn had died three years earlier, and Schumann was busy preparing for his move westward from the Saxon capital of Dresden, where he and his family had lived since December 1844 and where he composed his BACH fugues, to the Rhenish city of Düsseldorf. In or near Dresden in late July 1850, Schumann, however, heard not one but two different recitals that solemnized the hundredth anniversary of Bach's death, one of which was presided over by the previously mentioned Carl Kloss. Two years later, in December 1853, Schumann was treated to

Epilogue

a private performance of one or more of his BACH fugues in the Dutch city of Rotterdam, courtesy of Jan Albertus van Eijken, organist of the Zuiderkerk and organ instructor at the local conservatory. Schumann was then in Rotterdam on a wildly successful concert tour of the Netherlands, and Eijken (who, like Schaab, had studied with Becker at the Leipzig Conservatory) was an acquaintance from Schumann's years in Dresden. Holding forth at the organ of his church, Eijken naturally also played music by J. S. Bach, including the Fantasy and Fugue in G Minor, BWV 542. As we have seen earlier in this book, this was the same work played in Leipzig by Adolph Friedrich Hesse on his ill-fated organ crawl there in the winter of 1845 and the same one performed by Wilhelm Rust and company, in the guise of Rust's orchestration of the fantasy, on Palm Sunday in 1881 at the city's Thomaskirche.

Robert Schumann is hardly the only composer who has paid tribute to J. S. Bach by incorporating the B-A-C-H motive into one of their compositions. Indeed, the *Oxford Composer Companion* to Bach, published in 1999, lists over three hundred composers who have done so and over 400 such compositions.[6] Who knows what the actual totals are today? The most significant name on the list would have to be Ludwig van Beethoven, who left behind two such works, the humorous canon "Kühl, nicht lau," WoO 191, which resulted from some serious partying one night with the pianist Friedrich Kuhlau, and a fragmentary Overture on BACH. Bach, of course, was a decisive compositional influence on Beethoven, just as he was on Mendelssohn and Schumann. One is immediately reminded of Beethoven's celebrated pun on "Bach," which seems like an appropriate ending for the present monograph: "His name should not be *Brook* but *Ocean* because of his infinite and inexhaustible wealth of melodies and harmonies."

NOTES

Introduction

1. Russell Stinson, "Karl Gottlieb Freudenbergs *Erinnerungen aus dem Leben eines alten Organisten* und die Bach-Rezeption im 19. Jahrhundert," *Bach-Jahrbuch* 105 (2019): 237–51.
2. The music critic Alex Ross would definitely say for worse. To quote from his award-winning book *The Rest Is Noise*, published about fifteen years ago, "Classical music is widely mocked as a stuck-up, sissified, intrinsically un-American pursuit. The most conspicuous music lover in modern Hollywood film is the fey serial killer Hannibal Lecter, moving his bloody fingers in time to the *Goldberg Variations*." See Alex Ross, *The Rest Is Noise: Listening to the Twentieth Century* (New York: Picador, 2007), 560.

Chapter 1

1. "Aber Bach wurde um so tiefsinniger, je kleiner der Kreis war, an den er sich wendete." See Philipp Spitta, *Johann Sebastian Bach*, vol. 1 (Leipzig: Breitkopf & Härtel, 1873), 589.
2. See Kindscher's review of G. W. Körner's edition of the *Orgelbüchlein*, published in the 21 October 1847 issue of the *Neue Zeitschrift für Musik*, 196–98.
3. Peter Williams, *The Organ Music of J. S. Bach*, 2nd ed., (Cambridge: Cambridge University Press, 2003), 487.
4. Measure numbers according to the Neue Bach Ausgabe (NBA). For a detailed comparison of the two versions of "Herr Christ," see Russell Stinson, "Some Thoughts on Bach's Neumeister Chorales," *Journal of Musicology* 11, no. 4 (Fall 1993): 455–77, esp. 471–76.
5. Adolph Bernhard Marx, *Die Lehre von der musikalischen Komposition*, vol. 2 (Leipzig: Breitkopf & Härtel, 1842), 183–84.
6. Publication date according to Christine Blanken, Christoph Wolff, and Peter Wollny, *Thematisch-systematisches Verzeichnis der musikalischen Werke von Johann*

Sebastian Bach: Dritte, erweiterte Neuausgabe (Wiesbaden: Breitkopf & Härtel, 2022), 448 and 748.

7. See Russell Stinson, *Bach's Legacy: The Music as Heard by Later Masters* (New York: Oxford University Press, 2020), 6–33. On Hauser's catalogue in general and, specifically, the amount of time it took him to complete it, see Yoshitake Kobayashi, *Franz Hauser und seine Bach-Handschriften Sammlung* (Ph.D. diss., Georg-August-Universität Göttingen, 1973), 197–357, esp. 197.

8. Damcke's review appeared in volume 22 (pp. 29–36) of the periodical *Caecilia*. As I have also just recently discovered, Schelble's print is cited in an issue of *The Musical World* from 1838 (vol. 8, p. 260), in a long list of Bach publications that were circulating in England at the time. The citation reads, "Six Chorales, with Variations for the Organ, arranged for four hands, composed by John Sebastian Bach—F. P. Dunst, Frankfort." A further, slightly later citation of Schelble's print (although, again, he is not named as the transcriber) is found in Carl Ludwig Hilgenfeldt's Bach biography. See Hilgenfeldt, *Johann Sebastian Bach's Leben, Wirken und Werke: Ein Beitrag zur Kunstgeschichte des achtzehnten Jahrhunderts* (Leipzig: Friedrich Hofmeister, 1850), 142.

9. For a list of these hymnals, see p. 57 of Series II: Volume 2 of the Leupold Critical Urtext Edition of Bach's organ works (Colfax, North Carolina, 2018). This volume is in fact a very informative monograph by Mark Bighley on the chorales set by Bach in his organ compositions.

10. For a most interesting look at this *Orgelbüchlein* chorale, as well as the melody and tonality of its cantus firmus, see William Renwick, "Of Time and Eternity: Reflections on 'Das alte Jahr vergangen ist,'" *Journal of Music Theory* 50, no. 1 (Spring 2006): 65–76.

11. See NBA IV/1, Heinz-Harald Löhlein, ed., *Kritischer Bericht* to *Orgelbüchlein, Sechs Choräle von verschiedener Art (Schübler Choräle), Orgelpartiten*, 30.

12. "Der erste Band enthält zunächst die schon bekannten sechs Sonaten für zwei Claviere und Pedal, dann die berühmte Passacaille und eine Pastorale. Die Sonaten schrieb Bach nach Forkel für seinen ältesten Sohn Friedemann, um ihn damit zu dem grossen Orgelspieler vorzubereiten, der er nachmals geworden ist. Die Nägeli'sche Ausgabe führt den Titel: 'Orgelschule'; sie bilden auch eine eigentliche Schule, aber keinesweges zur Bildung der Anfänger, wie Mancher dann und wann noch irriger Weise glaubt und sie für diesen Zweck nicht tauglich hält, wohl aber eine solche für bereits ausgebildete Orgelspieler, die an diesen Sonaten ihre erlangte Fertigkeit immer in Schwunge erhalten können, da das Triospiel das übendste, aber auch schwerste auf der Orgel ist. Also sie bilden eine—Meisterschule." Schellenberg's review appeared in the 8 October 1845 issue of the *Allgemeine Musikalische Zeitung*, cols. 721–26; see especially col. 723.

13. "Weil aber Seb. Bach nicht nur beide Manuale gleichmässig, sondern auch das Pedal auf eine vortreffliche Weise behandelte, und sämmtliche Tonstücke in der Ausübung grösstentheils, mitunter sogar sehr schwierig, sind, so dürfte es nur denjenigen Orgelspielern empfohlen werden, welche bereits einen bedeutenden Grad von Fertigkeit haben, und eine vollkommene Ausbildung zu erreichen beabsichtigen, um in die Fusstapfen dieses grossen Meisters zu treten." Birnbach's

Notes

review appeared in the 26 March 1828 issue of the *Berliner Allgemeine Musikalische Zeitung*, 99. For a reprint with commentary, see Bach-Dokumente VI, 521–22.

14. *Johann Sebastian Bach: Six Trio Sonatas, BWV 525–530; Preludes and Fugues BWV 548 & 552* (Musica Omnia, 2014). Organists should study this recording, which may be regarded as a master class on the concept of the varied reprise, if only because of the added ornaments to the pedal line in the slow movement of the first sonata.

15. *Bach & Sons at the Organ* (Musica Omnia, 2016).

16. The presumably earliest extant organ transcription of the ricercar, that by the Bach pupil J. F. Agricola, has recently appeared in a modern edition. See Rüdiger Wilhelm, ed., *Johann Sebastian Bach: Ricercar à 6 c-Moll aus dem "Musikalischen Opfer" BWV 1079; Fassung für Orgel von Johann Friedrich Agricola* (Beeskow: Ortus Musikverlag, 2017).

17. For assistance with this source, I thank my longtime colleague and friend James A. Brokaw II.

18. See Siegmund Helms, "Johannes Brahms und Johann Sebastian Bach," *Bach-Jahrbuch* 57 (1971): 13–81, esp. 55 and 74.

19. Letter of 8 December 1855, cited in David Brodbeck, *Brahms: Symphony No. 1* (Cambridge Music Handbooks) (Cambridge: Cambridge University Press, 1997), 72–73. For the full, original text, see Berthold Litzmann, ed., *Clara Schumann—Johannes Brahms: Briefe aus den Jahren 1853–1896* (Leipzig: Breitkopf & Härtel, 1927), vol. 1, 160.

20. The ever-quotable Alex Ross describes the trajectory of the theme as winding "upward from the initial C before spiraling down an octave and a half to a bottom C that should be heard less as a note than as a minor earthquake." See his essay "Chacona, Lamento, Walking Blues: Bass Lines of Music History," in Alex Ross, *Listen to This* (New York: Picador, 2010), 22–54, esp. 42.

21. The Bach-Archiv (Leipzig) recently acquired a painting that may depict Bach as a teenage organist. For a reproduction with commentary, see Michael Maul, *Bach: Eine Bildbiographie* (Leipzig: Lehmstedt Verlag, 2022), 64–65.

22. The quoted passage at the beginning of this sentence is how Bach explained his lengthy absence from Arnstadt to the consistory there. See Hans T. David and Arthur Mendel, eds., *The New Bach Reader: A Life of Johann Sebastian Bach in Letters and Documents*, revised and enlarged by Christoph Wolff (New York: W. W. Norton, 1998), 46.

23. Mendelssohn never held a church-organ position and played very few formal organ recitals. Therefore, Yearsley considers him "the greatest *amateur* organist in history" (p. 228).

24. Marx's passacaglia is found on pages 408–9 of volume 2 of his treatise; he discusses Bach's passacaglia on pages 412–15. For a comparison of Mendelssohn's passacaglia and Bach's, see Russell Stinson, *The Reception of Bach's Organ Works from Mendelssohn to Brahms* (New York: Oxford University Press, 2006), 12–15.

25. Kerala J. Snyder, *Dieterich Buxtehude: Organist in Lübeck*, 2nd ed. (Rochester, NY: University of Rochester Press), 238.

26. "Das Thema oder der Tanz selbst, besteht wie gewöhnlich aus 4 Tacten, und 27mal wird dasselbe auf die mannigfachste Weise verändert. Der Baß jedoch, der, wie die Oberstimme, sehr sangbar gesetzt ist: [at this point, the ostinato theme is printed as a musical example] wird von dem Componisten beibehalten und tönt durch das Ganze fort. Wäre es für den Tonsetzer gewiß leicht gewesen, dieselben zahlreichen Veränderungen in derselben Tonart—D-Moll—auszuführen, so schaffte er doch seinem Werke neue Abwechselung, daß er nur sechsmal diese Tonart beibehielt, darauf in die verwandte Dur-Tonleiter—F-Dur—überleitete und sieben Veränderungen hier vorführte. Noch einmal schreitet er nach einer andern Tonart—A-Moll—und wieder erklingt das Thema in siebenfacher neuer Gestalt. Darauf gelangt der Meister zurück in seine Grund-Tonart und eben so lange, wie in den verwandten Klängen, verweilt er auch hier, um endlich sein Tonspiel zu Ende zu bringen." See Carl Ferdinand Becker, "Zur Geschichte der Hausmusik in früheren Jahrhunderten," *Neue Zeitschrift für Musik* 12, no. 7 (21 January 1840): 25–26, esp. 26. In the final installment of this essay, published in the very next issue of the *Neue Zeitschrift* (p. 30), Becker praised Bach's passacaglia as a "culmination point" in the history of theme-and-variations form. On Becker and the Andreas Bach Book, see NBA IV/5–6, Dietrich Kilian, ed., *Kritischer Bericht* to *Präludien, Toccaten, Fantasien und Fugen für Orgel*, 122–23.

27. Raymond Knapp, "The Finale of Brahms's Fourth Symphony: The Tale of the Subject," *19th-Century Music* 13, no. 1 (Summer 1989): 3–17, esp. 6–8.

28. As for any chronological concerns about Buxtehude's influence in this instance, there is no reason to doubt that Brahms already knew Buxtehude's passacaglia by the time he wrote his set of variations (which, incidentally, is based not on a theme by Haydn but on the "Chorale St. Anthoni"). Brahms's work was composed, in its original version for two pianos, during the summer of 1873. Apparently only later did he get acquainted with Buxtehude's two other ostinato-bass works for organ, the Chaconnes in C Minor and E Minor. See Knapp, "The Finale of Brahms's Fourth Symphony," 6, fn. 9.

29. On the composition date of this fugue, see my essay, "Toward a Chronology of Bach's Instrumental Music: Observations on Three Keyboard Works," *Journal of Musicology* 7, no. 4 (Fall 1989): 440–70, esp. 463–69; and my monograph, *The Bach Manuscripts of Johann Peter Kellner and His Circle: A Case Study in Reception History* (Durham and London: Duke University Press, 1989), 114–19.

30. See the discussion in Russell Stinson, *J. S. Bach at His Royal Instrument: Essays on His Organ Works* (New York: Oxford University Press, 2012), 120–28. According to Christoph Wolff, *Bach's Musical Universe: The Composer and His Work* (New York: W. W. Norton, 2020), 258, the Six Great are "a homogeneous set of pieces quite possibly intended by the composer to be an opus-like collection," but there is no hard evidence in support of this assertion. Essentially the same claim was made in passing by the nineteenth-century Bach biographer Philipp Spitta. See Spitta, *Johann Sebastian Bach*, vol. 1, p. 689, fn. 171.

This matter recalls a bold statement made by Wolff, on page 254 of his monograph, regarding the Great Eighteen organ chorales, BWV 651–668. Several scholars have hypothesized that Bach collected these works together with an eye to publishing

Notes

them, perhaps as a complement to Part 3 of the *Clavierübung*, another collection comprised mainly of organ chorales (BWV 669–689) that Bach published in 1739, that is, around the same time he was compiling the Great Eighteen. Wolff, however, maintains that "the rather haphazard choice of chorales and the duplication of a number of them would not have been suitable for a collection to be published." Wolff's first point may be well taken, but his second one is highly debatable, considering that all the chorales included in Part 3 of the *Clavierübung* are "duplicated" and that one of them ("Allein Gott in der Höh sei Ehr") is set three times.

31. To quote from the first page of Damcke's review, "Er [Schelble] selbst bearbeitete auf diese Art [for piano, four hands] mehrere, bis dahin ungedruckte Choralvorspiele [by Bach], und einer seiner Schüler arrangirte unter seiner Aufsicht die 6 grossen, sogenannten 'Wiener' Orgel-Präludien und Fugen. Beide Werke wurden in Frankfurt gedruckt."

32. Publication date according to Hilgenfeldt, *Johann Sebastian Bach's Leben, Wirken und Werke*, 142; and Max Schneider, "Verzeichnis der bis zum Jahre 1851 gedruckten (und der geschrieben in Handel gewesen) Werke von Johann Sebastian Bach," *Bach-Jahrbuch* 3 (1906): 84–113, esp. 105. See also Arthur Schanz, *J. S. Bach in der Klaviertranskription* (Eisenach: Karl Dieter Wagner, 2000), 513.

33. On Gleichauf and Mendelssohn, see Wm. A. Little, *Mendelssohn and the Organ* (New York: Oxford University Press, 2010), 107, 135, 271, 394, and 399.

34. The complete contents are given in Schanz, *J. S. Bach in der Klaviertranskription*, 512. An Internet search on Gleichauf's Bach transcriptions revealed a projected performance of several of them in 2019 by acclaimed keyboardists Anthony and Mary Jane Newman. See thesanctuaryseries.org/event/newman-and-newman-play-bach. According to that website, Gleichauf is thought to have made his transcriptions for Felix Mendelssohn and his sister Fanny, but there seems to be no real basis for such a claim.

35. The prelude was eventually published in Kittel's organ method, *Der angehende praktische Organist* (Erfurt, 1808).

36. See NBA IV/5–6, *Kritischer Bericht*, 132, 147, 364, 373–81, and 717.

37. Bach and his wife Anna Magdalena spent eight luxurious days in Kassel in conjunction with his examination of the organ at the Martinskirche there. They were put up at the finest hotel in town and provided with a servant, and Bach was extremely well paid for his efforts. The recital that Bach played on the instrument was attended by the prince of Hesse-Kassel, who was so impressed with the artist's pedal playing that he removed a ring from his finger and presented it to Bach as a sign of his admiration. For other particulars, see Christoph Wolff and Markus Zepf, *The Organs of J. S. Bach: A Handbook* (Urbana: University of Illinois Press, 2012), 39–40.

38. Stinson, *J. S. Bach at His Royal Instrument*, 7–8 and 115–16.

39. Publication date of the "earlier" Peters edition according to Christine Blanken et al., *Thematisch-systematisches Verzeichnis der musikalischen Werke von Johann Sebastian Bach: Dritte, erweiterte Neuausgabe*, 419 and 747.

40. See, for example, the review in the 4 November 1845 issue of the *Neue Zeitschrift für Musik*, 144. See also Annegret Rosenmüller, *Carl Ferdinand Becker*

(1804–1877): Studien zu Leben und Werk (Hamburg: von Bockel Verlag, 2000), 188 and 196.

41. Stinson, *J. S. Bach at His Royal Instrument*, 58–59. Interestingly, Schellenberg's piano transcription was once performed by the young Antonin Dvorak. See Jan Smaczny, "Bach's B-Minor Mass: An Incarnation in Prague in the 1860s and Its Consequences," in *Exploring Bach's B-Minor Mass*, ed. Yo Tomita, Robin A. Leaver, and Jan Smaczny (Cambridge: Cambridge University Press, 2013), 287–97, esp. 292–93.

42. See Schellenberg's report on Hesse's performance, published in the 18 January 1845 issue of the *Neue Zeitschrift für Musik*, 28.

43. The opening phrase of the subject, however, is slightly simplified for pedal performance, a detail that did not escape the attention of A. B. Marx. See *Die Lehre von der musikalischen Komposition*, vol. 4 (Leipzig: Breitkopf & Härtel, 1847), 17.

44. See Frederick George Edwards, "Bach's Music in England," *Musical Times* 37 (1896): 722–26, esp. 723; and Nicholas Thistlethwaite, *The Making of the Victorian Organ* (Cambridge: Cambridge University Press, 1990), 169–70.

45. Harvey Grace, *The Organ Works of Bach* (London: Novello, 1922), 225–32.

46. It may not have been until the turn of the twentieth century that the work catalogued as BWV 988, which Bach titled *ARIA mit verschiedenen Veraenderungen*, began to be known popularly as the "Goldberg Variations" (the nickname, of course, derives from a famous anecdote related by Forkel about Bach's pupil J. G. Goldberg and an insomniac patron of his). In any event, two of the greatest musical celebrities of the nineteenth century cited the piece in decidedly more generic terms: Franz Liszt referred to the work as Bach's "Variations originales," while Johannes Brahms called it Bach's "Variationen G dur." See, respectively, Michael Heinemann, *Die Bach-Rezeption von Franz Liszt* (Cologne: Studio, 1995), 40; and *Johannes Brahms: Briefwechsel*, vol. 8, ed. Max Kalbeck (Berlin: Deutsche Brahms-Gesellschaft, 1915), 218.

47. Williams, *The Organ Music of J. S. Bach*, 184.

48. See Jean M. Perreault, *The Thematic Catalogue of the Musical Works of Johann Pachelbel* (Lanham, MD: Scarecrow Press, 2004), 35–48.

49. So described in 1916 by the organist Herbert Hodge. For further discussion of the nickname and its origins, particularly with regard to Edward Elgar, see Stinson, *J. S. Bach at His Royal Instrument*, 97–98. Observe, too, the title used in 1925 by Oxford University Press for an orchestration of "Wir glauben" co-authored by another of the leading English composers of the day: *J. S. Bach: "Giant" Fugue, Transcribed for String Orchestra by Ralph Vaughan Williams and Arnold Foster*. The fugal component of the work is provided by the three manual voices, which form a fugue on the opening phrase of the chorale.

50. For valuable assistance with this source, I thank Paul Cary, Conservatory Librarian at Baldwin Wallace University.

51. The published catalogue of the Riemenschneider Bach Institute implies that the two editions are not bound together but are entirely separate sources. See Sylvia W. Kenney, *Catalog of the Emilie and Karl Riemenschneider Memorial Bach Library* (New York: Columbia University Press, 1960), 214 and 218. Furthermore, the

Notes

catalogue makes no mention of Rust's ownership of the Marx-Mendelssohn edition (on Mendelssohn as the co-editor of this publication, see Little, *Mendelssohn and the Organ*, 122–23). Finally, the catalogue makes no mention of any of the markings made by Rust that I will discuss here.

52. See the entries on Rust in *The New Grove Dictionary of Music and Musicians*, 2nd ed. (London: Macmillan, 2001), vol. 22, 36; and in Malcolm Boyd, ed., *J. S. Bach*, Oxford Composer Companions (Oxford: Oxford University Press, 1999), 422–23.

53. The registration indications inscribed by Rust at the beginning of the movement from the Pastorale are the following: Manual I—Bourdon 16′and Gedackt 4′′; Manual II—Gedackt 8′; and Manual III—Rohrflöte 8′and Fagotto 8′.

54. For an intriguing look at Rust in this regard, see Robert L. Marshall, "'Editore traditore': Suspicious Performance Indications in the Bach Sources," in Marshall, *The Music of Johann Sebastian Bach: The Sources, the Style, the Significance* (New York: Schirmer Books, 1989), 241–54.

55. Numerous authenticated examples of Rust's script are now available online, and the markings in the Riemenschneider score match these completely. For further comparison, see the facsimile reprint of Rust's manuscript copy of the newly discovered Bach organ chorale BWV 1128 in Stephan Blaut and Michael Pacholke. eds., *Johann Sebastian Bach: Choralfantasie für Orgel über "Wo Gott der Herr nicht bei uns hält," BWV 1128* (Beeskow: Ortus Musikverlag, 2008), xii–xiii.

56. Becker's review appeared in the 28 October 1845 issue of the *Neue Zeitschrift für Musik*, 137–39; Schellenberg's review appeared in the 28 January 1846 issue of the *Allgemeine Musikalische Zeitung*, cols. 721–26. See Chapter 2 of the present book for a detailed discussion.

57. For the fugue that follows, as may be seen on the bottom system of the page, Rust likewise prescribed two different manuals—along with manual changes galore— but with the letters "O" (for Oberwerk) and "U" (for Unterwerk). Thus, the right hand presumably begins on the Unterwerk for the first statement of the subject, switches to the Oberwerk on beat two of measure 2, and switches back to the Unterwerk in measure 3 for the statement of the subject there. The left hand plays only on the Unterwerk.

58. For particulars on these manuscripts, see Hans-Joachim Schulze, ed., *Katalog der Sammlung Manfred Gorke: Bachiana und andere Handschriften und Drucke des 18. und frühen 19. Jahrhunderts* (Leipzig: Musikbibliothek der Stadt Leipzig, 1977), 79. The entire Sammlung Gorke is now available online at sachsen.digital/sammlungen/bach-archiv-leipzig-sammlung-manfred-gorke. Included in the set of parts for Rust's orchestration of the G minor fantasy is an autograph organ part not found in the score. The part contains numerous detailed performance indications, including organ registrations.

59. Actually, the orchestration has ninety-nine measures versus the forty-nine in the organ version; it is twice as long, plus one beat. To prepare for and extend the final cadence, Rust changed the antepenultimate pedal note from an eighth note to a quarter and did likewise for the dominant-seventh chord that follows, causing him to assign this chord its own measure, in $\frac{3}{8}$ time. Rust made no such alterations in his edition of the fantasy for the BG.

146 Notes

60. Inexplicably, the inscription was later crossed out.
61. The other markings here, on beats three and four, were made by Rust for the sake of organ performance. They comprise two brackets between the top two staves indicating that the left hand plays all of that material.
62. In addition to the rather cryptic half rest drawn to the right of the "Fag" indication, Rust made one other inscription in measure 39 of the Riemenschneider score. Situated between the two quarter rests in the middle staff, the inscription consists of a treble clef followed by a g–g′ octave written in half notes and possibly the abbreviation "Viol" written above. Although the G octave certainly agrees with the harmony here, there is no corresponding passage in any of the string parts at this juncture in the orchestration (mm. 77–78).
63. The markings made by Rust in measure 40 are not limited to these two inscriptions. For example, at the beginning of the bar, below the top staff, he apparently inscribed "Pos" (for "Posaune," or trombone) followed by a half note on d′, and on beats three and four, below the alto line and in parallel motion with it, he added note heads on e′, d′, and e′. While no such trombone note ever materialized (even though it fits with the harmony), the last two note heads equate to how the second violin part reads in measure 80 of the orchestration. Witness also the "x" written above the last note of the middle staff, signifying exactly where the cello statement of the sixteenth-note motive begins.
64. The first of these markings is followed by an additional, indecipherable inscription.
65. Stinson, *The Reception of Bach's Organ Works*, 155–56.
66. The relevant documentation on Brahms and Rust regarding the position of Thomaskantor is found in Stefan Altner, *Das Thomaskantorat im 19. Jahrhundert* (Leipzig: Passage-Verlag, 2006), 54–88.
67. "Wir erleben immer neuen Kummer hier, immer Enttäuschungen. Hiezu gehört, daß Rust am Palmsonntag die g moll-Orgelfuge, für Orchester arrangiert, in der Thomaskirche spielen läßt, sowie er Choralvorspiele für vier Stimmen aussetzt und Text unterlegt, und den haben Sie uns empfohlen!!" Letter of 27 March 1881. See Max Kalbeck, ed., *Johannes Brahms im Briefwechsel mit Heinrich und Elisabet Herzogenberg* (Berlin: Deutsche Brahms-Gesellschaft, 1907), vol. 1, 144.
68. On the dating of that manuscript, and for other particulars, see Schulze, *Katalog der Sammlung Manfred Gorke*, 20. Another Bach transcription by Rust is his arrangement for two pianos of the double-choir motet "Ich lasse dich nicht, du segnest mich den," BWV 1164 (formerly BWV Anh. 159). See *Katalog der Sammlung Manfred Gorke*, 43.
69. See the 14 April 1881 issue of that publication, p. 196. According to the *Leipziger Tageblatt* (daily newspaper), the work in question was Bach's "G-moll-Orgelpräludium für Orchester bearbeitet von Rust, Wilhelm." See Altner, *Das Thomaskantorat im 19. Jahrhundert*, 83, fn. 314. It is immaterial that this citation refers to the piece as a "prelude" rather than a "fantasy," for these two terms were used casually and interchangeably. Indeed, the autograph of Rust's orchestration of the G-minor fantasy is titled "Orgel-Fantasie in Gmoll," while his edition of the work in BG 15 is titled "Praeludium (Fantasia)."
70. Stinson, *The Reception of Bach's Organ Works*, 68–69.

Notes

71. Altner, *Das Thomaskantorat im 19. Jahrhundert*, 162.
72. See Hermann Abert, *Johann Joseph Abert (1832–1915): Sein Leben und seine Werke* (Leipzig: Breitkopf & Härtel, 1916), 92–93, 192–96, and 201.
73. Renate Hofmann and Kurt Hofmann, *Johannes Brahms als Pianist und Dirigent: Chronologie seines Wirkens als Interpret* (Tutzing: Hans Schneider, 2006), 137–38 and 232.
74. See Hofmann, *Johannes Brahms als Pianist und Dirigent*, 151; and Stinson, *The Reception of Bach's Organ Works*, 138.
75. For a comprehensive discussion, see Stinson, *The Reception of Bach's Organ Works*, 126–81.
76. Valerie Woodring Goertzen, "Brahms's Performances of Bach's Organ Works," *American Brahms Society Newsletter* 37, no. 2 (Fall 2019): 1–5. On Brahms and the G-major fantasy, see also Russell Stinson, "Clara Schumann's Bach Book: A Neglected Document of the Bach Revival," *Bach: Journal of the Riemenschneider Bach Institute* 39, no. 1 (2008): 1–67.
77. See David et al., *The New Bach Reader*, 438. Forkel's Bach biography, titled *Über Johann Sebastian Bachs Leben, Kunst und Kunstwerke*, appeared in 1802.
78. Letter of 9 June 1827. See A. D. Coleridge, *Goethe's Letters to Zelter* (London: George Bell and Sons, 1887), 291.
79. "Am herrlichsten, am kühnsten, in seinem Urelemente erscheint er aber nun für allemal an seiner Orgel. Hier kennt er weder Maß noch Ziel und arbeitet auf Jahrhunderte hinaus." See the 14 May 1839 issue of the *Neue Zeitschrift für Musik*, 153–54.
80. Grace, *The Organ Works of Bach*, 303–4.

CHAPTER 2

1. See the entry on Rochlitz in *The New Grove Dictionary of Music and Musicians*, 2nd ed. (London: Macmillan, 2001), vol. 21, 484–85.
2. See Hans T. David and Arthur Mendel, and Christoph Wolff, eds., *The New Bach Reader: A Life of Johann Sebastian Bach in Letters and Documents*, revised and enlarged by Christoph Wolff (New York: W. W. Norton, 1998), 492.
3. For a recent discussion of Schicht's activities in Leipzig, see Jeffrey S. Sposato, *Leipzig after Bach: Church and Concert Life in a German City* (New York: Oxford University Press, 2018), 204–30.
4. This is also the conclusion reached in Bach-Dokumente VI, 347. See Bach-Dokumente VI, 344–46, for a reprint of the review under consideration here.
5. For the complete contents of Schicht's edition, see Bach-Dokumente VI, 528–29. See also NBA IV/2, Hans Klotz, ed., *Kritischer Bericht* to *Die Orgelchoräle aus der Leipziger Originalhandschrift*, 53.
6. "Es ist eine lobenswürdige Bemühung der Verlagshandlung, diese für die Orgelspielkunst so wichtigen Nachlässe des mit vollem Rechte zum klassischen Schriftsteller erhobenen J. S. Bach in Umlauf zu bringen. Der Geschmack hat sich zwar seit jenen Zeiten ziemlich verändert . . . jedoch was die Behandlung dieses königlichen Instruments betrifft, so werden die Bachschen Arbeiten jederzeit

Muster seyn und bleiben, und jeder Organist, der so viel Achtung und Gefühl für die Kunst hat, sich über das gemeine, blos mechanische Spiel zu erheben, wird ihnen die sorgfältigste Aufmerksamkeit widmen, die sie, wahrlich! verdienen. Zugegeben, dass nur ein fertiger und in den Bachischen Stil eingeweihter Spieler, nur auf einem guten Instrumente, und nur vor einem kunstverständigen Auditorium davon Gebrauch machen könne . . . in Hinsicht auf Kulturgeschichte der Musik für diese Gattung Epoche machende Denkmäler seyen, als auch in Hinsicht auf die Behandlung der Orgel, und insbesondere in Hinsicht auf des Verf. eigenthümliche Schöpfungskraft der melodischen und harmonischen Formen auf derselben—so lange Muster der Kunst bleiben und die lehrreichste Schule für alle sich vollendende Organisten seyn werden . . . Sämtliche Vorspiele sind in gebundenem Stile geschrieben, bald mehr, bald weniger streng."

7. "No. 1. ist der ausgeführte Choral: *Wachet auf, ruft uns die Stimme*—im Tenor. Die ermahnende und warnende Stimme eines Freundes. In der Oberstimme ist eine liebliche, einfache, auf wenige Figuren gebaute Altpartie." In comparing this work to "the admonishing voice of a friend," Rochlitz is alluding to the main message of the chorale text, which is, in accordance with the Parable of the Ten Virgins, to be prepared for Judgment Day.

8. "No. 2. ein kleines, kunstvolles, dreystimmiges Gewebe, wozu der Choral: *Meine Seele erhebt den Herrn*, als vierte Stimme im Sopran eintritt."

9. "No. 3. ist ein Duett im gebundenen Stile, wo die Oberstimme 8 Fusston und die Unterstimme 16 Fusston einen einzigen Takt zum Thema haben, und darüber 32 Takte lang mit einander concertieren, indess der Choral: *Wo soll ich fliehen hin*— auf dem Pedale 4 Fusston in Absätzen eintritt. Das ängstliche Suchen der Ruhe ist meisterhaft gemalt, und der Effekt ganz wunderbar und einzig." By "anxious search for peace," Rochlitz is again alluding to the chorale text, which deals with the burden of sin and how to escape from it. All three of the organ registration markings appear in the score of Schicht's edition, just as they do in the original print of the Schübler Chorales. The latter dates from around 1747/48.

10. "No. 4. ist ein Terzett auf dem Manual über den Choral: *Wer nur den lieben Gott lässt walten*—welcher vom Pedal dazu gespielt wird. Wiederum wahrhaft meisterlich behandelt! Die einzelnen Gedanken der Choralmelodie geben variirt den beyden Oberstimmen Stoff zu ihren mannichfaltigen Nachahmungen."

11. "No. 5. mit der Choralmelodie: *Ach bleib bey uns, Herr Jesu Christ*—in der Oberstimme, hat in der einfachen Tenorpartie mancherley lehrreiche Stellen und ist ein gutes Übungsstück, obgleich in Rücksicht auf Länge und Zweck etwas dagegen zu erinnern wäre."

12. "No. 6. mit dem Choral: *Kommst du nun Jesu vom Himmel* etc. in der Altstimme ¾ Takt, verlangt guten Vortrag, da die Oberpartie mit dem Basse ⅜ Takt spielt. Ist etwas zu lang jedoch unterhaltend und lehrreich." Bach-Dokumente VI, 345, erroneously reads "mit dem Basse ⅝ Takt spielt."

13. "No. 7. hat die Melodie *Allein Gott in der Höh' sey Ehr*—in der Mitte zweyer meisterhaft concertirenden Stimmen. Man vergisst über dieser schönen, gebundenen Arbeit die Länge. Jedoch scheint dem Rec. der Choral zu sehr im Hintergrunde zu stehen."

Notes 149

14. "No. 8. ein prächtiges, 124 Takte langes Trio über den vorigen Choral, worin die beyden Oberstimmen, neben dem, sich auf die Choralmelodie stützenden und brillanten Thema, noch den Choral wechselweise vortragen. Ein starkes Uebungsstück!"

15. "No. 9. ist eine niedliche Fughette über ebendemselben Choral; wozu der Anfang der ersten und dann der zweyten Zeile der Melodie den Grundstoff geben muss."

16. "No. 10. ist ein Meisterstück der Kunst über die alte Melodie: *Wir glauben all an einen Gott*—für das volle Werk. Das Thema, aus der Melodie genommen, führen die drey obern Stimmen in Fugenstile durch, wozu das Pedal sein eignes Contrathema ebenfalls durcharbeitet. Ein einzigsmal ergreift der Tenor dies Gegenthema."

17. "No. 11. eine artige Fughette über die vorige Melodie im sogenannten französischen Stile."

18. "No. 12. eine dreistimmige niedliche Fughette über die Melodie *Lob sey dem allmächtigen Gott*."

19. "No. 13. Hier sind drey Stimmen auf dem Manual geschäftig, die Melodie: *Ach Gott und Herr*—auf mannigfaltiche Art vorzutragen."

20. "No. 14. enthält eine Menge von Kunstäusserungen über den vorigen Choral, welcher in der Oberstimme als Cantus firmus erscheint und von den untern Stimmen in verkleinerten Noten so vorgetragen wird, dass man durchaus nichts anders hört, als die einzelnen Theile der Melodie."

21. "No. 15. ein kleines Vorspiel mit figurirtem Canto fermo: *Wer nur den lieben Gott* etc."

22. "No. 16. ist der ganze Choral: *Durch Adams Fall ist* etc im Stilo alla capella vierstimmig fugirt."

23. "No. 17. ist eine freundliche Ausführung des Chorals: *Schmücke dich, o liebe Seele*."

24. "No. 18. ist eine vierfache Behandlungsart der Melodie: *Liebster Jesu wir sind hier.*— wovon die beyden letzten fünf stimmig den Choral in den beyden Oberstimmen canonisch alla Quinta vortragen mit kleinen unbedeutenden Veränderungen in den übrigen beyden Mittelstimmen." The first work cited here by Rochlitz, BWV 706, actually consists of two settings of "Liebster Jesu." The first of these settings might be considered a "melody chorale," a type of organ chorale in which the hymn tune appears as a continuous melody in the soprano voice, with little or no ornamentation. The second is merely a harmonization, and a primitive one at that. The "two *middle* voices" referred to by Rochlitz, in conjunction with the two *Orgelbüchlein* settings of "Liebster Jesu," are obviously the two voices played by the left hand.

25. "No. 19. der Choral: *Allein Gott in der Höh* etc. mit einem einfachen Unter-Contrapunkte der dritten Gattung, ist etwas steif und wegen der Länge ermüdend."

26. "No. 20. ist ein herrliches, lehrreiches Trio über die vorige Melodie. Die Länge von 96 Takten übersieht man gern bey Betrachtung eines so kunstvoll behandelten Stoffs."

27. "No. 21. und 22. enthält den Choral: *Ich hab mein Sach Gott* etc. mit dreymaliger Veränderung der Harmonie, nebst einem Vorspiel, worin dieser Choral, fugirt, 140 Takte so durchgeführt wird, dass auch diese Melodie in der Oberstimme per

augmentationem erscheint, und von einem andern Instrumente dazu vorgetragen werden kann. Mit den durchgehenden Noten geht's aber hier ziemlich herbe zu."

28. "No. 23. ist wiederum ein treffliches Vorspiel im gebundenen Stile mit zwey sich immer nachahmenden Oberstimmen und dem Canto fermo im Pedale."

29. "No. 24. ist eine niedliche Fughette über den Choral: *Gelobet seyst du Jesu Christ."*

30. On the authorship of the third work (BWV 759), see NBA IV/10, Reinmar Emans, ed., *Kritischer Bericht* to *Orgelchoräle aus unterschiedlicher Überlieferung*, 475–78; and Peter Williams, *The Organ Music of J. S. Bach*, 2nd ed. (Cambridge: Cambridge University Press, 2003), 495.

31. Williams, *The Organ Music of J. S. Bach*, 321.

32. Bach's pupil Johann Ludwig Krebs made this same designation for his teacher's setting of "Christ lag in Todesbanden," BWV 718, writing the word "Übungsstück" on his manuscript copy of the piece. But Krebs surely had in mind both the right- and left-hand parts of this fantasy-like composition. See Felix Friedrich, "Johann Ludwig Krebs als Vertreter einer frühen Bach-Rezeption? Grundlegende Gedanken zum Symposium am 15. April 2000 in Altenberg," *Freiberger Studien zur Orgel* 7 (2002): 5–9, esp. 8; and Russell Stinson, *J. S. Bach at His Royal Instrument: Essays on His Organ Works* (New York: Oxford University Press, 2012), 19.

33. Williams, *The Organ Music of J. S. Bach*, 405.

34. For more discussion of this work as a specimen of a technique I have termed "the varied Stollen," see Stinson, *J. S. Bach at His Royal Instrument*, 38–39.

35. Letter of 15 May 1809. See Philip Olleson, ed., *The Letters of Samuel Wesley: Professional and Social Correspondence, 1797–1837* (Oxford: Oxford University Press, 2001), 108–9.

36. Letter of 16 February 1810. See *The Letters of Samuel Wesley*, 139. The nickname of "the old wig" may have originated with Bach's son Johann Christian, who spent a good deal of his career in London. At any rate, Johann Christian, whose own nickname was "the London Bach," is rumored to have referred to his father in this manner. See *The New Bach Reader*, 379.

37. For information on this source, I thank Michael Mullen, Assistant Librarian at the Royal College of Music.

38. Russell Stinson, *The Reception of Bach's Organ Works from Mendelssohn to Brahms* (New York: Oxford University Press, 2006), 78.

39. Samuel Wesley would doubtless have agreed with this assessment. In a letter of 1809 to the organist Benjamin Jacob, Wesley proposed to "electrify" Jacobs by playing this work either for or with him. See *The Letters of Samuel Wesley*, 105–6. This piece was also one of the works from Schicht's edition "recommended" by Wesley in a letter written a few weeks earlier to William Crotch, as cited earlier.

40. NBA IV/10, *Kritischer Bericht*, 112–13. On Rust's transcription, see also Hans-Joachim Schulze, ed., *Katalog der Sammlung Manfred Gorke: Bachiana und andere Handschriften und Drucke des 18. und frühen 19. Jahrhunderts* (Leipzig: Musikbibliothek der Stadt Leipzig, 1977), 20.

41. "Bach hat den regern Dreivierteltakt gewählt und den Cantus firmus hier und da, doch sehr mässig, verziert. Es gefällt zunächst die Schlankheit und Elastizität, mit der er seine Figuralstimme einführt, beim Eintritt des Cantus firmus heftiger

bewegt, gleichsam hin und her schüttelt, und dann wieder in die erste gehaltnere Weise zurückkehrt. Der obige Stoff genügt ihm zu einer—die Wiederholung ungerechnet—63 Takte langen Ausführung. Durch die Zwischenspiele der Figuralstimme, aushaltende Schlusstöne jeder Strophe des Cantus firmus, gleichartige Behandlung der einander entsprechenden Theile, und Zurückgehn auf den Anfang wird die ganze Arbeit hindurch Einheit und Klarheit erhalten. Die Modulation ist, wie immer bei Bach, einfach und kräftig, immer auf das Nächste gerichtet und immer weiter führend.

Sehr ergötzlich spielt die Figuralstimme selbst den Cantus firmus vor . . . aber in ihrer Weise mit harmonischen Beitönen und andern Hülfstönen harmonisch und melodisch ausführend. Festigend tritt das Achtelmotiv zwischen die Sechszehntel, und freisinnig wird vom dritten Takt an die rhythmische Ordnung der ersten Takte umgekehrt—dadurch aber Auftakt und Uebergangsakkord nett bezeichnet. Mit dem Eintritte der Choralstimme wird die Figuralstimme blosse, aber reich und lebhaft gestaltete Begleitung." See Adolph Bernhard Marx, *Die Lehre von der musikalischen Komposition*, vol. 2 (Leipzig: Breitkopf & Hartel, 1842), 181.

42. Stinson, *The Reception of Bach's Organ Works*, 156, 158, and 170–71.

43. On the composition date of BWV 707, see NBA IV/10, *Kritischer Bericht*, 190.

44. "Rec. erlaubt sich nach dieser gedrängten und in vielem Betracht zu kurzen Anzeige, noch folgende Aeusserungen für diejenigen, welche die Bachischen Werke dieser Gattung studiren und sich danach bilden wollen. Man wage sich nicht an die Bachischen Arbeiten, ohne Fertigkeit und hinlängliche Einsichten in die Harmonie zu haben, weil man sonst Gefahr läuft, entweder den Vortrag zu verfehlen, oder gar durch die Härten der durchgehenden Noten davon abgeschreckt zu werden. Man lerne aus diesen originellen Produkten des grossen Kunstgenies die feine Verarbeitung des Stoffs . . . Insbesondere beherzige man, dass ein Stück im strengen, gebundenen Stile den besten Effekt machen kann, wenn es auf verschiedenen Instrumenten vorgetragen wird, und hingegen, wenn es auf der Orgel oder dem Pianoforte gespielt wird, in den Stellen, wo die einzelnen Stimmen einander überspringen, oder in einander eingreifen, oder die durchgehenden Noten theils widrige Querstände machen, theils sich unter einander zerreiben, wegen der gleichen Tonfarbe zur blossen Augenmusik wird."

45. See Ulrich Leisinger, "Bachian Fugues in Mozart's Vienna," *Bach Notes* 6 (Fall 2006): 1–7, esp. 6. Such transcriptions also survive from around this time in London, where in 1807 Charles Frederick Horn published string-quartet arrangements of twelve keyboard fugues by Bach. For a complete list, see *The Letters of Samuel Wesley*, 78, fn. 2.

46. See the discussion of Becker's life in Annegret Rosenmüller, *Carl Ferdinand Becker (1804–1877): Studien zu Leben und Werk* (Hamburg: von Bockel Verlag, 2000), 11–20.

47. See the discussion of Schellenberg's life in Hermann J. Busch, "Organisten an St. Nikolai," in *Die Nikolaikirche zu Leipzig und ihre Orgel*, ed. Hermann J. Busch (Leipzig: Evangelische Verlagsanstalt, 2004), 29–35, esp. 33.

48. Although Mendelssohn respected Schellenberg's expertise as a proofreader, he refused to accept any of Schellenberg's proposed changes to his editions. See

Mendelssohn's letter to Breitkopf & Härtel of 9 June 1845, published in Uta Wald, ed., *Felix Mendelssohn Bartholdy: Sämtliche Briefe*, vol. 10 (Kassel: Bärenreiter, 2016), 480–81.

49. Another arrangement of a Bach organ work for four hands and four feet that deserves to be mentioned here is that by the Danish composer Niels Gade (1817–1890) of the partita on "Sei gegrüsset, Jesu gütig," BWV 768. Gade served under Felix Mendelssohn as assistant conductor of the Leipzig Gewandhaus orchestra from 1843 to 1847, and no doubt he got to know Bach's partita through Mendelssohn's edition of the piece (like Mendelssohn, he was also an organist). Gade's arrangement dates from 1859. For a modern edition, see Klaus Uwe Ludwig, ed., *Niels Wilhelm Gade: Variationen über den Choral "Sey gegrüsset Jesu gütig" von Johann Sebastian Bach* (Wiesbaden: Breitkopf & Härtel, 1996).

50. For particulars on these two transcriptions, see Arthur Schanz, *Johann Sebastian Bach in der Klaviertranskription* (Eisenach: Karl Dieter Wagner, 2000), 474 and 513.

51. The "Adagio" by Becker was presumably one of the twelve he had published in 1834 under the title *12 Adagio [sic] für Orgel zur Beförderung des wahren Orgelspiels*. For further data on that collection, see Rosenmüller, *Carl Ferdinand Becker*, 106–7 and 130. The works by Schellenberg were a pastorale, a fantasy on BACH, and a fantasy on "Ein feste Burg ist unser Gott."

52. "Nun folgte die so reizende und zugleich so mächtig ergreifende Fantasie und Fuge (G-moll) von J. S. Bach, von Hrn. Schellenberg zu vier Händen und doppeltes Pedal eingerichtet. Wir wüßten kein Tonstück für die Orgel zu nennen, das sich mit diesem hinsichtlich der Pracht und Kraft vergleichen dürfte, und empfehlen dieses Werk, welches in dieser eigenthümlichen Gestalt so eben bei Breitk. u. Härtel die Presse verlaßen hat, allen Orgelspielern, die auf Virtuosität Anspruch zu machen glauben. Der Vortrag dieser Nummer, wo der Concertgeber von Hrn. Org. Becker unterstürzt wurde, war dem Werke würdig." The review, whose author identified himself only as "C," appeared in the 4 November 1845 issue of the *Neue Zeitschrift*, 144. The title of Schellenberg's arrangement of BWV 542, as published in 1845 by Breitkopf & Härtel, reads *Johann Sebastian Bach: Fantasie und Fuge g-Moll für die Orgel. Für den Concertgebrauch zu vier Händen und doppeltes Pedal eingerichtet von Hermann Schellenberg*. See Rosenmüller, *Carl Ferdinand Becker*, 188. Curiously, there is no mention of Schellenberg's recital in Anselm Hartinger's comprehensive study, *"Alte Neuigkeiten": Bach-Aufführungen und Leipziger Musikleben im Zeitalter Mendelssohns, Schumanns und Hauptmanns 1829 bis 1852* (Wiesbaden: Breitkopf & Härtel, 2014).

53. *Allgemeine Musikalische Zeitung*, 8 October 1845, col. 726.

54. "Gestern Abend dirigirte ich hier im Gewandhause meine 6te Sinfonie, die ausgezeichnet ging, und nach jedem Satz lebhaften Beifall erhielt." For the complete text of this missive, see the online edition of the Spohr letters maintained by the Spohr Museum in Kassel (www.spohr-briefe.de).

55. "Herr Musikdir. Ad. Hesse aus Breslau, der rühmlich bekannte Orgelvirtuos, verweilte in letzter Woche einige Tage in unserer Stadt, um die Aufführung seiner neusten (6ten) Symphonie zu leiten, und benutzte den letzten Tag seines Hierseins, den Freunden des Orgelspiels auf seinem großartigen Instrumente einen Genuß

Notes

zu verschaffen. Ein gewählter Kreis von Künstlern und Kunstfreunden hatte sich am Freitag den 10. Nachmittags in unserer prächtigen Nicolaikirche eingefunden, und Diejenigen, denen H.'s Spiel noch neu, waren besonders gespannt auf des Künstlers weitbekannte Leistungen und auf die Behandlung des Instruments unter seinen Fingern. Hesse spielte auf der trefflichen Nicolaiorgel einige größere Tonstücke und ein sehr schönes Trio seiner Composition, und gab dadurch Gelegenheit, sein meisterhaftes Spiel, seine großartige Schreibweise für das volle Werk, wobei namentlich seine Behandlung des doppelten Pedals Erwähnung verdient, zu bewundern. Nach den gehörten eigenen Compositionen wollte H. nun auch einige von Bach's Kunstschöpfungen vorführen, aber, o Schade! ein Pedalclaves der sonst so solid gebauten Orgel versagte seine Dienste; eine winzige Kleinigkeit, das Brechen eines Abstractenhakes, welcher aber ohne das nöthige Material und die nöthigen Instrumente augenblicklich zu ersetzten nicht möglich war, führte auf die unbarmherzigste Weise das plötzliche Ende eines so seltenen Vergnügens herbei. Des Meisters Vorschlag, die angefangene Unterhaltung auf der Thomasorgel fortzusetzten, wurde mit Vergnügen angenommen; die ganze Versammlung setzte sich nach der Thomaskirche in Bewegung, die Bälgetreter wurden aus der Nicolaikirche mitgenommen, und so waren wir bald am Ziele und harrten der Fortsetzung des eben unterbrochenen Kunstgenusses. Die Orgel der Thomaskirche ist beim vollen Werke von großer Wirkung, aber für den Spieler ist es doppelt schwer, mit ihr zurecht zu kommen; ein heilloses Durcheinander der Registeranlage, so daß Untersatz und andere Pedalstimmen zwischen Manualstimmen, Stimmen der drei Claviere in bunter Reihe bald hier bald da zu suchen sind, machen einen schnellen Ueberblick geradezu unmöglich; dazu kommt eine abscheuliche schwerfällige Spielart der Manuale und des Pedals, um den Spieler vollends alle Lust zu benehmen. Heuler sind zwar in der jetzigen Jahreszeit auch in den besten Orgeln zu erwarten. Die fanden sich auch hier vor, hatten sich vielleicht erst nachdem das letztemal darauf gespielt wurde gebildet, und traten nun zum Leidwesen Aller hemmend in den Weg. Nimmt man dies alles zusammen, so können wir Hesse's Aufopferung und Kraft nicht genug anerkennen, welche bei solchen Umständen eines der größten Orgelstücke Bach's, die große Phantasie und Fuge in G-Moll (Nr. 4 im 2. Bde. der neuen Peters'schen Ausgabe), so wie noch einige seiner eigenen großen Compositionen auszuführen sich hingab und mit solcher Ausbauer vermochte. Obgleich häufig durch Heulen etlicher Claves zum einstweiligen Aufhören gezwungen, setzte H. sein Spiel doch bis zur einbrechenden Dunkelheit fort, und wiewohl seinen Zuhörern der Genuß durch dergleichen Störungen geschmälert wurde, da sie die Tonstücke nicht in einem Zuge hören konnten, so sind wir ihm und gewiß im Namen aller derer, die ihn hörten, zu doppeltem Danke verpflichtet, da wir den Willen für die That nehmen." *Neue Zeitschrift für Musik*, 18 January 1845, 28. See also the "Aufführungsverzeichnisse" (CD-ROM) in Hartinger, *"Alte Neuigkeiten,"* 190.

56. In reference to the organ at the Thomaskirche, cold dry air can cause cracks in the wind chests of organs with tracker action, resulting in ciphers. On some instruments with tracker action, especially those built before the invention of the pneumatic system known as the Barker lever, the organist must apply more

pressure to a key as more stops are used. When one is playing full organ, particularly when two or more manuals are coupled, this can result in extraordinarily stiff key action.

57. Hans Jürgen Seyfried, *Adolph Friedrich Hesse als Orgelvirtuose und Orgelkomponist* (Regensburg: Gustav Bosse, 1965), 12–13, 23–24, and 27. Hesse's recital on 29 June 1832 at the Peterskirche in Leipzig, which included three fugues by Bach (presumably from the Well-Tempered Clavier), a "Präludium und Fuge über den Namen Hesse," and a fugal improvisation on a theme supplied by Friedrich Rochlitz, was attended by the twelve-year-old Clara Wieck. See the "Aufführungsverzeichnisse" in Hartinger, *"Alte Neuigkeiten,"* 174; and Gerd Nauhaus and Nancy B. Reich, eds., *Clara Schumann: Jugendtagebücher 1827–1840* (Hildesheim: Georg Olms Verlag, 2019), 122.

58. See Seyfried, *Adolph Friedrich Hesse*, 19–20, 23, 26, and 33; and David Yearsley, *Bach's Feet: The Organ Pedals in European Culture* (Cambridge: Cambridge University Press, 2012), 236. The preface to volume 2 of the Peters edition, edited by F. C. Griepenkerl, is dated October 1844.

59. Yearsley, *Bach's Feet*, 232–33.

60. On Mendelssohn's whereabouts at that time, see R. Larry Todd, *Mendelssohn: A Life in Music* (New York: Oxford University Press, 2003), 485–87.

61. "Die Orgel ist die Königin der Instrumente und Bach's Werke ihr Schmuck." Becker himself encloses this sentence in quotation marks, which would seem to indicate that the wording is not his own. Perhaps he is quoting what was a popular aphorism at the time, but whose authorship is unknown.

62. Becker's reviews were published in the 1 July 1845 (pp. 2–3) and 28 October 1845 (pp. 137–39) issues of the *Neue Zeitschrift für Musik*; Schellenberg's reviews were published in the 8 October 1845 (cols. 721–26) and 28 January 1846 (cols. 59–62) issues of the *Allgemeine Musikalische Zeitung*. Excerpts from all four reviews are found in Bach-Dokumente VI, 510–14.

63. BECKER: "Präludium und Fuge, fünfstimmig mit dreifachen Tactwechsel, Es-Dur. Großartig und geistreich, jedoch wohl allen Verehrern Bach's aus dem 3. Theil der Clavierübungen bekannt."

SCHELLENBERG: "Präludium und Fuge in Es dur, aus den Clavierübungen entnommen. Die Fuge besonders ist ein unbestreitbar köstliches Werk; das Präludium enthält, die etwas altmodischen Schlüsse abgerechnet, sehr Werthvolles, und verlangt seiner eigenthümlichen Schreibweise wegen einen sicheren gewählten Vortrag und einen erfahrenen umsichtigen Spieler."

64. See the discussion in Stinson, *J. S. Bach at His Royal Instrument*, 50–53. See also Hartinger, *"Alte Neuigkeiten,"* 441–42, and the accompanying "Aufführungsverzeichnisse," 194.

65. BECKER: "Toccate und Fuge, F-Dur. Zwar schon früher bei Peters erschienen, doch hier mit verschiedenen Abschriften verglichen. Muß man die Fuge in ihren ruhigen, sicheren Schritten für ächt orgelgemäß anerkennen, so werden uns doch Manche beistimmen, wenn wir das Präludium für minder bedeutend halten, obgleich wir den Fleiß, den Bach an diesen Satz gewendet, fast durchgängig ein zweistimmiger Canon in der Octave, zu schätzen wissen."

Notes   155

SCHELLENBERG: "Toccate und Fuge in F dur (schon früher bei Peters gedruckt). Ein höchst grossartiges Werk, das, wenn man erst die beiden langen Orgelpuncte auf der Tonica und Dominante nebst dem Pedalsolo im Rücken hat, dem Spieler Freude machen muss."

66. Stinson, *The Reception of Bach's Organ Works*, 22–23, 28, and 64–65.

67. NBA IV/5–6, Dietrich Kilian, ed., *Kritischer Bericht* (*Präludien, Toccaten, Fantasien und Fugen für die Orgel*), 260–61. Publication date of the earlier Peters edition according to Christine Blanken, Christoph Wolff, and Peter Wollny, *Thematisch-systematisches Verzeichnis der musikalischen Werke von Johann Sebastian Bach: Dritte, erweiterte Neuausgabe* (Wiesbaden: Breitkopf & Härtel, 2022), 419 and 747.

68. "Der auf den optischen Eindruck bedachte Organist hob bei solchen Pedalsoli gern die Hände in die Höhe, um dem stauenden Publikum zu zeigen, daß er wirklich mit den Füßen spiele." Gotthold Frotscher, *Geschichte des Orgelspiels und der Orgelkompositionen* (Berlin: Max Hesse, 1935), 1176, fn. 2.

69. BECKER: "Toccate und Fuge, D-Moll. Ebenfalls schon bei Peters gestochen und verglichen mit Abschriften. In dem Vorwort dieser Ausgabe wird das Werk mit "dorisch" bezeichnet. Die dorische Tonart sucht man jedoch vergeblich, und der Mangel der Vorzeichnung in den älteren Abschriften rührt nur daher, daß man in dem 18. Jahrh. in den Molltonreihen die sechste Stufe nicht oder nur selten mit einem Erniedrigungszeichen—da eben so häufig die kleine wie die große sechste Stufe im Laufe eines Tonstücks benuzt wird—zu bemerken pflegte. Aus diesem Grunde findet man D-Moll ohne Vorzeichnung; G-Moll mit einem b, C-Moll mit zwei b in den alteren Musikalien. Wir führen dies nur an, um nicht den Unkundigen in dieser Sache in Ungewißheit zu lassen, und daß er nicht meine, er habe hier ein ächt dorisches Tonstück, eine Composition aus einer Kirchentonart oder gar einer alt-griechischen Tonreihe erhalten, woran Bach nicht im Entferntesten gedacht hatte."

SCHELLENBERG: "Toccate und Fuge in D moll, dorisch? (schon durch die frühere Peters'sche Ausgabe bekannt). Um den Effect zu erreichen, den die allgemein geschätzte Toccate bietet, lassen die Orgelvirtuosen gewöhnlich die Fuge weg, da sie nicht zu dessen Vermehrung, sondern zum Gegentheil beitragen möchte."

70. On this feature of the manuscript sources, see NBA IV/5–6, *Kritischer Bericht*, 375.

71. George B. Stauffer, *The Organ Preludes of Johann Sebastian Bach* (Ann Arbor: UMI Research Press, 1980), 27.

72. According to the composer and music historian Hubert Parry, writing at the turn of the twentieth century, the fugue, at least, was known in England as the one "in modo Dorico." See C. Hubert H. Parry, *Johann Sebastian Bach: The Story of the Development of a Great Personality* (New York and London: G. P. Putnam's Sons, 1909), 67.

73. "So wurde mit einem Werk des großen, tiefdenkenden, unerreichbaren Sebastian, wahrhaft sebastianisch, d.h. ehrwürdig, die durchweg religiose Festaufführung geschlossen." See *Euterpe* 2, no. 12 (December 1842), 200.

74. "So ist diese großartige Fuge mit einem der großartigsten Themen, die je geschrieben wurden, weder ein Liebling der Hörer noch der Spieler." See Keller, *Die*

Orgelwerke Bachs: Ein Beitrag zu ihrer Geschichte, Form, Deutung und Wiedergabe (Leipzig: Edition Peters, 1948), 91.

75. BECKER: "Präludium und Fuge, D-Moll. Nach einer Abschrift. Weder die Fuge noch das kurze Vorspiel vermögen wir für eine Originalcomposition zu halten. . . . Das vorangestellte Präludium scheint nicht dieser Fuge anzugehören und wurde schwerlich von Bach oder einem andern Orgelspieler beigefügt, da kein Orgelkenner auf das Pedal bei einer Orgelcomposition freiwillig verzichten wird."

SCHELLENBERG: "Präludium und Fuge in D moll. Von diesem Werke spricht der Verfasser: 'Sehr merkwürdig ist, dass die Fuge von Bach selbst auch noch für die Violine bearbeitet wurde. Sie findet sich in dieser Gestalt in der ersten der bekannten sechs Sonaten für Violine allein, und ist hier in G moll transponirt, weil sie aus D moll auf der Violine nicht gespielt werden konnte.' . . . Sollte denn Bach diese Fuge wirklich für die Orgel bestimmt haben? Nein, es ist keine Spur von Sebastian'schem Orgelstyl darin zu finden; das Präludium ist vollends ohne Zweifel für das Clavier geschrieben; würde denn Bach, abgesehen davon, dass das Präludium sehr unbedeutend ist, bei einer Orgelcomposition die Anwendung des Pedals gänzlich umgangen haben, wie hier? Abermals nein!"

76. NBA IV/5–6, *Kritischer Bericht*, 268. On Mendelssohn and this edition, see Wm. A. Little, *Mendelssohn and the Organ* (New York: Oxford University Press, 2010), 122–25.

77. See the discussion in Williams, *The Organ Music of J. S. Bach*, 70–74; and Stauffer, *The Organ Preludes of Johann Sebastian Bach*, 89–90 and 121–22.

78. BECKER: "Präludium und Fuge, G-Moll. Nach der früheren Ausgabe von Peters und einigen Abschriften. So schön auch die Fuge genannt werden muß und so dankbar sie für den Spieler ist, so wenig Geschmack können wir dem Präludium mit seiner riesenhaften, hier noch, um einige Tacte abgekürzten, wohl clavier-, aber nicht orgelmäßen Rosalie abgewinnen."

SCHELLENBERG: "Präludium und Fuge in G moll (schon früher bei Peters erschienen). Das Präludium besteht zumeist aus Laufwerk, und enthält nichts Besonderes; die Fuge dagegen ist ächt Bachisch."

79. BECKER: "Fantasie und Fuge, C-Moll. Zum erstenmal und gewiß zur Freude der sämmtlichen Verehrer Bach's nach einer Abschrift, an deren Richtigkeit sich kaum zweifeln läßt, hier mitgetheilt."

SCHELLENBERG: "Fantasie und Fuge in C moll. Wird zum ersten Male mitgetheilt, und zwar nach einer Abschrift aus Krebs' Nachlasse. Der Verfasser zählt dieses Werk zu den vortrefflichsten von Bach; doch möchte dies nur von der Fuge gesagt werden."

80. NBA IV/5–6, *Kritischer Bericht*, 257–60 and 329–30. Publication date of Körner's edition according to Christine Blanken et al., *Thematisch-systematisches Verzeichnis der musikalischen Werke von Johann Sebastian Bach: Dritte, erweiterte Neuausgabe*, 417 and 745. For a recent assessment of Körner's editions of organ music, see Karen Lehmann, " 'Boten des Aufschwunges'—Gotthilf Wilhelm Körners Editionen und die Thüringer Orgellandschaft seiner Zeit," in *"Diess herrliche, imponirende Instrument": Die Orgel im Zeitalter Felix Mendelssohn Bartholdys*, ed. Anselm

Hartinger, Christoph Wolff, and Peter Wollny (Wiesbaden: Breitkopf & Härtel, 2011), 389–401.

81. See Pieter Dirksen's stimulating comments on this matter in volume 3 of *Johann Sebastian Bach: Sämtliche Orgelwerke* (Wiesbaden: Breitkopf & Härtel, 2016), 23–24 and 146. See also Stinson, *J. S. Bach at His Royal Instrument*, 5–6.

82. Kindscher described the fantasy in these terms: "Zu den vollen und dicken des 1sten Bandes gehören natürlich Seb. Bach, Phantasie und Fuge C-Moll grandios auf das große Pedal-C das thematische Gebäu mit seinen unendlich bunten Verschlingungen setzend." His review appeared in the 10 October 1849 issue of the *Neue Zeitschrift für Musik*, 158–59. See also Bach-Dokumente VI, 520.

83. BECKER: "Präludium und Fuge, C-Dur. Das Thema dieser Fuge ist so durch und durch trocken und dem Bach'schen Geist so entgegen, daß man trotz der zahlreichen Abschriften, die der Ausgabe zum Grunde gelegt wurden, zweifelhaft bleibt, ob Bach wirklich dasselbe erfunden habe. Ein zweites Thema, welches nach einem claviermäßigen Mittelsatz eintritt, ist aber noch geringfügiger, und die Durchführung beider dürfte nicht für nachahmungswürdig anerkannt werden. Das Präludium ist dieser Fuge gegenüber zu kurz und nicht ideenreich genug, um zu interessiren."

SCHELLENBERG: "Präludium und Fuge in C dur. Nach Abschriften zum ersten Male gedruckt. Das Präludium, obwohl einige Bach'sche Züge enthaltend, ist höchst unbedeutend; die Fuge behandelt zwei Themata, von denen das erste wohl aus einer besonderen Laune des Componisten hervorgegangen sein mag; das zweite, nach einem Zwichensatze, belehrt zur Genüge, dass Bach dieses Tonstück nicht für die Orgel geschriebenen haben kann. Wo die Orgelvirtuosen Gelegenheit finden sollen, in diesem Werk ihr Instrument von der glänzendsten Seite zu zeigen, da eine reiche Abwechselung der Stimmen und Claviere sowohl durch den Geist als durch die äussere Einrichtung begründet wäre, wie der Verfasser meint, vermögen wir nicht zu entdecken."

84. BECKER: "Toccate und Fuge, C-Dur. Nach zwei Abschriften. Die Toccate ist nicht ohne eigenthümliche Züge und stellt die Fuge mit ihrem waldhornmäßigen Thema, mehren harten, bei Bach ganz fremden Tonfolgen, z. B. [at this point, Becker illustrates measures 93–94 of the fugue] dürftigen Wiederholungen und unpracticablen Sätzen, z. B. S. 81, Tact 15 u. 16. u. dgl., bedeutend in Schatten. Würde Bach, wenn die Fuge wirklich von ihm componirt wurde, ohne Pedal schließen, und hat er dies irgendwo in einer Orgelfuge gethan?"

SCHELLENBERG: "Toccata und Fuge in C dur. (Nach Abschriften.) Derselbe Vorwurf trifft diese Nummer; die ganz claviermässig geschriebene Toccata und die Fuge mit ihrem Trompetenthema beweisen hinlänglich, dass man in diesen Tonstücken keine Orgelcompositionen Bach's vor sich hat."

85. Körner advertised his edition of BWV 564 in the March 1845 issue (p. 56) of the periodical *Euterpe*; Griepenkerl's preface is dated May 1845.

86. Hentschel described the piece as "eine Tonschöpfung, die allein schon ausreichend sein würde, von dem Riesengeiste Bach's Zeugniß zu geben, wenn auch sonst keine Note von diesem hohen Meister vorhanden wäre." See *Euterpe* 5, no. 8 (August 1845), 140.

87. Essentially the same material is found, but in different keys, in measures 25–26 and 49–50.

88. On Brahms and these fifths, see Stinson, *The Reception of Bach's Organ Works*, 141–44. For Keller's mention of them, see his *Die Orgelwerke Bachs*, 77. Keller also pointed out a pair of what he considered "really unbeautiful" parallel octaves between the bottom two voices in measure 114. Did Griepenkerl have these same passages in mind when, toward the end of his preface (p. iii), he admitted that Bach was occasionally guilty not only of "harsh harmonies" but also of parallel fifths and octaves?

89. BECKER: "Präludium und Fuge, A-Moll. Früher schon bei Peters erschienen und mit einer Handschrift verglichen. Ein zwar kleines Werk, aber eines Bach's nicht unwürdig. Präludium und Fuge, E-Moll. Nach einigen Abschriften. Beide Sätze von geringer Bedeutung und durchaus nicht geeignet, den Geschmack des Orgelspielers zu läutern."

SCHELLENBERG: "Präludium und Fuge in A moll. Präludium und Fuge in E moll. Beiden Sätzen, wovon der erste durch eine Peters'sche alte Ausgabe schon bekannt, können wir auch nichts weiter nachrühmen, als dass sie von Bach sein sollen, und wenn dies der Fall ist, wohl hier am unrechten Platze stehen."

90. Russell Stinson, "Clara Schumann's Bach Book: A Neglected Document of the Bach Revival," *Bach: Journal of the Riemenschneider Bach Institute* 39, no. 1 (2008): 1–66, esp. 7–8 and 38.

91. BECKER: "Haben wir somit die einzelnen Bestandtheile dieses Bandes angedeutet, so können wir nicht umhin, die H. H. Herausgeber aufzufordern, in dem hoffentlich bald erscheinenden vierten Band nur Tonstücke aus Bach's Werken zu wählen, die von diesem Heroen der Tonkunst auch recht eigentlich für die Orgel, d. h. auch für die Kirche bestimmt waren. Nicht jede Fuge mit Pedal ist für die Orgel berechnet. Manche der Bach'schen Fugen eignen sich nach unserm Dafürhalten nur für das Zimmer, und müssen, ihrer Sphäre entrissen, gänzlich ihren Zweck verfehlen. Nicht unwahrscheinlich ist es, daß einige der hier mitgetheilten Sätze in einer heiteren Stunde entworfen und ausgeführt wurden—hatte doch jedes Clavier sein ihm zugehöriges Pedal—und da sind auch Themen zu benutzen und leicht und flüchtig zu bearbeiten, die der Kirche zwar unangemessen—wie z. B. das skurrile zu der 10ten Fuge [BWV 533], das langgedehnte und an die Zöpfe des siebenjährigen Kriegs erinnernde zu der 7ten [BWV 566], das Horn- und Trompetenthema der 8ten [BWV 564]—aber für das häusliche Kreise zur Vermehrung der Heiterkeit, ganz geeignet sind. . . . Wir glauben daher, daß es sehr nothwendig sei, den Charakter eines Werkes sorgfältig zu berücksichtigen, und bei einer Auswahl von Tonstücken für die Orgel aus dem 18. Jahrhundert um so schärfer, da das Hausinstrument (das Clavier, Positiv, Portativ u. a.) mit dem in der Kirche (die eigentliche Orgel) hinsichtlich eines Pedals genau übereinstimmte. Man thut älteren Tonmeistern nicht ohne solche Berücksichtigung wahrhaft unrecht. Wer aber wollte sich an einem Bach, der so scharf die Kirche von dem Hause zu trennen wußte, versündigen und ihn der Geschmacklosigkeit zeihen?"

SCHELLENBERG: "Wir legen den Herren Herausgebern der Bach'schen Orgelcompositionen dringend an's Herz, mit der Wahl der Tonstücke höchst

Notes 159

behutsam zu Werke zu geben; Bach, der uns nur in den Nummern 1 [BWV 552], 2 [BWV 540], 3 [BWV 538], 5 (Fuge) [BWV 535], 6 (Fuge) [BWV 537], wie wir ihn sonst kennen und verehren, entgegentritt, wird Niemand Verirrungen zeihen wollen, wie sie uns in den Tonstücken unter Nr. 7 [BWV 566], 8 [BWV 564], 9 [BWV 551], 10 [BWV 533] zu Gesicht kommen; spricht doch Forkel selbst, dass dieser Meister Kirche und Haus, Clavier und Orgel wohl von einander zu trennen wusste, dass er für beide Instrumente ein Anderer war,—wie könnten daher Sätze, wie die zuletzt genannten, als von ihm für die Orgel bestimmte angenommen werden?"

92. Becker makes a serious blunder in stating that all these instruments commonly included a pedalboard. The portativ never had one, and any instrument other than the large church organ that did was quite rare.

93. Translation from *The New Bach Reader*, 437–38.

94. In this connection, see also August Gottfried Ritter's review of volume 4 of the Peters edition, published in the 7 May 1847 issue of the *Neue Zeitschrift für Musik*, 157–58. Ritter maintained that such fast figuration as that found in the opening and closing sections of the Fantasy in G Major, BWV 572, was incompatible with the organs of Bach's time.

95. The Bach biographer Philipp Spitta, writing about thirty years later, offered a rather different assessment of this theme: "The fugue subject, which is at first timid and trembling but then goes on its quiet way, is of infinite charm" ("Gleich das Thema, schwebend und schüchtern, dann still seinen Weg wandelnd, ist von unendlichem Zauber"). See Spitta, *Johann Sebastian Bach*, vol. 1 (Leipzig: Breitkopf & Härtel, 1873), 402.

CHAPTER 3

1. "Von der hohen Kunst des deutschen Bach'schen Orgelspiels hatte Baini keine Ahnung, und der römische Organist Frescobaldi, ein Zwerg im Verhältnis zu Bach's Riesengeist, war sein Ideal." Karl Gottlieb Freudenberg, *Erinnerungen aus dem Leben eines alten Organisten*, ed. F. W. Viol (Breslau: F. E. C. Leuckart, 1870), 81.

2. All the biographical information on Freudenberg presented here is drawn from this publication.

3. "Seb. Bach hielt Beethoven sehr in Ehren; nicht Bach, sondern Meer sollte er heißen, wegen seines unendlichen unausschöpfbaren Reichthums von Toncombinationen und Harmonien." See Freudenberg, *Erinnerungen*, 42.

4. "Tüchtige Meister, unserer Zeit näher stehend, schufen auch in dieser Gattung der Composition herrliche Werke, doch haben sie einen Bach übertroffen? Sicher nicht, und selbst ein Beethoven, der Schöpfer der 36 Variationen—120. Werk—würde nur ihm den Kranz reichen, ihm, den er nicht einen Bach, sondern ein 'Meer' nannte." See Carl Ferdinand Becker, "Zur Geschichte der Hausmusik in früheren Jahrhunderten," *Neue Zeitschrift für Musik* 12, no. 8 (24 January 1840): 29–30.

5. See the 9 August 1850 issue of the *Neue Zeitschrift für Musik*, 63–64. See also Bach-Dokumente VI, 188–90. The above-quoted C. F. Becker played various Bach works on the piano at this event.

160   Notes

6. See the discussion in Russell Stinson, *Bach's Legacy: The Music as Heard by Later Masters* (New York: Oxford University Press, 2020), 77 and 86–88.

7. "Als ich sagte, daß Beethoven über Bach gesagt: Bach sei kein Bach, sondern ein Meer, meinte er, Beethoven habe ihn doch nicht gehörig erkennen können, da er zu sehr mit eigner Produktion beschäftigt war, und zu seiner Zeit von Bach nur das temperirte Klavier und einige Motetten bekannt waren." See Elisabeth Schmiedel and Joachim Draheim, eds., *An den Rhein und weiter: Woldemar Bargiel zu Gast bei Robert und Clara Schumann; Ein Tagebuch von 1852* (Sinzig: Studio Verlag, 2011), 39–40.

8. Rosenmüller, *Carl Ferdinand Becker*, 38 and 199.

9. See Schmiedel and Draheim, *An den Rhein und weiter*, 13.

10. "Wie ich neulich zu einem guten Freunde von mir komme, und er mir den Betrag von dem, was für die Tochter des unsterblichen Gott's der Harmonie gesammlet worden, zeigt, so erstaune ich über die geringe Summe, die Deutschland und besonders ihr Deutschland dieser mir verehrungswürdigen Person durch ihren Vater, anerkannt hat, das bringt mich auf den Gedanken, wie wär's, wenn ich etwas zum besten dieser Person herausgäbe, auf *praenumeration*? Schreiben sie mir geschwind wie das am besten möglich sey, damit es geschehe, ehe unß *diese Bach* stirbt, oder ehe *dieser Bach* austrocknet und wir ihn nicht mehr tränken können—daß sie dieses werk verlegen müßten, versteht sich von selbst." See Bach-Dokumente VI, 135–36.

11. See Wm. A. Little, *Mendelssohn and the Organ* (New York: Oxford University Press, 2010), 25–32; and Russell Stinson, *The Reception of Bach's Organ Works from Mendelssohn to Brahms* (New York: Oxford University Press, 2006), 8–11.

12. Andreas Sieling, *August Wilhelm Bach (1796–1869): Kirchenmusik und Seminarmusiklehrerausbildung in Preußen im zweiten Drittel des 19. Jahrhunderts* (Cologne: Studio, 1995), 148–50; and NBA IV/5–6, Dietrich Kilian, ed., *Kritischer Bericht* to *Präludien, Toccaten, Fantasien und Fugen für Orgel*, 153.

13. On Mendelssohn's role in this publication, see Little, *Mendelssohn and the Organ*, 122–23.

14. "Bach lehrte das Orgelspiel; er war ein tüchtiger Fugenmacher und gewandter Organist, hatte aber nicht die idealistische Anschauung über das Choralspiel, wie Klein in Schmiedeberg. Sonst war er eine gemütliche Natur. Das Aufsteigen des kleinen Felix machte ihn stutzig und neidisch. Mendelssohn wollte eine ungedruckte Bach'sche Fuge von ihm haben, er gab sie ihm aber nicht, und zu mir, der ich sie aufgeschrieben hatte, äußerte er: 'Was braucht der Judenjunge Alles zu haben, er hat ohnedem genug, geben Sie ihm die Fuge nicht.' Ich gab aber gerade dem liebenswürdigen Felix, der mit uns so kindlich anmuthsvoll verkehrte, diese Bachreliquie, worüber er jubelte und mir die Hand schüttelte: 'Freudenberg, das Geschenk vergesse ich Ihnen in meinem Leben nicht!'" See Freudenberg, *Erinnerungen*, 25. Freudenberg's reference to this prelude-fugue pair as merely a "fugue" is typical of nineteenth-century practice.

15. "In Breslau veranstaltete der Organist Freudenberg am letzten Sonntage eine Gedächtnißfeier Mendelssohns; er spielte zwei von den Orgelsonaten des dahingeschiedenen Meisters, zwei Choräle von Bach, und die eigene Bearbeitung

Notes

161

eines alten Kirchenliedes. In der Breslauer Zeitung wird angefragt: ob nicht außerdem noch eine große, den Manen Mendelssohns würdige Feier herzustellen wäre?" See *Urania* 5 (1848): 29–30.

16. Freudenberg, *Erinnerungen*, 28.

17. A. W. Bach included the fugue in his anthology *Orgel-Stücke für das Konzert*, which appeared in 1829. Publication date according to Christine Blanken, Christoph Wolff, and Peter Wollny, *Thematisch-systematisches Verzeichnis der musikalischen Werke von Johann Sebastian Bach: Dritte, erweiterte Neuausgabe* (Wiesbaden: Breitkopf & Härtel, 2022), 420 and 746. In this collection, the fugue is preceded not by the famous Fantasy in G Minor, BWV 542/1, but by an "Introduction" composed by A. W. Bach himself. See Andreas Sieling, "'Selbst den alten Vater Sebastian suchte man nicht mehr so langstielig abzuhaspeln': Zur Rezeptionsgeschichte der Orgelwerke Bachs," in *Bach und die Nachwelt, Band 2: 1850–1900*, ed. Michael Heinemann and Hans-Joachim Hinrichsen (Laaber: Laaber-Verlag, 1999), 299–339, esp. 307–8 and 337.

18. "Die uns gestellten Aufgaben waren schwieriger und gesteigerter als sonst: zunächst eine Choralausführung für zwei Claviere und Pedal, triomäßig durchgeführt, mit Berücksichtigung des reinen Satzes; zwei Präludien auf ein Trauerlied und einen Lob- und Dank-Psalm ex capite, ein Präludium, prima vista zu spielen, und eines, das vorher eingeübt war, in welchem nicht nur Hand und Fuß, sondern auch Kopf und Herz ein Wort mitzusprechen hatten. Das letztere wählte ich mir aus Sebastian Bach's Meisterwerken; es war ein Stück höherer Ordnung, eine lange fünfstimmige Fuge, die aus einem Largo mit breiten, ernsten, erhabenen Accordfolgen, einem bewegteren Fugato mit langathmigem Thema und einem Presto-Schlusse mit allen contrapunktischen Chicanen bestand, eine mächtige Composition, die ich wegen ihres poetischen, mannigfach wechselnden Inhalts mit Herzenslust spielte und gelungen ausführte." See Freudenberg, *Erinnerungen*, 108. The "Voigt" mentioned by Freudenberg is not to be confused with Carl Voigt, who was cited in Chapter 1 of the present book for his four-hand piano transcriptions of Bach's Six Great Preludes and Fugues for organ, BWV 543–548.

19. Karl Goedeke and Edmund Goetze, *Grundrisz zur Geschichte der deutschen Dichtung*, 2nd ed., vol. 7 (Dresden: Ehlermann, 1900), 436.

20. Within the Christian church, the Rogation days are characterized by solemn prayer and fasting.

21. "Das letzte haarsträubende Rencontre mit meinem nörgelnden Kircheninspicienten muß ich noch mittheilen, obwohl es den Leser in gerechtes Erstaunen über die Verwegenheit eines Organisten und Unterkirchenbeamten versetzen wird. Mein vielgeliebter Consistorialrath besucht mich beim Nachmittagsgottesdienste auf dem Orgelchor, während ich gerade zu meiner Freude ein großartiges Präludium von Seb. Bach mit technischer Gewandtheit und begeisterter Auffassung spiele. Nach Beendigung desselben erwarte ich von Herrn Fischer ein aufmunterndes Bravissimo! für meine wirklich gelungene Ausführung des schönen Tonstücks. Statt dessen muss ich aus seinem Munde hören: 'Mein Gott, wie können Sie den Glauben in Dur schließen!'—Ich bin wie aus den Wolken gefallen, daß das Präludium für den Glauben gehalten wurde und erkläre ihm dieses Mißverständniß. 'Nein, ich

meine heute früh beim Hauptgottesdienste an Jubilatefest.'—'Ach so—nun, weil der Glaube als dorische Tonart diesen Schluß zuläßt und der Mollschluß das Jubilate in eine Rogatestimmung verwandelt haben würde.'—'Aber, mein Gott, was sollen denn diese ungewohnten Neuerungen!' Nun rissen die Saiten meiner Geduld, sie mussten endlich reißen nach so vielen unsinnigen Quärgeleien, und wären sie so dick wie Schiffstaue gewesen. Die Freudenberg'sche Natur zeigte sich in der vollen Heftigkeit einer vulkanischen Eruption; wie bei einem feuerspeienden Berge flogen die Zornesteine aus dem Munde heraus und das erhitzte Blut verwandelte sich in einen glühenden Lavastrom. 'Mein Gott, was bekümmern Sie sich denn so viel um mein Orgelspiel, von dem Sie ja gar nichts verstehen. Die Kanzel ist Ihr Reich, die Orgel das meinige. Soll das nicht sein, so werde ich Ihnen die Dispositionen zu Ihren Predigten vorschreiben und dann erst mir Ihre unverständigen Einwürfe in mein Organistenamt gefallen lassen.'—'Nein, das ist unerhört, so einen groben Organisten, wie Sie, hat St. Magdalena seit ihrem 500jährigen Bestehen nicht gehabt.'—'Und so einen Kunstignoranten, wie Sie, hat die Kirche wol auch noch nicht in ihren Mauern gesehen; der liebe Gott hat Sie im Zorn zum Kircheninspector gemacht!' Es befanden sich mehrere unberufene Zuschauer und Zuhörer auf dem Chore, die ich sofort Alle hinunterfegte. 'Da muß ich wol auch gehen?'—frug der Herr Consistorialrath.—'Natürlich!—Hier oben hat Niemand etwas zu suchen, als ich.'—Und er ging; ich blieb. Die Zornesglut erlosch allgemach, so daß ich meinen Gottesdienst in ruhiger Stimmung beenden konnte." See Freudenberg, *Erinnerungen*, 118–19. In Fischer's defense, the fact that he authored a booklet on the organ of the Magdalenenkirche suggests that he was hardly a "musical ignoramus." His *Geschichte und Beschreibung der großen Orgel in der Haupt- und Pfarr-Kirche zu St. Maria Magdalena in Breslau* appeared in 1821.

22. Freudenberg's discussion of Mosewius is found on pages 134–42 of the *Erinnerungen*.

23. See the "Nachwort" to Johann Theodor Mosewius, *Johann Sebastian Bachs "Matthäus-Passion"/Johann Sebastian Bach in seinen Kirchen-Kantaten und Choralgesängen*, ed. Michael Heinemann (Hildesheim: Georg Olms Verlag, 2001).

24. This publication was preceded in 1845 by Mosewius's fifty-seven-page study of Bach's church cantatas and chorale harmonizations, titled *Johann Sebastian Bach in seinen Kirchen-Kantaten und Choralgesängen*.

25. "Neben angestrengter Geisteshätigkeit hatte auch er im häuslichen Leben manchen Kummer, manche Sorge und Schmerz zu ertragen; ein Ausflug in Gottes schöne Natur, der Umgang mit gleichgestimmten, durch Kunst und Wissenschaft mit ihm verbrüderten Seelen richteten ihn wieder auf und gaben ihm neue Kraft, neuen Muth zum Ausbaue des hohen Kunsttempels. Selbst bei Trauerfeierlichkeiten, z. B. bei Beerdigung seines geliebten Kindes, konnte sich seine trübe Stimmung in eine feste zuversichtliche verwandeln, als ich ihm seinen Lieblingschoral aus der 'Passion': 'Was mein Gott will, g'scheh allzeit, sein Wille der ist der beste,' beim Durchtragen des die theure Hülle bergenden Sarges in der Begräbnißkirche auf der Orgel spielte, ohne daß ich eine Note weg- noch zugethan habe." See Freudenberg, *Erinnerungen*, 139–40.

26. "Ein lieblicher, anmuthiger Knabe starb ihm nach langen Leiden an einer abzehrenden Krankheit wenige Jahre nach dem Tode seiner Frau. Mit der

Notes

sorglichsten Liebe und tiefem Schmerz eilte er an das Krankenbett des Kindes, so oft sein Beruf ihm eine freie Stunde ließ, und der Verlust desselben entlockte ihm noch nach langen Jahren Thränen der Wehmuth, so oft die Erinnerung ihm denselben zurückrief." See Anna Kempe, *Erinnerungen an Ernst* [!] *Theodor Mosewius* (Breslau: Joh. Urban Kern, 1859), 30–31. On the death of Frau Mosewius, see pages 12–13 of these memoirs.

27. "Bach's Bearbeitung hat sich an den Text der ersten Strophe angeschlossen; im Ganzen spricht sie festes Vertrauen auf Gott, Entschlossenheit und Ergebung in Leid und Ungemach aus.—Schon der feste positive Schluss der ersten Zeile ergreift mächtig; dann muss auf den tiefen Ausdruck im Schlusse der fünften Zeile bei 'fromme Gott' aufmerksam gemacht werden. Die kostbaren Zeilen 'und züchtiget mit Maassen,' mit der schönen Schlussfigur im Tenor, nach dem Ausdrucke sanfter Ergebung in dem Portamento der abwärts gehenden Scala; dann wieder die Rückkehr des Positiven in 'Wer Gott vertraut, fest auf ihn baut,' mit dem kräftigen Schluss, dann endlich die herrliche ausdrucksvolle Führung der Mittelstimmen zu 'den wird er nicht lassen.'—Wieder ein grosses Meisterstück im poetisch tiefen Ausdrucke des Gedichtes." See Johann Theodor Mosewius, *Johann Sebastian Bach's "Matthäus-Passion"* (Berlin: Verlag von J. Guttentag, 1852), 36–37. With regard to the death date of Mosewius's son, his biographer Anna Kempe gives the death date of his wife as 1826, which would imply that the boy died in the late 1820s. See Kempe, *Erinnerungen*, 12–13.

28. "Es kann nicht oft genug wiederholt werden, dass, auf einem Instrumente gespielt, diese Arbeiten [that is, the four-part chorales within the St. Matthew Passion] niemals das aussagen können, was sie gesungen entfalten. Wer sie in Gesangsweise in Herz und Gemüth aufgefasst hat, dem werden sie sich dann auch am Instrumente offenbaren. Aber ohne Anschauung ihrer Gesangsweise bleibt ihr Inhalt verschlossen, wie denn überhaupt Seb. Bach, der poetisch Tonkünstler, anders aufgesucht werden muss, als der unbegreifliche Techniker, der gewandteste, grossartigste aller musikalischen Baumeister." See Mosewius, *Johann Sebastian Bach's "Matthäus-Passion,"* 37.

29. Marx had hoped for a premiere earlier that year in Leipzig, presumably at the Gewandhaus under Mendelssohn's direction, but Mendelssohn, much to Marx's dismay, had decided to have nothing to do with the work. See R. Larry Todd, *Mendelssohn: A Life in Music* (New York: Oxford University Press, 2003), 394.

30. On Freudenberg's social interactions with Mendelssohn, see pages 26–27 of the *Erinnerungen*.

31. Freudenberg, *Erinnerungen*, 166–67.

32. Adolph Bernhard Marx, *Die Lehre von der musikalischen Komposition*, vol. 1 (Leipzig: Breitkopf & Härtel, 1837), 24 (emphasis added).

33. "Im Jahre 1841 erschien Adolf Bernhard Marx, der berühmte Theoretiker in Breslau, um sich durch Aufführung seines Oratoriums 'Moses' am 2. Dec. auch als praktischer Musiker Geltung zu verschaffen. . . . Ihm zu Ehren hatte ich in der St. Magdalenenkirche ein Orgelconcert veranstaltet; bei seinem Eintritt in die Kirche empfing ich ihn mit einem imposanten Orgelpräludium zu dem Liede: 'Triumph, Triumph, Er kommt mit Pracht' aus seinem Choral- und Orgelbuche. Außer

der Bach'schen Toccata in F-dur und einigen anderen Piecen spielte ich zum Schlusse mein Präludium zu dem Luther'schen Liede: 'Eine feste Burg ist unser Gott,' dem Marx seine volle Anerkennung zu Theil werden ließ." See Freudenberg, *Erinnerungen*, 148–50. The exceedingly festive prelude composed by Marx on the Easter hymn "Triumph! Triumph! es kommt mit Pracht" is No. 195 in his *Evangelisches Choral- und Orgelbuch: 235 Choräle mit Vorspielen*, published in 1832.

34. On Hesse's activities as a concert organist, see Hans Jürgen Seyfried, *Adolph Friedrich Hesse als Orgelvirtuose und Orgelkomponist* (Regensburg: Gustav Bosse, 1965), 10–39.

35. The most detailed account of Liszt's sojourn in Breslau is Michael Saffle, *Liszt in Germany 1840–1845: A Study in Sources, Documents, and the History of Reception* (Stuyvesant, NY: Pendragon Press, 1994), 151–53. See also Peter Raabe, *Liszts Leben*, 2nd ed. (Tutzing: Hans Schneider, 1968), 282.

36. "Hesse und ich machten ihm den ersten schuldigen Besuch und wurden ebenfalls von der Leutseligkeit des jungen berühmten Virtuosen eingenommen. Hesse lud ihn zu einem Orgelconcert in der Bernhardinkirche ein. A propos, sagte Liszt zu mir, Sie als Oberorganist könnten mir doch auch Ihre Orgel vorreiten! Ich, obschon kein so kühner Reiter wie College Hesse, hoffte doch den Ritt zu bestehen und kam seinem Wunsche entgegen, wobei sich Freund Hesse's Wangen wie die eines gesottenen Krebses rötheten, da er bei dergleichen Gelegenheiten nur allein das Privilegium zu besitzen meinte, sein Licht vor fremden Künstlern leuchten zu lassen. Zu meinem Orgelvortrage in der Magdalenenkirche hatten sich ungewohnter Weise auch mehrere Damen aus höheren Ständen eingefunden, die sonst gerade nicht für sogenannte gelehrte Orgelmusik schwärmen und ihre Augen mehr auf Liszt richteten, als ihre Ohren meinem Spiel zuneigten. Ich führte mehrere Bach'sche Orgelcompositionen vor, darunter ein Orgeltrio zu dem Liede: 'Schmücke dich, o liebe Seele' mit vielen Trillern und Fiorituren, die Liszt wegen der durch das Instrument gebotenen Schwerfälligkeit belächelte und bewitzelte." See Freudenberg, *Erinnerungen*, 151–52. About midway through this passage, Freudenberg obviously alludes to Matthew 5:16 ("Let your light so shine before men, that they may see your good works, and glorify your father, which is in heaven"), as translated by Martin Luther ("So laßt euer Licht leuchten vor den Leuten, damit sie eure guten Werke sehen und euren Vater im Himmel preisen").

37. "Ich bin viel mit ihm umgegangen; er hörte hier auch meine letzte Sinfonie, auch gab ich ihm 2 Orgelkonzerte." Letter of 19 May 1843. For the complete text of this missive—and on the identification of the symphony performed—see the online edition of the Spohr letters maintained by the Spohr Museum in Kassel (www.spohr-briefe.de). I am indebted to Karl Traugott Goldbach of the Spohr Museum for his assistance with this source. See also Seyfried, *Adolph Friedrich Hesse*, 28.

38. Seyfried, *Adolph Friedrich Hesse*, 32.

39. "Nach Tisch spielte uns Hesse auf seiner Orgel, mit der uns bekannten Delikatesse Reinlichkeit und Beherrschung, mehreres von sich, Bach und eine freie Fantaisie vor. Er ist unstreitig der erste jetzt lebende Organist." Diary entry for 12 March 1836. See Gerd Nauhaus and Nancy B. Reich, eds., *Clara Schumann: Jugendtagebücher 1827–1840* (Hildesheim: Georg Olms Verlag, 2019), 218.

Notes

40. "Vor dem Theater hatten wir einen Genuß der ganz mit diesem in Contrast steht, wir hörten Hesse aus Breslau in der Garnison-Kirche die Orgel spielen—meisterhaft, wie sie Keiner spielt. Er spielte Variationen von sich die reitzend waren, dann Fugen von Bach, von sich Concertstück ect: Die Orgel übt doch einen ganz unbeschreibbaren Zauber aus, und stimmt Einen so andächtig." Diary entry for 27 November 1839. See Nauhaus and Reich, *Clara Schumann: Jugendtagebücher*, 353. See also Seyfried, *Adolph Friedrich Hesse*, 27.

41. On Liszt and Bach's organ works, see Stinson, *The Reception of Bach's Organ Works*, 102–25.

42. For particulars on Hesse's recital repertoire, see Seyfried, *Adolph Friedrich Hesse*, 12–39.

43. It was also Liszt's rendition of this fugue (along with its prelude) that "revealed" the music of Bach to Richard Wagner. See Martin Geck, "Richard Wagner und die ältere Musik," in *Die Ausbreitung des Historismus über die Musik*, ed. Walter Wiora (Regensburg: Gustav Bosse, 1969), 123–46, esp. 128; Carl Dahlhaus, "Wagner und Bach," in *Klassische und romantische Musikästhetik*, by Carl Dahlhaus (Laaber: Laaber Verlag, 1999), 440–58, esp. 440; and Christian Thorau, "Richard Wagners Bach," in *Bach und die Nachwelt, Band 2, 1850–1900*, ed. Michael Heinemann and Hans-Joachim Hinrichsen, 163–99 (Laaber: Laaber-Verlag, 1999), 163–99, esp. 171.

44. See Saffle, *Liszt in Germany*, 138, 188, 248, and 252; and Michael Heinemann, *Die Bach-Rezeption von Franz Liszt* (Cologne: Studio, 1995), 71.

45. With regard to the temperature in the church, Liszt told Freudenberg that his hands and feet were "freezing." See Freudenberg, *Erinnerungen*, 152.

46. On the authorship of BWV 759 and BWV Anh. 74, see NBA IV/10, Reinmar Emans, ed., *Kritischer Bericht* to *Orgelchoräle aus unterschiedlicher Überlieferung*, 475–79; and Peter Williams, *The Organ Music of J. S. Bach*, 2nd ed. (Cambridge: Cambridge University Press, 2003), 495.

47. The Great Eighteen chorale had been in print for several years, but only as a four-hand piano transcription by Johann Nepomuk Schelble (1789–1837). It is one of six works contained in Schelble's exceedingly obscure collection, *VI VARIERTE CHORÄLE für die Orgel von J. S. Bach für das Pianoforte zu vier Händen eingerichtet*, which appeared in 1831. Publication date according to Christine Blanken et al., *Thematisch-systematisches Verzeichnis der musikalischen Werke von Johann Sebastian Bach: Dritte, erweiterte Neuausgabe*, 448 and 748. On Felix Mendelssohn's encounter with these transcriptions, see Stinson, *Bach's Legacy*, 7–33. For the complete contents of Schicht's edition, see Bach-Dokumente VI, 528–29. See also NBA IV/2, Hans Klotz, ed., *Kritischer Bericht* to *Die Orgelchoräle aus der Leipziger Originalhandschrift*, 53.

48. It has been recorded, though, by the organist Franz Haselbock, who included the work on his disc from 1991, *Organ Works of the Bach Family* (hänssler Classic).

49. The version published in Christoph Albrecht, ed., *Gottfried August Homilius: Choralvorspiele für Orgel* (Wiesbaden: Breitkopf & Härtel, 1988), 116–18, is considerably less ornate, as it is based not on Schicht's print but on the manuscript sources for the piece (see Albrecht's note on page 165 of his edition).

50. The editor was Friedrich Wilhelm Viol, a music critic in Breslau and founder of the city's "Verein für klassische Musik."

51. "Die Bach-Musik zu dem: 'Schmücke dich, o liebe Seele,' ist ein Evangelium aus seiner musikalischen Bibel, wer das nicht glaubt, ist ein unmusikalischer Thomas, und er soll ja nicht mit seiner Musikkenntniß und mit seinem Musikgefühl für das Schöne prahlen." See Freudenberg, *Erinnerungen*, 217.

52. For particulars, see Russell Stinson, *J. S. Bach's Great Eighteen Organ Chorales* (New York: Oxford University Press, 2001), 116–17.

53. On Mendelssohn, Schumann, and this piece, see Russell Stinson, *J. S. Bach at His Royal Instrument: Essays on His Organ Works* (New York: Oxford University Press, 2012), 43–45.

54. Mendelssohn described Bach in this manner in a letter of 18 January 1838 to the administrative committee of the Lower Rhenish Music Festival, in hopes of being allowed to conduct a work by Bach at the festival that spring (no Bach work had ever been performed at the festival in its nineteen-year history). He succeeded, conducting on 4 June what he billed as an Ascension Day cantata by Bach, but what was in fact a hodgepodge of movements from three different Bach cantatas. For particulars, see Todd, *Mendelssohn: A Life in* Music, 365–66. The pertinent passage of the letter reads as follows: "Hierzu halte ich es nun wirklich für nothwendig, den Namen Sebastian Bach auf dem Programm zu haben, wenn auch nur mit einem kurzen Stück; aber es ist gewiß Zeit, daß bei diesen Festen, denen [G. F.] Händel so viel Glanz verliehen hat, auch der andere *unsterbliche Meister, der in keinem Stück unter einem andern Meister, in vielen über allen steht*, nicht länger vergessen werde." See Uta Wald, *Felix Mendelssohn Bartholdy: Sämtliche Briefe*, vol. 5 (Kassel: Bärenreiter, 2012), 464.

CHAPTER 4

1. See the website www.imdb.com, last accessed on 9 September 2022.

2. On the identification of Rota as the other composer represented in this scene, see Franco Sciannameo, *Nino Rota's "The Godfather Trilogy": A Film Score Guide* (Lanham, MD: Scarecrow Press, 2010), 97–100 and 116. As Sciannameo makes clear, Rota based his organ music in this scene on the two Bach organ works used in it. Rota paid additional homage to Bach in 1972 (the year of *The Godfather's* release) with the publication (Edition Carisch) of his piano work *Variazione e fuga nei dodici toni sul nome di Bach*.

3. Royal S. Brown, *Overtones and Undertones: Reading Film Music* (Berkeley and Los Angeles: University of California Press, 1994), 80.

4. Brown, *Undertones and Overtones*, 80–81.

5. Nonetheless, Roland Petit chose Ottorino Respighi's orchestration of this piece for his dark, existentialist ballet from 1946, *Le jeune homme et la mort*. No doubt the most famous performance of this ballet, albeit a drastically abbreviated one, is that by Mikhail Baryshnikov in the opening scene of Taylor Hackford's 1985 film *White Nights*.

Notes

6. On this point, see also Sciannameo, *Nino Rota's "The Godfather Trilogy,"* 116. For a detailed discussion of how the D-major prelude is integrated into this scene, see Russell Stinson, *J. S. Bach at His Royal Instrument: Essays on His Organ Works* (New York: Oxford University Press, 2012), 113–14.

7. For an enlightening discussion of this film's score, see Neil Lerner, "The Strange Case of Rouben Mamoulian's Sound Stew: The Uncanny Soundtrack in *Dr. Jekyll and Mr. Hyde*," in *Music in the Horror Film: Listening to Fear*, ed. Neil Lerner (New York: Routledge, 2010), 55–79. See also Stinson, *J. S. Bach at His Royal Instrument*, 138–39.

8. Thomas Harris, *The Silence of the Lambs* (New York: St. Martin's Press, 1988), 185.

9. Thomas Fahy, "Killer Culture: Classical Music and the Art of Killing in *Silence of the Lambs* and *Se7en*," *Journal of Popular Culture* 37, no. 1 (2003): 28–42, esp. 32. See also Kristi Brown-Montesano, "Terminal Bach: Technology, Media, and the *Goldberg Variations* in Postwar American Culture," *Bach: Journal of the Riemenschneider Bach Institute* 50, no. 1 (2019): 81–117.

10. Andrew Ford, *The Sound of Pictures: Listening to the Movies, from Hitchcock to High Fidelity* (Collingwood: Black Inc.: 2010), 87.

11. Fahy, "Killer Culture," 28–31.

12. *Silence of the Lambs*, 215–16.

13. Carlo Cenciarelli, "Dr Lecter's Taste for 'Goldberg,' or: The Horror of Bach in the Hannibal Franchise," *Journal of the Royal Musical Association* 137 (2012): 107–34, esp. 119–20.

14. Christoph Wolff, "Bach's *Handexemplar* of the Goldberg Variations: A New Source," *Journal of the American Musicological Society* 29 (1976): 224–41, esp. 227–28.

15. "Dr Lecter's Taste for 'Goldberg,'" 120–21.

16. According to Nicholas Kenyon, *The Faber Pocket Guide to Bach* (London: Faber and Faber, 2011), 31, the movement played is either the Bourrée I or Bourrée II from this suite.

17. Ford, *The Sound of Pictures*, 87.

18. First in 1718 and then in 1720, Bach accompanied his patron Prince Leopold of Cöthen to the Bohemian spa city of Karlsbad, today, the city of Karlovy Vary in the Czech Republic. See the discussion in Robert L. Marshall and Traute M. Marshall, *Exploring the World of J. S. Bach: A Traveler's Guide* (Urbana: University of Illinois Press, 2016), 156–58.

19. Naomi Mandel, *Against the Unspeakable: Complicity, the Holocaust, and Slavery in America* (Charlottesville: University of Virginia Press, 2006), 72. On page 71 of her study, Mandel misidentifies the pianist in this scene as the "young man" hiding in the piano.

20. Michael H. Kater, *The Twisted Muse: Musicians and Their Music in the Third Reich* (New York: Oxford University Press, 1997), 173.

21. Kater, *The Twisted Muse*, 171–76; and Michael Gerhard Kaufmann, *Orgel und Nationalsozialismus: Die ideologische Vereinnahmung des Instruments im "Dritten Reich"* (Kleinblittersdorf: Musikwissenschaftliche Verlags-Gesellschaft, 1997), 131.

22. "Die meisten Orgelwerke Bachs sind für die Feiergestaltung ohne weiteres verwendbar, man denke etwa an den Mittelteil der G-Dur-Fantasie, die Einleitung

168   Notes

des Es-Dur-Präludiums, das C-Moll-, das D-Dur-Präludium und vieles andere aus den grossen Präludien, Fugen, Toccaten und Fantasien des Meisters. . . . Alle diesen . . . Stücke haben ihren Platz als Einleitung der Feier, als Zwischenspiele etwa zwischen zwei Sprechern oder Sprecher und Chor usw. und am Schluss." See Kaufmann, *Orgel und Nationalsozialismus*, 190.

23. According to Alfred Reichling, "Orgelklänge unter dem Hakenkreuz: Feiern-Feirräume-Feierorgeln," *Acta Organologica* 28 (2004): 411–44, esp. 434 n. 49, the E-flat prelude and fugue was commonly used to open Nazi festivals where an organ was present.

24. Constructed in 1933–1936 and substantially damaged by Allied bombing in 1945, this structure housed in its "Consecration Hall" a massive three-manual Steinmeyer organ. The building was privately criticized by Nazi propaganda minister Joseph Goebbels as a "collection of kitsch." See Reichling, "Orgelklänge unter dem Hakenkreuz," 434–35.

25. "Den Schluss bildete Bachs Fantasie in G-Dur, die Karl August von Kotzebue auf der Orgel vollendet spielte. In dem gewaltigen zweiten Teil erklang die Orgel unter seinen Händen wie ein ferngrollendes Gewitter." See Reichling, "Orgelklänge unter dem Hakenkreuz," 436.

26. Donal Henahan, "Film Music Has Two Masters," *New York Times*, July 19, 1987, cited in James Wierzbicki, *Film Music: A History* (New York: Routledge, 2009), 223–24. The title of Henahan's column, with its allusion to the New Testament, implies an uneasy power struggle of sorts between filmmaker and composer.

27. To clarify, it is not Casals who is heard in this film but the Danish cellist Erling Bengtsson.

CHAPTER 5

1. See volume 2 of *Johann Sebastian Bach: Sämtliche Orgelwerke* (Wiesbaden: Breitkopf & Härtel, 2014), 14 and 132–36.

2. *Bach 333* is a co-production of Deutsche Grammophon and Decca Classics, in collaboration with the Bach-Archiv (Leipzig). The contents also include a DVD of John Eliot Gardiner's wonderful documentary *Bach: A Passionate Life*; a book containing essays on Bach's life written by staff members of the Bach-Archiv; another book containing elegant program notes by Nicholas Kenyon; and a booklet listing not only all the compositions according to the numbering and titling of the new third edition of the BWV but also all the individual performers and ensembles represented, which number between six and seven hundred. The $500 price tag may be off-putting at first, but the price per disc is only $2.25.

3. CD 218 (*Inspired by Bach: Gounod to Pärt*) includes Max Reger's Prelude and Fugue in G Major for Solo Violin, Op. 117, No. 5. The program notes and the track listing correctly identify Reger's prelude as a transcription of the opening section of the Fantasy in G Major, BWV 572, but nowhere is it mentioned that the subject of the fugue is taken from another Bach organ work in G major, the Fugue in G Major, BWV 541/2. On the source of the fugue subject, see Russell Stinson, *J. S. Bach at His*

Notes 169

Royal Instrument: Essays on His Organ Works (New York: Oxford University Press, 2012), 142.

4. This adaptation by Siloti is represented by two different recordings in *Bach 333*; see CD 160 (*Piano Legends 1959–1993*, Emil Gilels) and CD 220 (*Bach & The Virtuoso Piano: The 20th Century,* Vikingur Ólafsson). See also Charles F. Barber, *Lost in the Stars: The Forgotten Musical Life of Alexander Siloti* (Lanham, MD: Scarecrow Press, 2002), 256–59.

5. For a recent edition, see Charles F. Barber, ed., *The Alexander Siloti Collection: Editions, Transcriptions and Arrangements for Piano Solo* (New York: Carl Fischer, 2003).

6. The new Breitkopf & Härtel edition of BWV 535 (ed. David Schulenberg) is the first to propose, on the basis of two early manuscript copies, exactly where the hands trade off.

7. Sean Carroll, *The Big Picture: On the Origins of Life, Meaning, and the Universe Itself* (New York: Dutton, 2016), 429.

8. A more legitimate organist known for his interpretation of the F-major toccata is Cameron Carpenter. Carpenter—who is surely the greatest "pedalist" in the world today—performs the toccata in the outrageously difficult key of F-sharp major. His rationale for doing so is explained in the liner notes to his recording *Cameron Live!* (Telarc, 2010).

9. "Unter den Toccaten zeichnet sich hauptsächlich die in *F* aus. Sie ist ein prachtvolles Werk und gehört der glänzendsten Periode von Bach's Künstlerleistungen an." See Carl Ludwig Hilgenfeldt, *Johann Sebastian Bach's Leben, Wirken und Werke: Ein Beitrag zur Kunstgeschichte des achtzehnten Jahrhunderts* (Leipzig: Friedrich Hofmeister, 1850), 130.

10. Peter Williams, *The Organ Music of J. S. Bach*, 2nd ed. (Cambridge: Cambridge University Press, 2003), 76.

11. Arthur Schanz, *Johann Sebastian Bach in der Klaviertranskription* (Eisenach: Karl Dieter Wagner, 2000), 491. Despite its many mistakes, Schanz's tome remains a valuable resource. Another handy guide is Klaus Schneider, *Lexikon "Musik über Musik:" Variationen—Transkriptionen—Hommagen—Stilimitationen—B-A-C-H* (Kassel: Bärenreiter, 2004). This 421-page catalogue, devoted exclusively to instrumental works, lists over 8,000 examples of musical borrowings throughout history by almost 3,000 individuals. Included are 270 works that incorporate the famous B-A-C-H motive and roughly 200 transcriptions, for various instruments, of organ works by Bach.

12. H. Heathcoate Statham, *The Organ and Its Position in Musical Art* (London: Chapman and Hall, 1909), 75 and 92–96.

13. Albert Schweitzer, *J. S. Bach*, vol. 1 (Leipzig: Breitkopf & Härtel, 1911), 319–20.

14. See the discussion in Stinson, *J. S. Bach at His Royal Instrument*, 100–101.

15. It was presumably one of these performances that prompted the following diatribe from the pen of Heathcoate Statham: "The Toccata in F, an orchestral arrangement of which was played in London not long since, was a most mistaken choice, since in character and *genre* it is, from the very first bar, emphatically *keyboard* music; and moreover the long 'drone bass' on the pedal, at the commencement, is an effect which only the organ can give." See H. Heathcoate Statham, "The Aesthetic

Treatment of Bach's Organ Music," *Proceedings of the Royal Musical Association* 27 (1900–1901): 131–61, esp. 133.

16. Hannah French, *Sir Henry Wood: Champion of J. S. Bach* (Woodbridge: Boydell Press, 2019), 25, 156–58, and 280–81.

17. Williams, *The Organ Music of J. S. Bach*, 76.

18. Hermann Keller, *Die Orgelwerke Bachs: Ein Beitrag zu ihrer Geschichte, Form, Deutung und Wiedergabe* (Leipzig: Edition Peters, 1948), 93.

19. In what is clearly a case of compositional borrowing, Mendelssohn begins the coda of his Fugue in F Minor for organ (see mm. 59–60 of the revised version) with exactly the same harmonies as in measures 424-25 of Bach's toccata. See the discussion in Russell Stinson, *The Reception of Bach's Organ Works from Mendelssohn to Brahms* (New York: Oxford University Press, 2006), 21–23 and 65–66.

20. Keller, *Die Orgelwerke Bachs*, 94.

21. Nicholas Thistlethwaite, *The Making of the Victorian Organ* (Cambridge: Cambridge University Press, 1990), 172–73. The other three orchestrations are by Bernhard Scholz (prelude only, 1874), Arnold Schoenberg (1929), and Frederick Stock (unpublished, but first recorded in 1941). Schoenberg's orchestration is included on CD 217 (*Bach Orchestrated—Reger to Stokowski*) of *Bach 333*.

22. For a modern edition containing both Wesley's "Introduction" and Novello's arrangement of the fugue, see Michael Gassmann, ed., *Orgelmusik aus England und Amerika, Band 15: Samuel Wesley (1766–1837), Vierhändige Orgelwerke* (Sankt Augustin: J. Butz, 2005). See also Philip Olleson, *The Letters of Samuel Wesley: Professional and Social Correspondence, 1797–1837* (Oxford: Oxford University Press, 2001), 225–27.

23. See the discussion in Albrecht Riethmüller, "Zur Geschichte eines Musikwerks: Die Interpretation von Präludium und Fuge ('St. Anne') für Orgel Es-Dur (BWV 552) zwischen Bach und Schönberg," in *Berliner Orgel-Colloquium*, ed. Hans Heinrich Eggebrecht (Kleinblittersdorf: Musikwissenschaftliche Verlags-Gesellschaft, 1990), 31–44, esp. 39–40.

24. For a recent re-creation of Mendelssohn's recital in which music by the avant-garde composer Hans-Joachim Hespos is substituted in place of the *Freie Phantasie*, see the recording by Oliver Kluge, *Luftschattengelichte: Bach und Hespos* (Rondeau Production, 2013).

25. See page 182 of the "Aufführungsverzeichnisse" (CD-ROM) in Anselm Hartinger, *"Alte Neuigkeiten": Bach-Aufführungen und Leipziger Musikleben im Zeitalter Mendelssohns, Schumanns und Hauptmanns 1829 bis 1852* (Wiesbaden: Breitkopf & Härtel, 2014).

26. The final ritornello statement is shorter by one bar, for reasons involving the modulation from C minor back to the tonic key in measures 174–77.

27. Anton Felix Schindler, *Beethoven as I Knew Him*, ed. Donald W. MacArdle (Chapel Hill: University of North Carolina Press, 1966), 380.

28. With regard to the original publication dates of Bach's oeuvre, by far the most authoritative (and convenient) source is now the third edition of the BWV. See Christine Blanken, Christoph Wolff, and Peter Wollny, *Thematisch-systematisches*

Verzeichnis der musikalischen Werke von Johann Sebastian Bach: Dritte, erweiterte Neuausgabe (Wiesbaden: Breitkopf & Härtel, 2022).

29. As Beethoven told Freudenberg, "auch ich . . . spielte in meiner Jugend viel die Orgel, aber meine Nerven vertrugen die Gewalt dieses Rieseninstrumentes nicht." See Karl Gottlieb Freudenberg, *Erinnerungen aus dem Leben eines alten Organisten*, ed. Friedrich Wilhelm Viol (Breslau: F. E. C. Leuckart, 1870), 42.

30. See volume 4 of *Johann Sebastian Bach: Sämtliche Orgelwerke*, ed. Jean-Claude Zehnder (Wiesbaden: Breitkopf & Härtel, 2012), 23.

31. Harvey Grace, *The Organ Works of Bach* (London: Novello, 1922), 27–28.

32. See David Owen Norris, ed., *A Bach Book for Harriet Cohen: Transcriptions for Pianoforte from the Works of J. S. Bach; With an Introduction by David Owen Norris* (Oxford: Oxford University Press, 2013). Three of the transcriptions from Gray's recording, including Bax's arrangement of BWV 572, may be found on CD 220 (*Bach & The Virtuoso Piano—The 20th Century*) of *Bach 333*.

33. Statham, "The Aesthetic Treatment of Bach's Organ Music," *Proceedings of the Royal Musical Association* 27 (1900–1901): 145.

34. John R. Near, *Widor on Organ Performance Practice and Technique* (Rochester, NY: University of Rochester Press, 2019), 28–29.

35. For a detailed discussion, see Russell Stinson, "Clara Schumann's Bach Book: A Neglected Document of the Bach Revival," *Bach: Journal of the Riemenschneider Bach Institute* 39, no. 1 (2008): 1–67, esp. 20–27.

36. See Valerie Woodring Goertzen, "Brahms's Performances of Bach's Organ Works," *American Brahms Society Newsletter* 37, no. 2 (Fall 2019): 1–5. See also the preface to Goertzen's edition for the new Brahms Gesamtausgabe, *Johannes Brahms: Arrangements von Werken anderer Komponisten für Klavier zu zwei Händen oder für die linke Hand allein* (Munich: G. Henle Verlag, 2017). My thanks to Prof. Goertzen for sharing her research with me.

37. Goertzen, "Brahms's Performances of Bach's Organ Works," 5. Zellner was reporting on a piano recital given by Brahms in Vienna on 17 March 1867.

38. Robert Hill, "Die Herkunft von Bach's 'Thema Legrenzianum,'" *Bach-Jahrbuch* 72 (1986): 105–7.

39. See, for example, page 327 of Alfred Dürr and Yoshitake Kobayashi, eds., *Bach-Werke-Verzeichnis: Kleine Ausgabe* (Wiesbaden: Breitkopf & Härtel, 1998).

40. Rodolfo Zitellini, "Das 'Thema Legrenzianum' der Fuge BWV 574—eine Fehlzuschreibung?" *Bach-Jahrbuch* 99 (2013): 243–59.

41. Most recently, the *Orgelbüchlein* setting of "Ich ruf zu dir, Herr Jesu Christ" (BWV 639), as transcribed for piano by Ferruccio Busoni, was featured in *All Quiet on the Western* Front, a film released in October 2022. For a comprehensive discussion of the reception history of the *Orgelbüchlein*, see Russell Stinson, *Bach: The Orgelbüchlein* (New York: Oxford University Press, 1999), 145–68.

42. "Die Orgeltonwerke dieses Heros weichen ihrem Inhalte und ihrer Gestaltung nach so sehr von den Tonsätzen seiner Vorgänger und Zeitgenossen ab . . . Ein blick auf die Choralvorspiele: Aus tiefer Noth, Wenn wir in höchsten Nöten sein, auf die großen Bearbeitungen des Kyrie, auf die *Ricercarta a 6* im musikalischen Opfer und die canonischen Veränderungen über das Weihnachtslied: 'Vom Himmel hoch

da komm' ich her' gewiß das Höchste, was der menschliche Geist in tiefsinnigen Combinationen zu leisten vermag—lehrt uns neben der Allgewalt der Technik des Meisters nicht minder die Tiefe des Ausdrucks bewundern, der uns mitten durch die labyrinthischen Tongeflechte entgegentönt, wie uns gleicherweise Bach in jenen Choralvorspielen, die weniger, oder gar keine höheren contrapunktischen Combinationen enthalten, wie z. B. Schmücke dich, o liebe Seele, Das alte Jahr vergangen ist, Ich ruf' zu dir, Herr Jesu Christ, O Mensch, bewein' dein Sünde groß, aus dem vorwiegend melodischen Elemente heraus in einer religiösen Hoheit und Würde erscheint, daß Kenner wie Laien gleich mächtig davon berührt werden ... so bleibt uns doch kein Zweifel, daß der Genius Bach's, sie alle überstrahlt. Dieser war es, welcher den Orgeltonsatz nach allen Richtungen durchdrang, sich überall neu offenbarte und auf diesem Felde, wo er in den Präludien und Fugen in C-Moll, F-Moll, G-Moll, A-Moll, E-Moll, H-Moll etc. seine höchste Kraft und Weihe niederlegte, unerreicht blieb." Schellenberg's essay appeared in the 26 July 1850 issue of the *Neue Zeitschrift für Musik*. See also Bach-Dokumente VI, 160–63.

It should be pointed out that the first and last works in the second group of chorale preludes cited by Schellenberg (BWV 654 and 622, respectively) likewise exemplify the ornamental chorale. The setting of "Schmücke dich" (from the Great Eighteen Chorales), as discussed at the end of Chapter 3 of the present book, was absolutely revered by both Mendelssohn and Schumann. The setting of "O Mensch bewein," a third ornamental chorale from the *Orgelbüchlein*, was one of six Bach organ works published by Schumann, in his capacity as editor, in the *Neue Zeitschrift für Musik*. Schellenberg would have known the ricercar from the Musical Offering primarily as an organ duet, in the arrangement by his teacher Carl Ferdinand Becker. As mentioned in Chapter 1 of the present book, Schellenberg and Becker played that arrangement in concert.

43. See pages 179 and 186–87 of the "Aufführungsverzeichnisse" in Hartinger, *"Alte Neuigkeiten."*

44. See Schellenberg's review of volumes 1 and 2 of the Peters edition of Bach's complete organ works, published in the 8 October 1845 issue of the *Allgemeine Musikalische Zeitung*, cols. 721–26, esp. 725. In that critique, he also hailed the Fugue in A Minor, BWV 543/2, as a "magnificent" work.

45. See column 725 of Schellenberg's review of the first two volumes of the Peters edition. There, Schellenberg ranked the F-minor above the Prelude and Fugue in A Major, BWV 536, and the Prelude and Fugue in C Minor, BWV 546.

46. See Schanz, *Johann Sebastian Bach in der Klaviertranskription*, 525–29. Ferruccio Busoni's gorgeous transcription of "Ich ruf zu dir" is included on CD 219 (*Bach & The Virtuoso Piano—Liszt and Busoni*) of Bach 333.

47. Grace, *The Organ Works of Bach*, vii. Newman's mention of *Tristan und Isolde* as a kind of landmark in music history comes as no surprise, considering that he had already authored two books on Richard Wagner.

48. Albert Schweitzer, *Out of My Life and Thought: An Autobiography* (London: Allen & Unwin, 1933), 30–31. By "descriptive," Schweitzer obviously means Bach's use of musical symbolism in setting *sacred* texts, whether actual or, as in the case of organ

Notes   173

chorales, implied. Schweitzer's autobiography was first published, in German, in 1931.

49. Interestingly enough, Bach's other organ setting of this chorale, from the Neumeister Collection (BWV 1117), was chosen by Ingmar Bergman—a filmmaker known for his love of Bach—as the music for the closing credits of his last film, *Saraband*, released in 2003. The work is played there (full organ!) by fellow Swede Hans Fagius, and it serves to underscore the dark subject matter of the plot.

50. Released on the Hyperion label in 2001, the disc *Bach Arrangements* also contains Hewitt's own transcription of the *Orgelbüchlein* setting of "Das alte Jahr."

51. Hugh Morris, "Finishing Bach's Organ Music, with Help from 118 Composers," *New York Times*, 25 October 2022.

52. Christoph Wolff, *Bach's Musical Universe: The Composer and His Work* (New York: W. W. Norton, 2020), 256–57. On page 359 of this study, note 10, Wolff identifies the "friend" as someone who copied for J. S. Bach from 1742 to 1750 and later for C. P. E. Bach in Berlin. On the religious implications of Bach's choice of this chorale at this point in his life, see Reiner Marquard, "'Vor deinen Thron tret ich hiermit' (BWV 668): Erwägungen zum Verständnis der Frömmigkeit bei Johann Sebastian Bach," *Bach-Jahrbuch* 107 (2021): 185–221.

53. Griffith made these comments in his program notes to a concert of works by Gubaidulina and Bach at Columbia University in 2015.

54. See, for example, the choral arrangement by The Theatre of Early Music on the disc *The Voice of Bach* (RCA Red Seal, 2008). As recently as 2021, the work was performed by the Danish National Girls Choir, accompanied by the Danish String Quartet. In that arrangement, the choir sings the soprano line, and the quartet plays the lower parts.

55. Arnold Schoenberg would have faced this challenge had he carried through with his idea for an arrangement for "four solo singers" of Bach's organ chorale "Herr Gott, dich loben wir," BWV 725. See page xxvi of the preface to Rudolf Stephan and Tadeusz Okuljar, eds., Arnold Schönberg: Bearbeitungen I/II, Arnold Schönberg Gesamtausgabe, Abteilung VII, Reihe B, Band 25/26 (Mainz: B. Schott's Söhne, 1988).

56. See Felix Oberborbeck, ed., *Johann Sebastian Bach: Choral "Vor deinen Thron tret ich hiermit"* (Wolfenbüttel: Möseler Verlag, 1950). Fifty years later, in the Bach year of 2000, the same press issued Heribert Breuer's choral arrangement of the work.

57. On a somewhat lighter note, the musicologist Eric Blom (1888–1959) is said to have requested "Vor deinen Thron" for his funeral, referring to the work as the "Bach cho-rale." Unfortunately, though, Blom was misunderstood, and the laughably incongruous "Bar-ca-rolle" from Offenbach's *The Tales of Hoffmann* was played instead! For this information, I am indebted to my friend and colleague Michael Oriatti.

58. Keller's original designation reads "Arnstädter Gemeindechoräle." See, respectively, Hermann Keller, *Die Orgelwerke Bachs*, 141–43; and Hermann Keller, *The Organ Works of Bach: A Contribution to Their History, Form, Interpretation and Performance*, trans. Helen Hewitt (New York: C. F. Peters, 1967), 185–89.

59. Schanz, *Johann Sebastian Bach in der Klaviertranskription*, 536.

174 Notes

60. Hewitt's recording is included on her *Bach Arrangements* disc; Fergus-Thompson's recording has been reissued on CD 220 (*Bach & The Virtuoso Piano—The 20th Century*) of *Bach 333*.

61. See the preface by David Owen Norris to Michael Aston. ed., *Bach Transcriptions for Piano: Twentieth-Century Arrangements from Choral and Instrumental Works* (Oxford: Oxford University Press, 2013). Salmon's transcription is found on pages 19–21 of this publication. According to Norris's preface to the OUP reprint of *A Bach Book for Harriet Cohen* (p. 6), one "Dorothy Sellen" also published a piano transcription of BWV 729 in 1932. But surely Norris means Dorothea Salmon.

62. Accordingly, the piece takes pride of place as the opening work in Robert Gower, ed., *The Oxford Book of Christmas Organ Music* (Oxford: Oxford University Press, 1995).

63. Still, the Duets captured the attention of two of the most important composers of the twentieth century: Béla Bartók taught and performed the works as a piano pedagogue and concert pianist, and Paul Hindemith cribbed the main theme of the second Duet for his opera *Cardillac*. See, respectively, László Somfai, "Bartók's Transcription of J. S. Bach," in *Studien zur Musikgeschichte: Eine Festschrift für Ludwig Finscher*, ed. Annegrit Laubenthal (Kassel: Bärenreiter: 1995), 689–96, esp. 692–93; and Günther Metz, "Hindemith und die alte Musik," in *Alte Musik im 20. Jahrhundert: Wandlungen und Formen ihrer Rezeption*, ed. Giselher Schubert (Mainz: Schott, 1996), 93–112, esp. 107–8. Incidentally, the "transcription" referred to in the title of Somfai's essay has nothing to do with the Duets but is Bartók's piano arrangement of Bach's sixth trio sonata for organ (BWV 530).

64. See Joachim Stutschwesky, ed., *J. S. Bach: Four Duets for Violin and Cello* (New York: International Music Company, 1947).

65. See Christine Blanken, *Die Bach-Quellen in Wien und Alt-Österreich* (Hildesheim: Georg Olms Verlag, 2011), 158, 302–3, 675, 994, and 1082; and NBA V/ 9.2, Uwe Wolf, ed., *Kritischer Bericht* to *Sechs kleine Praeludien, einzeln überlieferte Klavierwerke I* (Kassel: Bärenreiter, 2000), 326.

66. See page 162 of the "Aufführungsverzeichnisse" in Hartinger, "*Alte Neuigkeiten*."

EPILOGUE

1. The main source for my discussion here is, in addition to my own previous writings on Bach reception, the "Aufführungsverzeichnisse" (CD-ROM) in Anselm Hartinger, "*Alte Neuigkeiten*": *Bach-Aufführungen und Leipziger Musikleben im Zeitalter Mendelssohns, Schumanns und Hauptmanns 1829 bis 1852* (Wiesbaden: Breitkopf & Härtel, 2014).

2. See Felix Mendelssohn Bartholdy/Rudolf Lutz, *Sonate in d über "O Haupt voll Blut und Wunden" für Orgel* (Stuttgart: Carus-Verlag, 2013). A recording by Lutz of his reconstruction may be found on the CD *Leipziger Orgeln um Felix Mendelssohn Bartholdy* (Genuin, 2009).

3. See Bach-Dokumente VI, 668.

4. On Schaab and Mendelssohn's recital, see Anselm Hartinger, "Das Orgelkonzert nach 1800—Erscheinungsbild, Protagonisten und Transformation einer

Notes

Aufführungsgattung," in *"Diess herrliche, imponirende Instrument"*: *Die Orgel im Zeitalter Felix Mendelssohn Bartholdys*, ed. Anselm Hartinger, Christoph Wolff, and Peter Wollny (Wiesbaden: Breitkopf & Härtel, 2011), 257–84, esp. 274–76 and 284.

5. See Klaus Schubert, "Johann Sebastian Bachs Präludium und Fuge c-Moll für Orgel BWV 546 und die beiden Orgeltriosätze c-Moll nach Johann Friedrich Fasch BWV 585: Ein bislang unbekannte Werkbeziehung," in *Perspectives on Organ Playing and Musical Interpretation: Pedagogical, Historical, and Instrumental Studies (A Festschrift for Heinrich Fleischer at 90)*, ed. Ames Anderson, Bruce Backer, David Backus, and Charles Luedtke (New Ulm, MN: Martin Luther College, 2002), 108–37.

6. See Malcom Boyd, ed., *J. S. Bach*, Oxford Composer Companions (Oxford: Oxford University Press, 1999), 50–55.

REFERENCES

Abert, Hermann. *Johann Joseph Abert (1832–1915): Sein Leben und seine Werke.* Leipzig: Breitkopf & Härtel, 1916.

Albrecht, Christoph, ed. *Gottfried August Homilius: Choralvorspiele für Orgel.* Wiesbaden: Breitkopf & Härtel, 1988.

Altner, Stefan. *Das Thomaskantorat im 19. Jahrhundert.* Leipzig: Passage-Verlag, 2006.

Aston, Michael, ed. *Bach Transcriptions for Piano: Twentieth-Century Arrangements from Choral and Instrumental Works.* Oxford: Oxford University Press, 2013.

Barber, Charles F. *Lost in the Stars: The Forgotten Musical Life of Alexander Siloti.* Lanham, MD: Scarecrow Press, 2002.

Barber, Charles. F., ed. *The Alexander Siloti Collection: Editions, Transcriptions and Arrangements for Piano Solo.* New York: Carl Fischer, 2003.

Bartholdy, Felix Mendelssohn, and Rudolf Lutz. *Sonate in d über "O Haupt voll Blut und Wunden" für Orgel.* Stuttgart: Carus-Verlag, 2013.

Becker, Carl Ferdinand. "Zur Geschichte der Hausmusik in früheren Jahrhunderten." *Neue Zeitschrift für Musik* 12, nos. 7 and 8 (21 and 24 January 1840): 25–26 and 29–30, respectively.

Blanken, Christine. *Die Bach-Quellen in Wien und Alt-Österreich.* Hildesheim: Georg Olms Verlag, 2011.

Blanken, Christine, Christoph Wolff, and Peter Wollny. *Thematisch-systematisches Verzeichnis der musikalischen Werke von Johann Sebastian Bach· Dritte, erweiterte Neuausgabe.* Wiesbaden: Breitkopf & Härtel, 2022.

Blaut, Stephan, and Michael Pacholke, eds. *Johann Sebastian Bach: Choralfantasie für Orgel über "Wo Gott der Herr nicht bei uns hält," BWV 1128.* Beeskow: Ortus Musikverlag, 2008.

Boyd, Malcolm, ed. *J. S. Bach.* Oxford Composer Companions. Oxford: Oxford University Press, 1999.

Brodbeck, David. *Brahms: Symphony No. 1.* Cambridge Music Handbooks. Cambridge: Cambridge University Press, 1997.

Brown, Royal S. *Overtones and Undertones: Reading Film Music.* Berkeley and Los Angeles: University of California Press, 1994.

Brown-Montesano, Kristi. "Terminal Bach: Technology, Media, and the *Goldberg Variations* in Postwar American Culture." *Bach: Journal of the Riemenschneider Bach Institute* 50, no. 1 (2019): 81–117.

Busch, Hermann J. "Organisten an St. Nikolai." In *Die Nikolaikirche zu Leipzig und ihre Orgel*, edited by Hermann J. Busch, 29–35. Leipzig: Evangelische Verlagsanstalt, 2004.

Carroll, Sean. *The Big Picture: On the Origins of Life, Meaning, and the Universe Itself.* New York: Dutton, 2016.

Cenciarelli, Carlo. "Dr Lecter's Taste for 'Goldberg,' or: The Horror of Bach in the Hannibal Franchise." *Journal of the Royal Musical Association* 137 (2012): 107–34.

Coleridge, A. D. *Goethe's Letters to Zelter.* London: George Bell and Sons, 1887.

Dahlhaus, Carl. "Wagner und Bach." In *Klassische und romantische Musikästhetik*, by Carl Dahlhaus, 440–58. Laaber: Laaber Verlag, 1999.

David, Hans T., and Arthur Mendel, eds. *The New Bach Reader: A Life of Johann Sebastian Bach in Letters and Documents.* Revised and enlarged by Christoph Wolff. New York: W. W. Norton, 1998.

Dirksen, Pieter, ed. *Johann Sebastian Bach: Sämtliche Orgelwerke*, vol. 3 (*Fantasien / Fugen*). Wiesbaden: Breitkopf & Härtel, 2016.

Dürr, Alfred, and Yoshitake Kobayashi, eds. *Bach-Werke-Verzeichnis: Kleine Ausgabe.* Wiesbaden: Breitkopf & Härtel, 1998.

Edwards, Frederick George. "Bach's Music in England." *Musical Times* 37 (1896): 722–26.

Emans, Reinmar. NBA IV/10: *Kritischer Bericht* to *Orgelchoräle aus unterschiedlicher Überlieferung.* Kassel: Bärenreiter, 2008.

Fahy, Thomas. "Killer Culture: Classical Music and the Art of Killing in *Silence of the Lambs* and *Se7en*." *Journal of Popular Culture* 37, no. 1 (2003): 28–42.

Ford, Andrew. *The Sound of Pictures: Listening to the Movies, from Hitchcock to High Fidelity.* Collingwood: Black Inc.: 2010.

French, Hannah. *Sir Henry Wood: Champion of J. S. Bach.* Woodbridge: Boydell Press, 2019.

Freudenberg, Karl Gottlieb. *Erinnerungen aus dem Leben eines alten Organisten.* Edited by Friedrich Wilhelm Viol. Breslau: F. E. C. Leuckart, 1870.

Friedrich, Felix. "Johann Ludwig Krebs als Vertreter einer frühen Bach-Rezeption? Grundlegende Gedanken zum Symposium am 15. April 2000 in Altenberg." *Freiberger Studien zur Orgel* 7 (2002): 5–9.

Frotscher, Gotthold. *Geschichte des Orgelspiels und der Orgelkompositionen.* Berlin: Max Hesse, 1935.

Gassmann, Michael, ed. *Orgelmusik aus England und Amerika, Band 15: Samuel Wesley (1766– 1837), Vierhändige Orgelwerke.* Sankt Augustin: J. Butz, 2005.

Geck, Martin. "Richard Wagner und die ältere Musik." In *Die Ausbreitung des Historismus über die Musik*, edited by Walter Wiora, 123–46. Regensburg: Gustav Bosse, 1969.

Glöckner, Andreas, Anselm Hartinger, and Karen Lehmann, eds. *Ausgewählte Dokumente zum Nachwirken Johann Sebastian Bachs 1801–1850.* Bach-Dokumente VI. Kassel: Bärenreiter, 2007.

Goedeke, Karl, and Edmund Goetze. *Grundrisz zur Geschichte der deutschen Dichtung*, 2nd ed., vol. 7. Dresden: Ehlermann, 1900.

References

Goertzen, Valerie Woodring. "Brahms's Performances of Bach's Organ Works." *American Brahms Society Newsletter* 37, no. 2 (Fall 2019): 1–5.

Goertzen, Valerie Woodring, ed. *Johannes Brahms: Arrangements von Werken anderer Komponisten für Klavier zu zwei Händen oder für die linke Hand allein.* Johannes Brahms Gesamtausgabe, Serie IX, Band 1. Munich: G. Henle Verlag, 2017.

Gower, Robert, ed. *The Oxford Book of Christmas Organ Music.* Oxford: Oxford University Press, 1995.

Grace, Harvey. *The Organ Works of Bach.* London: Novello, 1922.

Harris, Thomas. *The Silence of the Lambs.* New York: St. Martin's Press, 1988.

Hartinger, Anselm. *"Alte Neuigkeiten": Bach-Aufführungen und Leipziger Musikleben im Zeitalter Mendelssohns, Schumanns und Hauptmanns 1829 bis 1852.* Wiesbaden: Breitkopf & Härtel, 2014.

Hartinger, Anselm. "Das Orgelkonzert nach 1800—Erscheinungsbild, Protagonisten und Transformation einer Aufführungsgattung." In *"Diess herrliche, imponirende Instrument": Die Orgel im Zeitalter Felix Mendelssohn Bartholdys,* edited by Anselm Hartinger, Christoph Wolff, and Peter Wollny, 257–84. Wiesbaden: Breitkopf & Härtel, 2011.

Heinemann, Michael. *Die Bach-Rezeption von Franz Liszt.* Cologne: Studio, 1995.

Helms, Siegmund. "Johannes Brahms und Johann Sebastian Bach." *Bach-Jahrbuch* 57 (1971): 13–81.

Henahan, Donal. "Film Music Has Two Masters." *New York Times,* 19 July 1987.

Hilgenfeldt, Carl Ludwig. *Johann Sebastian Bach's Leben, Wirken und Werke: Ein Beitrag zur Kunstgeschichte des achtzehnten Jahrhunderts.* Leipzig: Friedrich Hofmeister, 1850.

Hill, Robert. "Die Herkunft von Bach's 'Thema Legrenzianum.'" *Bach-Jahrbuch* 72 (1986): 105–7.

Hofmann, Renate, and Kurt Hofmann. *Johannes Brahms als Pianist und Dirigent: Chronologie seines Wirkens als Interpret.* Tutzing: Hans Schneider, 2006.

Kalbeck, Max, ed. *Johannes Brahms: Briefwechsel.* 10 vols. Berlin: Deutsche Brahms-Gesellschaft, 1908–1917.

Kater, Michael H. *The Twisted Muse: Musicians and Their Music in the Third Reich.* New York: Oxford University Press, 1997.

Kaufmann, Michael Gerhard. *Orgel und Nationalsozialismus: Die ideologische Vereinnahmung des Instruments im "Dritten Reich."* Kleinblittersdorf: Musikwissenschaftliche Verlags-Gesellschaft, 1997.

Keller, Hermann. *Die Orgelwerke Bachs: Ein Beitrag zu ihrer Geschichte, Form, Deutung und Wiedergabe.* Leipzig: Edition Peters, 1948.

Keller, Hermann. *The Organ Works of Bach: A Contribution to Their History, Form, Interpretation and Performance.* Translated by Helen Hewitt. New York: C. F. Peters, 1967.

Kempe, Anna. *Erinnerungen an Ernst Theodor Mosewius.* Breslau: Joh. Urban Kern, 1859.

Kenney, Sylvia W., ed. *Catalog of the Emilie and Karl Riemenschneider Memorial Bach Library.* New York: Columbia University Press, 1960.

Kenyon, Nicholas. *The Faber Pocket Guide to Bach.* London: Faber and Faber, 2011.

Kilian, Dietrich. NBA IV/5–6: *Kritischer Bericht to Präludien, Toccaten, Fantasien und Fugen für Orgel.* Kassel: Bärenreiter; Leipzig: Deutscher Verlag für Musik, 1978–1979.

Klotz, Hans. NBA IV/2: *Kritischer Bericht* to *Die Orgelchoräle aus der Leipziger Originalhandschrift*. Kassel: Bärenreiter; Leipzig: Deutscher Verlag für Musik, 1957.

Knapp, Raymond. "The Finale of Brahms's Fourth Symphony: The Tale of the Subject." *19th-Century Music* 13, no. 1 (Summer 1989): 3–17.

Kobayashi, Yoshitake. *Franz Hauser und seine Bach-Handschriften Sammlung*. PhD. diss., Georg-August-Universität Göttingen, 1973.

Lehmann, Karen. "'Boten des Aufschwunges'—Gotthilf Wilhelm Körners Editionen und die Thüringer Orgellandschaft seiner Zeit." In *"Diess herrliche, imponirende Instrument": Die Orgel im Zeitalter Felix Mendelssohn Bartholdys*, edited by Anselm Hartinger, Christoph Wolff, and Peter Wollny, 389–401. Wiesbaden: Breitkopf & Härtel, 2011.

Leisinger, Ulrich. "Bachian Fugues in Mozart's Vienna." *Bach Notes* 6 (Fall 2006): 1–7.

Lerner, Neil. "The Strange Case of Rouben Mamoulian's Sound Stew: The Uncanny Soundtrack in *Dr. Jekyll and Mr. Hyde*." In *Music in the Horror Film: Listening to Fear*, edited by Neil Lerner, 55–79. New York: Routledge, 2010.

Little, Wm. A. *Mendelssohn and the Organ*. New York: Oxford University Press, 2010.

Litzmann, Berthold, ed. *Clara Schumann–Johannes Brahms: Briefe aus den Jahren 1853–1896*. 2 vols. Leipzig: Breitkopf & Härtel, 1927.

Löhlein, Heinz-Harald, ed. NBA IV/1: *Kritischer Bericht* to *Orgelbüchlein, Sechs Choräle vonverschiedener Art (Schübler Choräle), Orgelpartiten*. Kassel: Bärenreiter; Leipzig: Deutscher Verlag für Musik, 1987.

Ludwig, Klaus Uwe, ed. *Niels Wilhelm Gade: Variationen über den Choral "Sey gegrüsset Jesu gütig" von Johann Sebastian Bach*. Wiesbaden: Breitkopf & Härtel, 1996.

Mandel, Naomi. *Against the Unspeakable: Complicity, the Holocaust, and Slavery in America*. Charlottesville: University of Virginia Press, 2006.

Marquard, Reiner. "'Vor deinen Thron tret ich hiermit' (BWV 668): Erwägungen zum Verständnis der Frömmigkeit bei Johann Sebastian Bach." *Bach-Jahrbuch* 107 (2021): 185–221.

Marshall, Robert L. "'Editore traditore': Suspicious Performance Indications in the Bach Sources." In *The Music of Johann Sebastian Bach: The Sources, the Style, the Significance*, by Robert L. Marshall, 241–54. New York: Schirmer Books, 1989.

Marshall, Robert L., and Traute M. Marshall. *Exploring the World of J. S. Bach: A Traveler's Guide*. Urbana: University of Illinois Press, 2016.

Marx, Adolph Bernhard. *Die Lehre von der musikalischen Komposition*. 4 vols. Leipzig: Breitkopf & Härtel, 1837–1847.

Maul, Michael. *Bach: Eine Bildbiographie*. Leipzig: Lehmstedt Verlag, 2022.

Metz, Günther. "Hindemith und die alte Musik." In *Alte Musik im 20. Jahrhundert: Wandlungen und Formen ihrer Rezeption*, edited by Giselher Schubert, 93–112. Mainz: Schott, 1996.

Morris, Hugh. "Finishing Bach's Organ Music, with Help From 118 Composers." *New York Times*, 25 October 2022.

Mosewius, Johann Theodor. *Johann Sebastian Bach's Matthäus-Passion*. Berlin: Verlag von J. Guttentag, 1852.

References 181

Mosewius, Johann Theodor. *Johann Sebastian Bachs Matthäus-Passion / Johann Sebastian Bach in seinen Kirchen-Kantaten und Choralgesängen*, edited by Michael Heinemann. Hildesheim: Georg Olms Verlag, 2001.

Nauhaus, Gerd, and Nancy B. Reich, eds. *Clara Schumann: Jugendtagebücher 1827–1840*. Hildesheim: Georg Olms Verlag, 2019.

Near, John R. *Widor on Organ Performance Practice and Technique*. Rochester, NY: University of Rochester Press, 2019.

Norris, David Owen, ed. *A Bach Book for Harriet Cohen: Transcriptions for Pianoforte from the Works of J. S. Bach; With an Introduction by David Owen Norris*. Oxford: Oxford University Press, 2013.

Oberborbeck, Felix, ed. *Johann Sebastian Bach: Choral "Vor deinen Thron tret ich hiermit."* Wolfenbüttel: Möseler Verlag, 1950.

Olleson, Philip, ed. *The Letters of Samuel Wesley: Professional and Social Correspondence, 1797–1837*. Oxford: Oxford University Press, 2001.

Parry, C. Hubert H. *Johann Sebastian Bach: The Story of the Development of a Great Personality*. New York and London: G. P. Putnam's Sons, 1909.

Perreault, Jean M. *The Thematic Catalogue of the Musical Works of Johann Pachelbel*. Lanham, MD: Scarecrow Press, 2004.

Pleasants, Henry, ed. *The Musical World of Robert Schumann: A Selection from His Own Writings*. London: Gollancz, 1965.

Raabe, Peter. *Liszts Leben*. 2nd ed. Tutzing: Hans Schneider, 1968.

Reichling, Alfred. "Orgelklänge unter dem Hakenkreuz: Feiern—Feirräume—Feierorgeln." *Acta Organologica* 28 (2004): 411–44.

Renwick, William. "Of Time and Eternity: Reflections on 'Das alte Jahr vergangen ist.'" *Journal of Music Theory* 50, no. 1 (Spring 2006): 65–76.

Riethmüller, Albrecht. "Zur Geschichte eines Musikwerks: Die Interpretation von Präludium und Fuge ('St. Anne') für Orgel Es-Dur (BWV 552) zwischen Bach und Schönberg." In *Berliner Orgel-Colloquium*, edited by Hans Heinrich Eggebrecht, 31–44. Kleinblittersdorf: Musikwissenschaftliche Verlags-Gesellschaft, 1990.

Rosenmüller, Annegret. *Carl Ferdinand Becker (1804–1877): Studien zu Leben und Werk*. Hamburg: von Bockel Verlag, 2000.

Ross, Alex. "Chacona, Lamento, Walking Blues: Bass Lines of Music History." In *Listen to This*, by Alex Ross, 22–54. New York: Picador, 2010.

Ross, Alex. *The Rest Is Noise: Listening to the Twentieth Century*. New York: Picador, 2007.

Saffle, Michael. *Liszt in Germany 1840–1845: A Study in Sources, Documents, and the History of Reception*. Stuyvesant, NY: Pendragon Press, 1994.

Schanz, Arthur. *Johann Sebastian Bach in der Klaviertranskription*. Eisenach: Karl Dieter Wagner, 2000.

Schindler, Anton Felix. *Beethoven as I Knew Him*. Edited by Donald W. MacArdle. Chapel Hill: University of North Carolina Press, 1966.

Schmiedel, Elisabeth, and Joachim Draheim, eds. *An den Rhein und weiter: Woldemar Bargiel zu Gast bei Robert und Clara Schumann; Ein Tagebuch von 1852*. Sinzig: Studio Verlag, 2011.

Schmieder, Wolfgang. *Thematisch-systematisches Verzeichnis der musikalischen Werke von Johann Sebastian Bach*. Rev. ed. Wiesbaden: Breitkopf & Härtel, 1990.

Schneider, Klaus. *Lexikon "Musik über Musik": Variationen—Transkriptionen—Hommagen—Stilimitationen—B-A-C-H*. Kassel: Bärenreiter, 2004.

Schneider, Max. "Verzeichnis der bis zum Jahre 1851 gedruckten (und der geschrieben in Handel gewesen) Werke von Johann Sebastian Bach." *Bach-Jahrbuch* 3 (1906): 84–113.

Schubert, Klaus. "Johann Sebastian Bachs Präludium und Fuge c-Moll für Orgel BWV 546 und die beiden Orgeltriosätze c-Moll nach Johann Friedrich Fasch BWV 585: Ein bislang unbekannte Werkbeziehung." In *Perspectives on Organ Playing and Musical Interpretation: Pedagogical, Historical, and Instrumental Studies (A Festschrift for Heinrich Fleischer at 90)*, edited by Ames Anderson, Bruce Backer, David Backus, and Charles Luedtke, 108–37. New Ulm, MN: Martin Luther College, 2002.

Schulenberg, David, ed. *Johann Sebastian Bach: Sämtliche Orgelwerke*, vol. 2 (*Präludien und Fugen II*). Wiesbaden: Breitkopf & Härtel, 2014.

Schulze, Hans-Joachim, ed. *Katalog der Sammlung Manfred Gorke: Bachiana und andere Handschriften und Drucke des 18. und frühen 19. Jahrhunderts*. Leipzig: Musikbibliothek der Stadt Leipzig, 1977.

Schweitzer, Albert. *J. S. Bach*. Translated by Ernest Newman. 2 vols. Leipzig: Breitkopf & Härtel, 1911.

Schweitzer, Albert. *Out of My Life and Thought: An Autobiography*. London: Allen & Unwin, 1933.

Sciannameo, Franco. *Nino Rota's "The Godfather Trilogy": A Film Score Guide*. Lanham, MD: Scarecrow Press, 2010.

Seyfried, Hans Jürgen. *Adolph Friedrich Hesse als Orgelvirtuose und Orgelkomponist*. Regensburg: Gustav Bosse, 1965.

Sieling, Andreas. *August Wilhelm Bach (1796–1869): Kirchenmusik und Seminarmusiklehrerausbildung in Preußen im zweiten Drittel des 19. Jahrhunderts*. Cologne: Studio, 1995.

Sieling, Andreas. "'Selbst den alten Vater Sebastian suchte man nicht mehr so langstielig abzuhaspeln': Zur Rezeptionsgeschichte der Orgelwerke Bachs." In *Bach und die Nachwelt, Band 2: 1850–1900*, edited by Michael Heinemann and Hans-Joachim Hinrichsen, 299–339. Laaber: Laaber-Verlag, 1999.

Smaczny, Jan. "Bach's B-Minor Mass: An Incarnation in Prague in the 1860s and Its Consequences." In *Exploring Bach's B-Minor Mass*, edited by Yo Tomita, Robin A. Leaver, and Jan Smaczny, 287–97. Cambridge: Cambridge University Press, 2013.

Snyder, Kerala J. *Dieterich Buxtehude: Organist in Lübeck*. 2nd ed. Rochester, NY: University of Rochester Press, 2007.

Somfai, László. "Bartók's Transcription of J. S. Bach." In *Studien zur Musikgeschichte: Eine Festschrift für Ludwig Finscher*, edited by Annegrit Laubenthal, 689–96. Kassel: Bärenreiter: 1995.

Spitta, Philipp. *Johann Sebastian Bach*. 2 vols. Leipzig: Breitkopf & Härtel, 1873–1879.

Sposato, Jeffrey S. *Leipzig after Bach: Church and Concert Life in a German City*. New York: Oxford University Press, 2018.

Statham, H. Heathcoate. "The Aesthetic Treatment of Bach's Organ Music." *Proceedings of the Royal Musical Association* 27 (1900–1901): 131–61.

Statham, H. Heathcoate. *The Organ and Its Position in Musical Art*. London: Chapman and Hall, 1909.

References

Stauffer, George B. *The Organ Preludes of Johann Sebastian Bach.* Ann Arbor: UMI Research Press, 1980.

Stephan, Rudolf, and Tadeusz Okuljar, eds. *Arnold Schönberg: Bearbeitungen I/II.* Arnold Schönberg Gesamtausgabe, Abteilung VII, Reihe B, Band 25/26. Mainz: B. Schott's Söhne, 1988.

Stinson, Russell. *Bach: The Orgelbüchlein.* New York: Oxford University Press, 1999.

Stinson, Russell. *The Bach Manuscripts of Johann Peter Kellner and His Circle: A Case Study in Reception History.* Durham and London: Duke University Press, 1989.

Stinson, Russell. *Bach's Legacy: The Music as Heard by Later Masters.* New York: Oxford University Press, 2020.

Stinson, Russell. "Clara Schumann's Bach Book: A Neglected Document of the Bach Revival." *Bach: Journal of the Riemenschneider Bach Institute* 39, no. 1 (2008): 1–67.

Stinson, Russell. *J. S. Bach at His Royal Instrument: Essays on His Organ Works.* New York: Oxford University Press, 2012.

Stinson, Russell. *J. S. Bach's Great Eighteen Organ Chorales.* New York: Oxford University Press, 2001.

Stinson, Russell. "Karl Gottlieb Freudenbergs *Erinnerungen aus dem Leben eines alten Organisten* und die Bach-Rezeption im 19. Jahrhundert." *Bach-Jahrbuch* 105 (2019): 237–51.

Stinson, Russell. *The Reception of Bach's Organ Works from Mendelssohn to Brahms.* New York: Oxford University Press, 2006.

Stinson, Russell. "Some Thoughts on Bach's Neumeister Chorales." *Journal of Musicology* 11, no. 4 (Fall 1993): 455–77.

Stinson, Russell. "Toward a Chronology of Bach's Instrumental Music: Observations on Three Keyboard Works," *Journal of Musicology* 7, no. 4 (Fall 1989): 440–70.

Stutschwesky, Joachim, ed. *J. S. Bach: Four Duets for Violin and Cello.* New York: International Music Company, 1947.

Thistlethwaite, Nicholas. *The Making of the Victorian Organ.* Cambridge: Cambridge University Press, 1990.

Thorau, Christian. "Richard Wagners Bach." In *Bach und die Nachwelt, Band 2: 1850–1900,* edited by Michael Heinemann and Hans-Joachim Hinrichsen, 163–99. Laaber: Laaber-Verlag, 1999.

Todd, R. Larry. *Mendelssohn: A Life in Music.* New York: Oxford University Press, 2003.

Wald, Uta, ed. *Felix Mendelssohn Bartholdy: Sämtliche Briefe,* vol. 5. Kassel: Bärenreiter, 2012.

Wald, Uta, ed. *Felix Mendelssohn Bartholdy: Sämtliche Briefe,* vol. 10. Kassel: Bärenreiter, 2016.

Wierzbicki, James. *Film Music: A History.* New York: Routledge, 2009.

Wilhelm, Rüdiger, ed. *Johann Sebastian Bach: Ricercar à 6 c-Moll aus dem Musikalischen Opfer BWV 1079; Fassung für Orgel von Johann Friedrich Agricola.* Beeskow: Ortus Musikverlag, 2017.

Williams, Peter. *The Organ Music of J. S. Bach.* 2nd ed. Cambridge: Cambridge University Press, 2003.

Wolf, Uwe. *NBA V/9.2: Kritischer Bericht* to *Sechs kleine Praeludien, einzeln überlieferte Klavierwerke I.* Kassel: Bärenreiter, 2000.

Wolff, Christoph. "Bach's *Handexemplar* of the Goldberg Variations: A New Source." *Journal of the American Musicological Society* 29 (1976): 224–41.

Wolff, Christoph. *Bach's Musical Universe: The Composer and His Work*. New York: W. W. Norton, 2020.

Wolff, Christoph, and Markus Zepf. *The Organs of J. S. Bach: A Handbook*. Urbana: University of Illinois Press, 2012.

Yearsley, David. *Bach's Feet: The Organ Pedals in European Culture*. Cambridge: Cambridge University Press, 2012.

Zehnder, Jean-Claude, ed. *Johann Sebastian Bach: Sämtliche Orgelwerke*, vol. 4 (*Toccaten und Fugen / Einzelwerke*). Wiesbaden: Breitkopf & Härtel, 2012.

Zitellini, Rodolfo. "Das 'Thema Legrenzianum' der Fuge BWV 574—eine Fehlzuschreibung?" *Bach-Jahrbuch* 99 (2013): 243–59.

INDEX

For the benefit of digital users, indexed terms that span two pages (e.g., 52–53) may, on occasion, appear on only one of those pages.

Abert, Hermann (1871-1927; musicologist), 40
Abert, Johann Joseph (1832-1915; composer, conductor)
  orchestration of works by Bach, 40
Agricola, Johann Friedrich (1720-1774; composer, organist)
  organ transcription of movement from BWV 1079, 141n.16
All Quiet on the Western Front, 171n.41
Altenstein, Karl vom Stein zum (1770-1840; politician), 80
Amsterdam Loecki Stardust Quartet, 107
Atkins, Ivor (1869-1953; organist), 109–10

Bach, Anna Magdalena, née Wilcke (1701-1760; wife of Johann Sebastian), 143n.37
Bach, August Wilhelm (1796-1869; organist), 74–75, 78–79, 80
Bach, Carl Philipp Emanuel (1714-1788; composer, son of Johann Sebastian), 11–12, 173n.52
Bach, Johann Christian (1735-1782; composer, son of Johann Sebastian), 150n.36
Bach, Johann Christoph (1671-1721; organist, brother of Johann Sebastian), 15–16, 119

Bach, Johann Sebastian (1685-1750; composer). See also *listing of works under BWV numbers*
  "Arnstadt Congregational Chorales," 130
  B Minor Mass, 83
  Christmas Oratorio, 83
  Die Kunst der Fuge, 121, 127–28, 134–35
  Goldberg Variations (BWV 988), 23, 97–100, 104, 113–14
  Orgelbüchlein, 6–10, 113–14, 120–27
  Schübler Chorales (BWV 645-650), 44–45, 46–47, 49–50, 52–53, 148n.9
  St. John Passion, 7
  St. Matthew Passion, 83–86, 117, 133–34
  Suites for Solo Cello, 103–4
  Well-Tempered Clavier, 17, 18–19, 44, 55, 90, 114, 154n.57
Bach, Regina Susanna (1742-1809; daughter of Johann Sebastian), 75–76, 78
Bach, Wilhelm Friedemann (1710-1784; composer, son of Johann Sebastian), 12
Bach 333, 106–7
Bachgesellschaft edition of J. S. Bach's complete works, 25–26, 38–39, 91–92, 145n.59, 146n.69
Baini, Giuseppe (1775-1884; church musician, musicologist), 75

Bargiel, Woldemar (1828-1897; composer, conductor), 77–78

Bartók, Béla (1881-1945; composer), 128, 174n.63
 piano transcription of BWV 530, 174n.63

Baryshnikov, Mikhail (b. 1948; dancer, actor), 166n.5

Bax, Arnold (1883-1953; composer)
 piano transcription of BWV 572, 117

Becker, Carl Ferdinand (1804-1877; organist, composer), 15–16, 21, 26–27, 55–73, 76, 121, 122, 134–36
 "Adagio" for organ, 56
 organ-duet arrangement of movement from BWV 1079, 21, 171–72n.42

Beethoven, Ludwig van (1770-1827; composer), 55, 74–78, 115, 137
 Diabelli Variations, Op. 120, 76
 "Kühl, nicht lau," WoO 191, 137
 Overture on BACH, 137
 Sonata in C Minor, Op. 13 ("Pathètique"), 115
 String Quartet in C-sharp Minor, Op. 131, 90

Bengtsson, Erling (1932-2013; cellist), 168n.27

Bergman, Ingmar (1918-2007; filmmaker), 103–4
 Saraband, 173n.49
 Through a Glass Darkly, 103–4

Berlioz, Hector (1803-1869; composer), 20–21

Berner, Friedrich Wilhelm (1780-1827; composer), 74–75

Bertini, Henri (1798-1876; composer, pianist)
 piano transcription of the Well-Tempered Clavier, 8–9

Best, William Thomas (1826-1897; organist), 117

Bighley, Mark S. (b. 1954; organist, musicologist), 140n.9

Birnbach, Heinrich (1782-1848; composer), 12–13

Blom, Eric (1888-1959; musicologist), 173n.57

Böhm, Georg (1661-1733; composer), 72–73

Böhme, Ullrich (b. 1956; organist), 129–30

Bononcini, Giovanni Maria (1642-1678; composer), 119

Brahms, Johannes (1833-1897; composer), 13–14, 38–41, 43, 53, 109, 118–19, 120, 144n.46
 Ein deutsches Requiem, 40–41
 "Herzlich tut mich erfreuen," Op. 122, No. 4, 53
 Octaven und Quinten, 69
 Symphony No. 4 in E Minor, 16–17
 Variations on a Theme by Haydn, Op. 56, 16–17

Breitkopf & Härtel editions of organ works by Bach, 25–39, 44–55, 56, 64, 67, 78–79, 91–92, 116, 157n.81

Brenner, Ludwig von (1833-1902; conductor, composer), 40

Breuer, Heribert (b. 1945; organist, conductor)
 choral transcription of BWV 668, 173n.56

Bright, Richard (1937-2006; actor), 95–96

Brown, Royal (b. 1940; film scholar), 95–97

Busoni, Ferruccio (1866-1924; composer, pianist), 108–9
 piano transcription of BWV 639, 171n.41

Butt, John (b. 1960; organist, conductor), 127

Buxtehude, Dietrich (ca. 1637-1707; composer), 15–16, 24, 67, 72–73
 Chaconne in C Minor, 142n.28
 Chaconne in E Minor, 16–17
 Passacaglia in D Minor, 15–17

BWV 225: "Singet dem Herrn ein neues Lied," 44

BWV 234: Mass in A Major, 39–40

BWV 288-289: "Das alte Jahr vergangen ist," 9–10

BWV 525-530: Trio Sonatas for Organ, 10–13

Index

BWV 525: Sonata No. 1 in E-flat Major, 10–11

BWV 530: Sonata No. 6 in G Major, 174n.63

BWV 532: Prelude and Fugue in D Major, 25, 96–97, 102

BWV 533: Prelude and Fugue in E Minor, 25, 64, 70, 78–80, 121–22

BWV 534: Prelude and Fugue in F Minor, 56, 120–22

BWV 535: Prelude and Fugue in G Minor, 61, 65, 106–7, 121–22

BWV 536: Prelude and Fugue in A Major, 172n.45

BWV 537: Fantasy and Fugue in C Minor, 66

BWV 538: Toccata and Fugue in D Minor ("Dorian"), 20, 61–63, 115

BWV 539: Prelude and Fugue in D Minor, 25–28, 64–65, 67–68

BWV 540: Toccata and Fugue in F Major, 20–21, 41, 60–61, 87–88, 102–3, 108–11

BWV 541: Prelude and Fugue in G Major, 122, 168–69n.3

BWV 542: Fantasy and Fugue in G Minor, 21, 25, 26, 56–59, 80, 120–22, 136–37

BWV 543-548: Six "Great" Preludes and Fugues for Organ, 18–19, 41–42, 90, 107, 121–22, 136

BWV 543: Prelude and Fugue in A Minor, 22–23, 41, 120–22, 136

BWV 544: Prelude and Fugue in B Minor, 41, 114, 120–22

BWV 546: Prelude and Fugue in C Minor, 102, 114, 120–22, 135–36

BWV 547: Prelude and Fugue in C Major ("9/8"), 17–19, 122

BWV 548: Prelude and Fugue in E Minor ("Wedge"), 114, 120–22

BWV 549: Prelude and Fugue in C Minor (originally D Minor), 121–22

BWV 550: Prelude and Fugue in G Major, 25–26, 107

BWV 551: Prelude and Fugue in A Minor, 61, 70, 121–22

BWV 552: Prelude and Fugue in E-flat Major ("St. Anne"), 23–24, 40–41, 60, 80–81, 102–3, 111–14, 122

BWV 564: Toccata, Adagio, and Fugue in C Major, 68–69

BWV 565: Toccata in D Minor, 25, 26, 62–63, 96–97, 114–15

BWV 566: Prelude and Fugue in C Major (originally E Major), 25, 64, 66–68

BWV 569: Prelude in A Minor, 25–26

BWV 572: Fantasy in G Major (*Pièce d'Orgue*), 41, 102–3, 116–19, 159n.94, 168–69n.3

BWV 574: Fugue in C Minor on a Theme by Bononcini, 111, 119

BWV 582: Passacaglia in C Minor, 12, 14–16, 24

BWV 590: Pastorale in F Major, 12, 25, 26, 41

BWV 599-644: *Orgelbüchlein*

BWV 601: "Herr Christ, der ein'ge Gottessohn," 8

BWV 603: "Puer natus in Bethlehem," 10

BWV 614: "Das alte Jahr vergangen ist," 8–9, 120–21, 122–23, 126–27

BWV 622: "O Mensch, bewein dein Sünde groß," 7–8, 120–21, 122–23

BWV 627: "Christ ist erstanden," 7

BWV 633-634: "Liebster Jesu, wir sind hier," 48

BWV 639: "Ich ruf zu dir, Herr Jesu Christ," 120–21, 122–23, 126–27

BWV 641: "Wenn wir in höchsten Nöten sein," 121

BWV 643: "Alle Menschen müssen sterben," 126

BWV 651-668: Great Eighteen Chorales, 106, 142–43n.30

BWV 654: "Schmücke dich, o liebe Seele," 90–93, 120–21

BWV 664: "Allein Gott in der Höh sei Ehr," 48–49, 50

BWV 668: "Vor deinen Thron tret ich hiermit," 120–21, 127–30

BWV 669-689: chorale settings from Part 3 of the *Clavierübung*, 142–43n.30

BWV 669-671: "Kyrie" settings, 120–21

BWV 675-677: "Allein Gott in der Höh sei Ehr," 47, 50–52, 111

BWV 680-681: "Wir glauben all an einen Gott," 24, 47–48, 52

BWV 686: "Aus tiefer Not schrei ich zu dir," 120–21

BWV 691: "Wer nur den lieben Gott lässt walten" (from the *Clavierbüchlein vor Wilhelm Friedemann Bach*), 48

BWV 692-693: "Ach Gott und Herr." *See* Walther, Johann Gottfried

BWV 697: "Gelobet seist du, Jesu Christ," 49

BWV 704: "Lob sei dem allmächtigen Gott," 48

BWV 705: "Durch Adams Fall ist ganz verderbt," 39–40, 48, 52, 55

BWV 706: "Liebster Jesu, wir sind hier," 48

BWV 707-708: "Ich hab mein Sach Gott heimgestellt," 49, 54

BWV 710: "Wir Christenleut," 49

BWV 711: "Allein Gott in der Höh sei Ehr," 48, 52–53

BWV 718: "Christ lag in Todesbanden," 150n.32

BWV 725: "Herr Gott, dich loben wir," 173n.55

BWV 729: "In dulci jubilo," 130–31

BWV 740: "Wir glauben all an einen Gott, Vater." *See* Krebs, Johann Ludwig

BWV 759: "Schmücke dich, o liebe Seele." *See* Homilius, Gottfried August

BWV 768: "Sei gegrüsset, Jesu gütig," 152n.49

BWV 769: Canonic Variations on "Vom Himmel hoch, da komm ich her," 44–45, 120–21

BWV 772-786: Two-Part Inventions, 131–32

BWV 802-805: Duets from Part 3 of the *Clavierübung*, 131–32

BWV 807: English Suite No. 2 in A Minor, 100–1

BWV 849: Prelude and Fugue in C-sharp Minor (Well-Tempered Clavier, Book 1), 40, 90

BWV 855: Prelude and Fugue in E Minor (Well-Tempered Clavier, Book 1), 107, 131–32

BWV 898: Prelude and Fugue on BACH, 134–35

BWV 903: Chromatic Fantasy and Fugue, 28–32

BWV 913: Toccata in D Minor, 115

BWV 961: Fughetta in C Minor, 131–32

BWV 1001: Sonata in G Minor for Solo Violin, 26–27, 64–65

BWV 1008: Suite No. 2 in D Minor for Solo Cello, 103–4

BWV 1079: Musical Offering, 13–14, 120–21

BWV 1091: "Das alte Jahr vergangen ist" (Neumeister Collection), 9–10

BWV 1117: "Alle Menschen müssen sterben" (Neumeister Collection), 173n.49

BWV 1128: "Wo Gott der Herr nicht bei uns hält," 145n.55

BWV 1164 (formerly BWV Anh. 159): "Ich lasse dich nicht, du segnest mich den," 146n.68

BWV Anh. 74: "Schmücke dich, o liebe Seele." *See* Homilius, Gottfried August

Calmus Ensemble, 129–30

Carpenter, Cameron (b. 1981; organist), 169n.8

Carroll, Sean (b. 1966; physicist), 108

Casals, Pablo (1876-1973; cellist), 103, 168n.27

Cenciarelli, Carlo (musicologist), 99–100

Cherubini, Luigi (1760-1842; composer), 25

Chronik der Anna Magdalena Bach, 114

Cohen, Harriet (1895-1967; pianist), 117, 130–31

Index

Conte, Richard (1910-1975; actor), 96
Coppola, Francis Ford (b. 1939; filmmaker)
  The Godfather, 95–97
Crotch, William (1775-1847; composer, organist), 50–51, 150n.39

Damcke, Bertold (1812-1875; composer), 8–9, 19
Danish National Girls Choir, 173n.54
Danish String Quartet, 173n.54
David, Hans T. (1902-1967; musicologist), 114–15
Demme, Jonathan (1944-2017; filmmaker)
  The Silence of the Lambs, 97–100
Diana, Princess of Wales (1961-1997; British princess), 134–35
Dirksen, Pieter (b. 1961; organist, musicologist), 157n.81
Doles, Johann Friedrich (1715-1797; composer), 44, 49–50
Dröbs, Johann Andreas (1784-1825; organist), 55
Dvorak, Antonin (1841-1904; composer), 144n.41

Eijken, Albertus van (1823-1868; organist), 136–37
Elgar, Edward (1857-1934; composer), 43, 109–10, 144n.49
Elizabeth II (1926-2022; British queen), 126–27, 134–35
Elvira Madigan, 103
Emerson, Keith (1944-2016; keyboardist), 108
Emerson, Lake & Palmer, 108
  "The Only Way" (from *Tarkus*), 108
Esser, Heinrich (1818-1872; conductor, violinist)
  orchestration of BWV 540/1, 109–10

Fagius, Hans (b. 1951; organist), 173n.49
Fahy, Thomas (scholar of pop culture), 97–98
Fasch, Johann Friedrich (1688-1758; composer), 136

Fergus-Thompson, Gordon (b. 1952; pianist), 130–31
Ficker, Johannes (1861-1944; church historian), 126
Fischer, Johann Wilhelm (1762-1850; clergyman), 81–83
Ford, Andrew (b. 1957; composer, broadcaster), 100–1
Forkel, Johann Nikolaus (1749-1818; Bach biographer), 12, 41–42, 71–72
Foster, Arnold (1898-1962; composer)
  orchestration of BWV 680, 144n.49
Franck, César (1822-1890; composer), 43
Frederick the Great, King of Prussia (1712-1786), 13–14
Freire, Nelson (1944-2021; pianist), 106
French, Hannah (musicologist, broadcaster), 110
Frescobaldi, Girolamo (1583-1643; composer), 74–75
Freudenberg, Karl Gottlieb (1797-1869; organist), 74–93, 115
  "Ein feste Burg ist unser Gott," 80, 87
  Erinnerungen aus dem Leben eines alten Organisten, 74–93
Frotscher, Gotthold (1897-1967; musicologist), 61

Gade, Niels (1817-1890; composer), 152n.49
  organ-duet arrangement of BWV 768, 152n.49
Gardiner, John Eliot (b. 1943; conductor), 129–30, 168n.2
Gleichauf, Franz Xaver (1801-1856; composer, pedagogue), 19
  piano transcriptions of organ works by Bach, 19
Goebbels, Joseph (1897-1945; Nazi politician), 168n.24
Goertzen, Valerie (musicologist), 118
Goethe, Johann Wolfgang von (1749-1832; writer), 41–42
Goldberg, Johann Gottlieb (1727-1756; harpsichordist, composer), 144n.46

Gould, Glenn (1932-1982; pianist), 97, 98, 104

Gower, Robert (b. 1952; organist), 174n.62

Grace, Harvey (1874-1944; organist, critic), 23–24, 42, 116–17, 123–24

Grainger, Percy (1882-1961; composer, pianist)
  piano transcription of BWV 540/1, 108–9

Gray, Antony (pianist), 117

Griepenkerl, Friedrich Conrad (1782-1849; editor)
  edition of organ works by Bach, 59–73, 158n.88

Griffiths, Paul (b. 1947; critic), 128–29

Gubaidulina, Sofia (b. 1931; composer), 128
  Meditation on the Bach Chorale "Vor deinen Thron tret ich hiermit," BWV 668, 128–29

Guest, Douglas (1916-1996; organist), 130–31

Haag, Herbert (1908-77; organist), 101–3

Hackford, Taylor (b. 1944; filmmaker)
  White Nights, 166n.5

Handel, George Frideric (1685-1759; composer), 25, 166n.54

Harris, Thomas (b. 1940; novelist)
  The Silence of the Lambs, 98

Hartinger, Anselm (b. 1971; musicologist), 113

Haselbock, Franz (b. 1939; organist), 165n.48

Haslinger, Tobias (1787-1842; publisher)
  violin-duet transcriptions of BWV 802-805 and 961, 131–32

Hauptmann, Moritz (1792-1868; composer), 113

Hauser, Franz (1794-1870; singer, Bach collector), 8–9

Haydn, Franz Joseph (1732-1809; composer), 142n.28

Hellmann, Diethard (1928-1999; church musician)
  choral transcription of BWV 705, 52

Henahan, Donal (1921-2012; critic), 103

Hentschel, Ernst Julius (1804-1875; composer, pedagogue), 69

Herzogenberg, Elisabeth von, née Stockhausen (1847-1892; pianist, singer), 38–40

Herzogenberg, Heinrich von (1843-1900; composer), 38–39

Hespos, Hans-Joachim (1938-2022; composer), 170n.24

Hesse, Adolph Friedrich (1809-1863; organist, composer), 20–21, 57–59, 87–90, 136–37
  Präludium und Fuge über den Namen Hesse, 154n.57
  Symphony No. 5, 89–90
  Symphony No. 6, 57

Hewitt, Angela (b. 1958; pianist), 130–31
  piano transcription of BWV 614, 173n.50
  piano transcription of BWV 643, 126

Hilgenfeldt, Carl Ludwig (1806–after 1852; Bach biographer), 108, 140n.8

Hill, Robert (b. 1953; harpsichordist, musicologist), 119

Hindemith, Paul (1895-1963; composer)
  Cardillac, 174n.63

Hitler, Adolf (1889-1945; Nazi dictator), 101–3

Hodge, Herbert (organist), 144n.49

Holst, Gustav (1874-1934; composer)
  Christmas Day, 130–31

Homilius, Gottfried August (1714-1785; composer), 49–50
  "Schmücke dich, o liebe Seele" (BWV 759 and BWV Anh. 74), 48, 49–51, 90–92, 93

Hopkins, Anthony (b. 1937; actor), 97

Horn, Charles Frederick (1762-1830; composer)
  string-quartet transcriptions of keyboard fugues by Bach, 151n.45

Hough, Stephen (b. 1961; pianist, composer), 127

Index

Jacob, Benjamin (1778-1829; organist), 150n.39
organ-duet arrangement of BWV 552/2, 23, 112–13
Jakob, Friedrich August Leberecht (1803-1884; organist), 63

Kater, Michael (b. 1937; Holocaust scholar), 101
Kauffmann, Georg Friedrich (1679-1735; composer), 54
Kayser, Bernhard Christian (1705-1778; organist), 116
Keller, Hermann (1885-1967; organist, editor), 63, 69, 110–11, 130
Kempe, Anna (nineteenth century; biographer of J. T. Mosewius), 84, 163n.27
Keneally, Thomas (b. 1935; novelist) *Schindler's Ark*, 100–1
Kenyon, Nicholas (b. 1951; critic, musicologist), 168n.2
Kilian, Dietrich (1928-1984; musicologist), 116
Kindscher, Louis (1800-1875; organist, composer), 6–7, 66
Kirnberger, Johann Philipp (1721-1783; composer, theorist), 18–19
Kittel, Johann Christian (1732-1809; organist, composer), 20, 55
Preludio pro Organo pleno, 20
Klein, Bernhard Joseph (1793-1832; composer), 74–75, 80
Klein, Christian Benjamin (1754-1825; organist), 74–75, 80
Kloss, Carl (1792-1853; organist), 134–35, 136–37
Kluge, Oliver (b. 1969; organist), 170n.24
Knapp, Raymond (b. 1952; musicologist), 16–17
Koopman, Ton (b. 1944; organist, conductor), 106
Körner, Gotthilf Wilhelm (1809-1865; organist)

editions of organ works by Bach, 66, 69, 139n.2
Kotzebue, Karl August von (twentieth century; organist in Bayreuth), 102–3
Krebs, Johann Ludwig (1713-1780; composer, organist), 49–50, 54, 56, 66, 135, 150n.32
"Ach Gott, erhöh mein Seufzen," 135
"Wir glauben all an einen Gott, Vater" (BWV 740), 8
Krebs, Johann Tobias (1690-1762; organist), 20–21, 66
Krüger, Eduard (1807-1885; organist, critic), 136
Kuhlau, Friedrich (1786-1832; pianist, composer), 137

Lampadius, Wilhelm Adolf (1812-1892; singer, writer), 76
Legrenzi, Giovanni (1626-1690; composer), 119
Trio Sonata No. 2 in G Minor, Op. 2, No. 11, 119
Leonhardt, Gustav (1928-2012; harpsichordist, conductor), 114
Leopold, Prince of Anhalt-Cöthen (1694-1728; German prince), 167n.18
Leupold edition of organ works by Bach, 140n.9
Liszt, Franz (1811-1886; composer), 8–9, 43, 88–91, 107, 108–9, 125–26, 144n.46
piano transcriptions of BWV 543-548, 90, 107
Prelude and Fugue on BACH, 134–35
Logier, Johann Bernhard (1777-1846; composer), 74–75
Lohmann, Heinz (1934-2001; organist, editor), 116
Lord Berners (1883-1950; composer) piano transcription of BWV 729, 130–31
Luther, Martin (1483-1546; theologian), 81–82, 87, 164n.36
Lutz, Rudolf (b. 1951; organist, conductor), 133–34

Index

Mamoulian, Rouben (1897-1987; filmmaker)
  Dr. Jekyll and Mr. Hyde, 96–97
Mandel, Naomi (b. 1969; Holocaust scholar), 101
Marx, Adolph Bernhard (1795-1866; theorist, composer), 52–53, 86–88, 144n.43
  Die Lehre von der musikalischen Komposition, 8–9, 15, 86–87
  editions of organ works by Bach, 25–39, 64, 67, 78–79
  Moses, 86–87
  Passacaglia in C Minor, 15
  "Triumph, Triumph, es kommt mit Pracht," 87
Mary of Teck (1867-1953; British queen), 126–27
Mendel, Arthur (1905-1979; musicologist), 114–15
Mendelssohn, Fanny (1805-1847; composer, pianist), 109, 143n.34
Mendelssohn, Felix (1809-1847; composer), 8–9, 15, 19, 25, 39–40, 41–42, 43, 58–59, 61, 76, 78–80, 86, 92–93, 109, 110–11, 113, 120, 133–37, 152n.49
  editions of organ works by Bach, 25–39, 56, 64, 67, 78–79, 92–93
  Fugue in F Minor, 170n.19
  Passacaglia in C Minor, 15
  Sonata in B-flat Major for Organ, Op. 65, No. 4, 135
Moscheles, Ignaz (1794-1870; pianist), 77–78
Mosewius, Johann Theodor (1788-1858; conductor, musicologist), 83–86
Mozart, Wolfgang Amadeus (1756-1791; composer), 44, 55, 100–1
  Die Zauberflöte, 88
  Fantasy in F Minor, K. 608, 111
  Piano Concerto No. 21 in C Major, 103
Mühly, Nico (b. 1981; composer), 127
Müller-Blattau, Josef (1895-1976; musicologist), 101–2

Musgrave, Thea (b. 1928; composer), 127

Nägeli, Hans Georg (1773-1836; composer, publisher)
  edition of BWV 525-530, 12–13
Neale, John Mason (1818-1866; hymn writer), 130–31
Near, John (organist, musicologist), 117
Neumeister Collection of organ chorales from the Bach circle, 8
Newman, Anthony and Mary Jane (keyboard duo), 143n.34
Newman, Ernest (1868-1959; critic, musicologist), 123–24
Norris, David Owen (b. 1953; pianist, broadcaster), 117, 174n.61
Novello, Vincent (1781-1861; publisher)
  orchestration and organ-duet arrangement of BWV 552, 111

Oberborbeck, Felix (1900-1975; conductor, composer)
  choral and instrumental transcriptions of BWV 668, 129
Offenbach, Jacques (1819-1880; composer)
  The Tales of Hoffmann, 173n.57

Pachelbel, Johann (1653-1706; composer), 24
Pacino, Al (b. 1940; actor), 95–96
Palestrina, Giovanni Pierluigi da (ca. 1525-1594; composer), 16–17, 74–75
Panufnik, Roxanna (b. 1968; composer), 127
Parry, Hubert (1848-1918; composer, historian), 155n.72
Peters editions of organ works by Bach, 12, 20–21, 26–27, 55–73, 92–93, 122, 124–25
Petit, Roland (1924-2011; dancer, choreographer)
  Le jeune homme et la mort, 166n.5
Piutti, Carl (1846-1902; organist), 39–40
Planyavsky, Peter (b. 1947; organist), 127
Plowright, Jonathan (b. 1959; pianist), 117

Prince Philip, Duke of Edinburgh (1921-2021; British prince), 134–35
Puzo, Mario (1920-1999; novelist)
The Godfather, 95

Raison, André (ca. 1640-1719; composer, organist), 24
Reger, Max (1873-1916; composer), 111
Prelude and Fugue in G Major for Solo Violin, Op. 117, No. 5, 168–69n.3
Reinecke, Carl (1824-1910; composer, conductor), 40
Resphigi, Ottorino (1879-1936; composer)
orchestration of BWV 582, 166n.5
Richter, Bernhard Friedrich (1850-1931; church musician)
choral transcription of BWV 705, 52
Richter, Ernst Friedrich (1808-1879; composer), 38–39
choral transcription of BWV 668, 129
Ritter, August Gottfried (1811-1885; organist, composer), 159n.94
Rochlitz, Friedrich (1769-1842; critic), 44–55, 77–78, 135–36, 154n.57
Rogg, Lionel (b. 1936; organist), 127
Roitzsch, Ferdinand (1805-1889; editor)
edition of organ works by Bach, 59
Ross, Alex (b. 1968; critic), 139n.2, 141n.20
Rossini, Gioachino (1792-1868; composer), 25
Rota, Nino (1911-1979; composer)
film score for *The Godfather*, 95–96
Variazione e fuga nei dodici toni sul nome di Bach, 166n.2
Roth, Daniel (b. 1942; organist), 124–25
Rust, Wilhelm (1822-1892; organist, editor, composer), 25–40, 129, 136–37
Am SeeM Tiberias, 39–40
choral transcription of BWV 705, 39–40, 52
edition of organ works by Bach, 25–26, 38–39, 69, 145n.59, 146n.69
orchestration of BWV 542/1, 28–40, 136–37

pedaliter arrangement of BWV 539/1, 26–28
piano transcription of BWV 1164, 146n.68
Rutter, John (b. 1945; composer), 127

Salmon, Dorothea (twentieth century)
piano transcription of BWV 729, 130–31
Scarlatti, Domenico (1685-1757; composer), 41–42
Schaab, Robert (1817-1887; organist, composer), 135–37
Prelude and Fugue on "Meine Hoffnung. steht auf Gott," Op. 68, 135
Schad, Joseph (1812-1879; pianist, composer), 131–32
Schanz, Arthur (musicologist), 108–9, 122–23, 126, 130–31
Schelble, Johann Nepomuk (1789-1837; conductor), 19
piano transcriptions of organ chorales by Bach, 8–9, 19, 165n.47
Schellenberg, Hermann (1816-1862; organist), 12, 21, 26–27, 55–73, 120–22
organ-duet arrangement and piano transcription of BWV 542, 21, 56
piano transcription of movement from Bach's St. Mattthew Passion, 56
Schicht, Johann Gottfried (1753-1823; composer, conductor), 55
edition of organ chorales by Bach, 44–55, 91–92
Schindler, Anton (1795-1864; associate and biographer of Beethoven), 115
Schmitt, Christian (b. 1976; organist), 106
Schnabel, Joseph Ignaz (1767-1831; composer), 74–75
Schoenberg, Arnold (1874-1951; composer), 173n.55
orchestration of BWV 552, 170n.21
Scholz, Bernhard (1835-1916; conductor, composer), 40–41
orchestration of BWV 552/1, 40–41, 170n.21

Schulenberg, David (b. 1955; musicologist), 106
Schumann, Clara, née Wieck (1819-1896; pianist), 14, 77, 89–90, 109, 134–36, 154n.57
Schumann, Robert (1810-1856; composer), 8–9, 41–42, 43, 51–52, 70, 77, 89–90, 92–93, 109, 113, 120, 133–37
Six Fugues on BACH, Op. 60, 111, 135, 136–37
Symphony No. 2 in C Major, 14
Schütz, Heinrich (1585-1672; composer), 16–17
Schweitzer, Albert (1875-1965; organist, humanitarian), 106, 109, 123–26, 129–31
Shore, Howard (b. 1946; composer)
film score for *The Silence of the Lambs*, 99
Siloti, Alexander (1863-1945; pianist), 107
piano transcription of BWV 535/1, 106, 107
piano transcription of BWV 855/1, 107
Spielberg, Steven (b. 1946; filmmaker)
Schindler's List, 100–1
Spitta, Philipp (1841-1894; Bach biographer), 6–7, 142–43n.30, 159n.95
Spohr, Louis (1784-1859; composer), 57, 89
Statham, Heathcote (1839-1924; organist, architect), 108–9, 169–70n.15
Stock, Frederick (1872-1942; conductor, composer)
orchestration of BWV 552, 170n.21
Stutschwesky, Joachim (1891-1982; cellist, composer)
violin-cello transcriptions of BWV 802-805, 131–32
Swingle Singers, 129

Tarkovsky, Andrei (1932-1986; filmmaker), 120
Solaris, 126–27
Tausig, Carl (1841-1871; pianist), 108–9
piano transcription of BWV 614, 8–9

The Crown, 126–27
The Theatre of Early Music, 173n.54
Thirty-Two Short Films about Glenn Gould, 104
Trier, Lars von (b. 1956; filmmaker), 120
Nymphomaniac, 126–27

Vaughan Williams, Ralph (1872-1958; composer)
orchestration of BWV 680, 144n.49
Viol, Friedrich Wilhelm (1817-1874; critic), 166n.50
Vivaldi, Antonio (1678-1741; composer), 22–23, 63
Vogler, "Abt" (1749-1814; composer, organist), 17
Voigt, Carl (1808-1879; conductor), 19, 161n.18
piano transcriptions of BWV 543-548, 19, 161n.18

Wagner, Cosima, née Liszt (1837-1930; wife of Richard Wagner), 125–26
Wagner, Richard (1813-1883; composer), 43, 125–24, 165n.43, 172n.47
Tristan und Isolde, 123
Walther, Johann Gottfried (1684-1748; composer)
"Ach Gott und Herr" (BWV 692-693), 48, 49–50
Watts, Isaac (1674-1748; hymn writer), 112–13
Wesley, Samuel (1766-1837; organist, composer), 50–51, 111–13, 150n.39
Wesley junior, Charles (1757-1834; organist, composer), 50–51
Whitehead, William (b. 1970; organist), 127
Whiteley, John Scott (b. 1950; organist), 127
Widor, Charles-Marie (1844-1937; organist, composer), 117, 124–26
Toccata from Organ Symphony No. 5 in F Minor, 117
Williams, Peter (1937-2016; musicologist), 8, 108, 110–11

Winterfeld, Carl von (1784-1852; musicologist), 80
Wolff, Christoph (b. 1940; musicologist), 6–10, 114–15, 127–28
Bach's Musical Universe: The Composer and His Work, 6–10, 142–43n.30
Wood, Henry (1869-1940; conductor), 110
orchestration of BWV 540/1, 110

Yearsley, David (b. 1965; musicologist, organist), 10–24
Bach's Feet: The Organ Pedals in European Culture, 10–24

organ transcription of movement from BWV 1079, 13

Zehnder, Jean-Claude (b. 1941; organist, musicologist), 171n.30
Zellner, Leopold Alexander (1823-1894; composer), 118–19
Zelter, Carl Friedrich (1758-1832; conductor, pedagogue), 41–42, 74–75, 80
Zimmerman, Jerry (d. 1995; pianist), 97
Zitellini, Rodolfo (musicologist), 119